WISDM'S

PARADISE

WISDOM'S PARADISE

The Forgotten Shakers of Union Village

by Cheryl Bauer
& Rob Portman

ORANGE FRAZER *PRESS*
Wilmington, Ohio

ISBN 1-882203-40-2

Additional copies of *Wisdom's Paradise: The Forgotten Shakers of Union Village* may be ordered directly from:

Orange Frazer Press
P.O. Box 214
Wilmington OH 45177

Telephone 1.800.852.9332 for price and shipping information.
Website: www.orangefrazer.com

Book Design and Layout: Tim Fauley
Cover Image: photographed by Robert A. Flischel at The Golden Lamb, Lebanon, Ohio

Robert A. Flischel photographs: 13, 18, 19, 44, 62, 67, 76, 103, 118, 121, 174, 175, 197, 219, 258
Golden Lamb Inn: 62, 76, 121, 142, 170, 175
Library of Congress, Geography and Map Division: 124, 126, 130, 131, 132, 134, 135, 137, 140
Library of Congress, Special Collections: 51, 66, 164, 196 (Realf)
Otterbein Lebanon, Ohio, Archives: 44, 54, 55, 67, 84, 89, 155, 169, 173, 184, 225, 236, 237, 253, 255
Warren County, Ohio, Historical Society and Museum: 22, 33, 38, 56, 85, 102, 112 (Otterbein Collection), 118, 143, 168, 179, 185, 189, 193, 196 (Hampton), 218, 227, 241, 243
Cheryl Bauer: 12, 259
Randy McNutt: 260, 263
Rob Portman: 230

Library of Congress Control Number: 2004115103

Acknowledgements

This book would not have been written without the influence of four people who are no longer with us. Hazel Spencer Phillips was a Shaker historian and author whose curiosity about the people of Union Village was contagious. Her encouragement started Rob Portman on this project more than 25 years ago. Rob's mother, Joan Jones Portman, and his grandparents, Virginia and Robert H. Jones, also led him to write this history. Their love of Shaker artistry and perfection, and their collections of Shaker artifacts and literature over the past 75 years have helped preserve the history of Union Village and introduced many other people to the Shakers.

Many thanks to three people who help to preserve that history today: Mary Lue Warner, Mary Klei, and Mary Payne. Your interest and encouragement made a challenging project seem manageable.

Several individuals took time to provide information, make suggestions, and simply talk with us about the Believers of Union Village. They were a great help: Oloye Adeyemon, Mary Allen, Debra Bauer, Martha Boice, Karen Campbell, Fred Compton, Dennis Dalton, Jerry Grant, Douglas Hamel, Melba Hunt, Jim Innis, Stephen Kelley, Charles Muller, Brian Thomas, James Thomas, Paul Resatar, Richard Spence, Darryl Thompson, and Cathy Winans.

A special debt is owed to the people who made this book a delight to read and look at: Dr. Elizabeth Pruden, who proofread the final manuscript, and Robert Flischel, who took wonderful photos.

Finally, our deepest gratitude goes to those people who today foster our love of history and encourage all our endeavors: Ruth Bauer, Randy McNutt, and Jane Portman.

Table of Contents

A Note on the Text: Spelling and punctuation from original documents have been retained as much as possible in the text. Minor changes have been made in a few cases to clarify meaning. Where multiple spellings of proper names exist, the most accepted version of that time is used.

WISDOM'S
PARADISE

Top: Trustees' Office at New Lebanon, New York

Arrival—
Salvation on the Frontier

Shortly before Shaker leader Ann Lee died in New York in 1784, she predicted that the next great wave of religious conversion would occur in what was then the southwest. When word of a massive revival in Ohio and Kentucky reached Shaker headquarters in the early 1800s, Lee's prediction seemed true. Her followers sent Issachar Bates, John Meacham, and Benjamin Seth Youngs—all respected Shaker elders—to seek converts and establish new communities in the southwest. On New Year's

Day, 1805, the three left New Lebanon, New York, for the Ohio frontier.

This is the beginning of our story about Union Village, which the missionaries founded. It is told through the Shakers' words, the writings of their contemporaries, and the discoveries of historians. It is long overdue. The last book to focus on Union Village's history was published in 1907, five years before the community disbanded. Our objective is to provide a largely chronological history that depicts life at Union Village and encourages further research, discussion, and publishing about one of America's great experiments in religious freedom.

Union Village has been called the "most turbulent and precocious" of all nineteenth-century Shaker communities.[1] During its 107 years, the Warren County village evolved into one of the most prominent communal societies in the United States. In 1805, the community became the frontier outpost of the United Society of Believers in Christ's Second Appearing. As the first Shaker village established west of the Alleghenies, Union Village parented settlements in West Union, Indiana; Pleasant Hill and South Union, Kentucky; and North Union, Watervliet, and Whitewater, Ohio.

All of these western Shaker communities had disbanded by the early 1900s. Their sites are now subdivisions, historic landmarks, a living museum at Pleasant Hill, and, in Union Village's case, a retirement community. Since the closings, a sort of legend has evolved about the western Shakers. They are often thought of as transplanted New England farmers who lived peacefully and left a legacy of graceful furniture and architecture. When they are praised, it is for their craftsmanship and egalitarian views. The religious beliefs that shaped their daily lives are often overlooked. This wasn't always so. In the nineteenth century, the western Shakers were at first persecuted for their beliefs, later ridiculed, and finally romanticized.

In reality, the Believers, as they called themselves, were as varied as any of their contemporary counterparts. They were moral and frugal farmers in the New England tradition, but they were also innovators, entrepreneurs, religious scholars and writers, and advocates of racial and sexual equality within the sect. Members became builders, poets, visionaries, and—sometimes—scoundrels. They were also survivors who weathered attacks from suspicious mobs and betrayals by their own members to become the most influential western Shaker village.

Union Village's ancestry dates to Lee, founder of the United Society in eighteenth-century England. Lee was born in 1736 to a blacksmith and his wife. She grew up in the industrial city of Manchester, where, as a matter of course, she attended the Anglican Church. Intelligent but illiterate, she joined many people of her time in seeking greater assurance of eternal salvation. Her search led her to James and Jane Wardley, former Quakers who had been influenced by the Camisards, a French group that sparked religious revivals throughout Europe in the late 1600s and early 1700s.

The Wardley Society, as the couple's followers were called, engaged in many of the practices that Ann Lee later incorporated into the United Society. Worship services featured meditation, public confession of sins, a divine message, and ultimately, ecstatic singing, shouting, and shaking to praise God, which led critics to mock them as the Shaking Quakers, or simply the Shakers. The Wardleys believed, as did the Camisards, that divine truths were revealed to the faithful in ongoing heavenly visions and dreams. They differed from mainstream Christian groups by looking for the imminent second coming of Christ to be in female form, and they believed that men and women were equal in God's sight.[2]

Lee, who had experienced visions since childhood, embraced these radical ideas and added one more tenet of faith—celibacy. She believed abstinence was crucial for salvation. Psychologists and scholars have speculated that events in her childhood and marriage, as well as eighteenth-century attitudes about sex, led her to embrace celibacy. She supposedly became concerned about the issue as a child when she begged her mother to practice abstinence. As an adult, she married at her father's insistence and suffered four difficult deliveries. Three of her children died as infants and a fourth died at age six. But Lee offered a different rationale for celibacy. The edict, she told friends, was not hers, but God's. She said she learned in a divine vision that God cast Adam and Eve out of the Garden of Eden for engaging in sex.[3] She and her later followers also interpreted many Biblical passages to support this belief. Eventually, celibacy became a barrier to growth both within the Shaker society and among potential converts who were otherwise drawn by Lee's principles.

Many people also had difficulty accepting the idea that God was both male and female. God the Father was revered as the Creator. Holy Mother Wisdom embodied knowledge. Shaker theologians argued that one would be incomplete without the other. This belief encouraged equal treatment and respect for each sex, and led to the concept of Christ also being present in a male and female body. Shakers believed that Jesus, a fully human man, was the first appearing of the Christ spirit in the flesh.[4]

Lee began to formulate this concept while imprisoned in England for heresy in 1773. While praying, she experienced a vision in which "the spirit of Christ suffused her being."[5] After years of prayer, self-deprivation, and mental anguish, she believed she had seen the way to salvation and had become one with Christ. Lee taught that all believers had the potential to do the same. By leading a sinless life, anyone could become a divine spirit. This concept evolved into an alternative view of Christ's role in salvation. Most Christians believed that Jesus' death was the atonement for the past, present, and future sins of humanity. Shakers, on the other hand, revered Jesus as a servant of God who attained salvation by refusing to yield to his sinful human nature. Rather, "he took that nature and crucified it, as an example to all souls; and that as many as took up the same cross, and followed him in that day, were a kind of first-fruits of his creatures."[6] For Believers, Jesus was the ultimate male role model on how to live a holy life. Lee became the ultimate female role model, and her followers began addressing her as Mother Ann.

The spiritual equality of the sexes opened the way for women to exercise more authority within the church. Many Christians, accustomed to primarily male leadership, condemned this as heresy. The principle contradicted traditional practice, and, perhaps more importantly, challenged the social order. Society reacted negatively. Lee and her followers were repeatedly harassed and beaten by opponents, and imprisoned by authorities. The persecution drove her and eight other Believers to seek tolerance and religious freedom in America in 1774. While Lee and her followers believed their views were the sure path to salvation, they supported religious choice because they wanted freedom to practice their faith. But America proved no more tolerant than England. The Believers continued to be attacked verbally and physically, hauled into court, and thrown into jail for their views on celibacy, the female Christ spirit, a communal economy, and pacifism.

With the colonies entering war, pacifism became an unavoidable issue in 1776. Believers took refuge in a remote location northwest of Albany, New York. Their Indian neighbors called the site Niskeyuna; they called it Watervliet. It became the first Shaker community in America. Members spent much time traveling in the area, and their pacifistic preaching soon became known to the public. Like the Quakers, the Believers were firmly committed to peace. They considered killing for any reason immoral and contrary to God's commandments and Jesus' example. As British immigrants, they were rumored to be Tory sympathizers. Lee and several of her followers were jailed in 1780 for preaching against war.[7]

Another controversial element, the communal economic system, began out of necessity in the sect's early days. Many members lived very modestly. Establishing a new church and combating persecution limited their ability to earn a living. Soon the Believers were meeting in members' homes, sharing a meal and the hearth, along with their new faith. Eventually, they pooled all their material resources into one concern, called the joint interest. At the same time, they dedicated their time and talents to spreading the Shaker message. Restructuring the family unit became a part of the system. Husbands, wives, and children no longer lived together. Biological relationships were dissolved as Believers learned to live in spiritual union as brothers and sisters. Husbands and wives might live separately in the same family dwelling, in different families within a Shaker community, or even in different communities. Children were raised together by several sisters in a group called the Children's Order. Many people condemned the dissolution of the biological family and attacked the Believers because of it.

Despite violent opposition at times, they continued to preach throughout New York and New England, gaining converts slowly but persistently. An enthusiastic group of converts gathered at New Lebanon, New York, not far from the Massachusetts border. New Lebanon became the central ministry of the United Society in 1788.[8] Despite Lee's death four years later, her followers continued to proselytize and form new communities. By 1800, Shaker communities existed in New York, Massachusetts, Connecticut, New Hampshire, and Maine.

The inception of Union Village in 1805 set the stage for the western expansion of the faith. During a revival that began in the 1830s, Union Village was given the spiritual name of Wisdom's Paradise, an appellation that seems to convey the hope and optimism that surrounded the community. In many ways, Union Village was one of America's more successful experiments in Christian communal life. It contributed to the Shaker faith through its books and music, and to the economy through its inventions and innovative industries. The village also served as a progressive role model to its secular neighbors in areas ranging from education to conservation. Yet there was also a troubled side to Union Village, one that is not fully understood today. Sometimes the frontier community strained the United Society's resources and authority, and individual egos disrupted harmony within the village. It was not an easy life.

We hope our book illuminates Union Village's challenges as well as its successes, and recognizes those hundreds of souls who carved a community out of the early Ohio frontier.

"*Many of the people here have been in expectation...that something extraordinary would take place this Summer.*"

—John Meacham,
Turtle Creek, Ohio, 1805

Top: Otterbein-Lebanon Shaker museum
Right: Hand-forged hardware in the basement of Marble Hall

⑤ Chapter One ⑤

Into the Miami Country—
Shaping a New Community

When Malcolm Worley answered the door on the night of March 22, 1805, cold air and new ideas swept into his cabin. Spring had just arrived in Turtle Creek, Ohio, but the three strangers on his doorstep were dressed for rough weather. White fur hats framed their faces. Their gray overcoats, blue waistcoats, and brown overalls looked old-fashioned, and their speech sounded different. But that wasn't what intrigued Worley. He had heard rumors about these men for some time, and he was eager to talk with

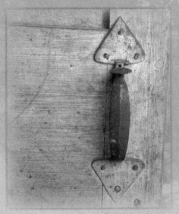

them personally. "Come in, Brethren, I was looking for you," he told Shaker missionaries Issachar Bates, John Meacham, and Benjamin Youngs.[1]

Friends in Kentucky, where Worley lived before moving to Ohio in 1802, had prepared him for the Shakers' arrival—and for their unusual religious views. The missionaries came at a time when Worley was searching for assurance of salvation. At age 43, the rugged, well-educated farmer had already experienced his share of heartaches. His wife had died during childbirth, leaving him with several young children. While questions of mortality and eternity preoccupied his thoughts, his Presbyterian faith still left him hungry for answers.

The Believers must have been quite persuasive (missionaries were sometimes called propagandists in those days). They recognized that Worley was ripe for change. Exuberant and confident of their faith, they offered him new hope. Worley and Bates sat up until 2 a.m. that first night, talking about salvation. By dawn, Worley was ready to accept the Shaker message. He quickly visited his pastor, Richard McNemar, who was stunned by the news.[2]

Worley wanted to change his life. He was starting over on a small farm in a new state, and beginning to prosper. His second wife, Peggy, had just given birth to twins. Not long ago he had spiritually uprooted his family to join McNemar in the New Lights sect but hadn't found peace of mind. By 1805, he was so distraught over his spiritual fate that not even his pastor could allay his concerns.

The Shakers hoped to achieve what McNemar could not. They had not sought out Worley by happenstance. Their leaders in New Lebanon, New York, had sent them to spread the message of the United Society of Believers in Christ's Second Appearing and to establish Shaker colonies on the frontier. They knew of Worley's prominence in the community, and therefore the value of his conversion. McNemar once described him as "a man of unspotted character, an independent fortune, and a liberal education."[3] With the backing of such a respected man, the missionaries figured, others might take notice.

Worley's ready acceptance of the Shakers shocked many New Lights. When he introduced McNemar to the missionaries, the pastor was also ready to listen. He was not familiar with the United Society, and it took some time for him to digest all of their ideas. "Some of their conversation I could not so well understand; a number of things appeared new," he wrote later.[4] Yet he was impressed with their apparent integrity, piety, and understanding of Christianity. He agreed to allow the missionaries to speak at the Turtle Creek church the next day. Benjamin Youngs read a message from the New Lebanon ministry, inviting the congregation to join the Shakers. He outlined the fundamental steps of joining the sect: members must believe in "the manifestation of Christ," confess their sins, and fight against all impurity, especially their sexual natures.

Youngs' talk set off a week of intense discussion at Turtle Creek. The sect was new to most people. Having separated from the Presbyterian Church, many of the New Lights were unsure of the future. The Shakers offered direction and structure for the revival spirit. As local people talked with the missionaries, they watched McNemar and Worley's reactions. Worley acted quickly. On

March 27, he officially converted, becoming the first western Shaker. His wife soon followed his example.

Worley hoped the missionaries' arrival was the next phase of a religious revival that had begun in Kentucky around 1800. At that time, revival affected many Christian denominations, including Methodist, Baptist, and Presbyterian. Many colonial religious leaders started reform movements that stressed the individual's personal relationship with God and proclaimed that eternal salvation was open to more than just a chosen few. The winning of the Revolutionary War re-energized such reforms, with more pastors and evangelists preaching that people could take an active role in securing salvation. Self-determination—politically, economically, and spiritually—was the new republic's ideal. People had thrown off the yoke of royal authority and a state church, and now some of them wanted to secede from established church authority. Adoption of the Bill of Rights in 1791 also fueled dissenters' desires to start their own sects. The First Amendment's inclusive command that the government not legislate religion or prohibit the free practice of religion encouraged experimentation.

As one of Kentucky's most effective evangelists, McNemar led sensational outdoor revival meetings in which he and Worley witnessed highly unusual behaviors that they finally attributed to a divine source. When McNemar exhorted crowds to repent, listeners became emotional to the point of hysteria, seeking God's salvation or pleading with loved ones to accept Christ as their savior. People cried, trembled, fainted, and appeared to go into trances. Thousands of people showed up at one revival in Blue Springs, Kentucky. The meeting took on a festival atmosphere with preaching, praying, and singing. Participants became more animated as the day continued. Some laughed and sang, some shook and danced. These behaviors were interpreted as spontaneous acts of praise to God. Other behaviors seemed almost grotesque. Some people vocalized a harsh sound described as a bark. Others experienced the "jerks," swaying back and forth so violently that their heads touched the ground in front and then in back of them. Other people rolled on the ground. Such acts or manifestations were considered gifts to mortify pride and prompt repentance.[5]

To conventional Christians, these acts seemed bizarre, or even blasphemous. To Shakers, the manifestations in Kentucky presented an exciting possibility. They hoped that a prediction by Mother Ann Lee, founder of the sect, was being fulfilled. Shortly before her death in 1784, Lee had spoken of a spiritual revival that was to occur in the southwest—in those days, the Ohio and Kentucky frontier. When Worley and McNemar moved to southwestern Ohio, the revival spirit accompanied them. McNemar became pastor of the Turtle Creek Presbyterian Church in 1802. Manifestations ensued, to the discomfort of some members. McNemar and a handful of sympathetic pastors broke away from the Presbyterian Church in 1803 and began calling themselves the New Lights. Many New Light philosophies appealed to the Shakers, or Believers, as they called themselves. New Lights rejected doctrine formulated by clergy, particularly John Calvin. Believers would receive "spiritual light" directly from God, which would create immediate harmony and allow all accepting souls to share equally in divine gifts. "Neither was there any distinction, as to age, sex, color, or anything of a temporary nature," McNemar wrote, "old and young, male and female, black and white, had equal privilege to minister the light."[6]

The Shakers espoused similar views. In 1804, their central ministry at New Lebanon corresponded about their circumstances and beliefs with New Lights in Kentucky and Ohio. The Shakers believed they were living in the era of Christ's second appearance on earth, and suggested that the New Lights join them. Like Worley, the Shakers had struggled for assurance of salvation before accepting Ann Lee's

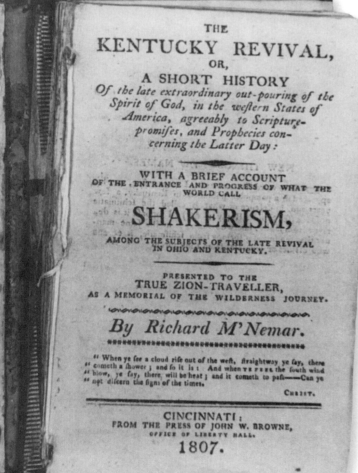

Title page of 1807 edition of *The Kentucky Revival*

admonition to forsake the life of the flesh to be reborn as Godly creations.[7] After more encouraging correspondence, the central ministry, headed by Mother Lucy Wright, sent the three missionaries west. They left New York on New Year's Day, 1805, and visited the Kentucky New Lights first but soon determined that the real leadership was at Turtle Creek in Warren County.

Although the schism separated the New Lights from the Presbyterian Church, most Christians were conventionally religious. They attended church and were concerned about their eternal lives. But they were also concerned about their temporal lives. Clashes with Indians had subsided barely a dozen years earlier. The community of Beedle's Station, the first white settlement in Warren County, had begun in 1795 as a blockhouse. That year, the Indian tribes signed the Treaty of Greenville, which restricted them to regions not yet settled by whites. With conflict seemingly quelled, the proposed county seat of Lebanon, five miles east of Turtle Creek, was founded in 1802. Warren County was formally established in 1803, the year Ohio became a state.

The country itself was still being formed. Ohio in 1805 was a frontier filled with challenge and opportunity. Revolutionary War veterans wanted to create new lives for themselves and their families. Southwestern Ohio was an uncommonly good place to do so. Turtle Creek lay in a fertile valley between the Great Miami and Little Miami rivers, where land was lush and plentiful for farming. Cincinnati, about 30 miles to the southwest on the Ohio River, was the area's major settlement, and a busy port. The makings of prosperity existed for anyone who had some capital and the capacity to work hard.

Lebanon promised at least a few civilized amenities. Dirt streets wrapped around a handful of houses and a tavern, the Sign of the Black Horse (later to be the Golden Lamb Inn). Subscription schools educated children whose families could afford the tuition. Baptists and Presbyterians held regular worship services.[8] Christianity was an integral part of the culture but the Believers, who considered themselves the true Christians, had a different set of priorities. Local people valued family, personal prosperity, and patriotism, while the Shakers preached celibacy, a communal economy, and pacifism. They were the first whites to establish a communal settlement in Ohio. The frontier setting attracted later groups coming from eastern cities, including the religious Separatists of Zoar in Tuscarawas County and the secular Fourierite Association of Utopia in Clermont County. But the Believers were the first "communists" to challenge the mores and laws of the region.

The steps to being accepted into the Shakers' Gathering Order, or newcomers' group, were few but life-changing. Prospective members confessed their sins to a church official called an elder, a position held by each of the missionaries. They then agreed to live celibately and follow the elders' guidance while learning more about the faith. Frontier conditions necessitated some modifications. Typically, Worley's wife, Peggy, would have confessed to an eldress, a female church leader. With an eldress unavailable, one of the men heard her confession. Children could not join the United Society until they came of age, so the Worley children merely abided by their parents' decision, and did not actually convert. There was no Gathering Order yet, so the missionaries informally tutored the Worleys in the faith while living with them.

During the weeks following Worley's conversion, interested people began to crowd into his cabin to talk about the faith. McNemar continued to allow the missionaries to speak in one of the three churches he led on respective Sundays. They influenced a former slave from Virginia, 19-year-old Anna Middleton. Little is recorded of Middleton except that she had, as a slave, moved to Ohio with her owner shortly before the missionaries arrived, and received her freedom upon entering the state. She became the second convert to Shakerism at Turtle Creek, and was accepted on equal terms with the white Believers. The few known facts of Middleton's life support the idea that the Shakers practiced racial equality as well as talked about it. In 1812, she signed Union Village's first formal covenant agreement, a step that showed her legal as well as spiritual involvement in the sect. Middleton lived in the First Family, the most prominent group within a Shaker community, and she remained a Believer her entire life.[9]

S uch equality was highly unusual on the western frontier. Both Middleton's sex and race made her a second-class citizen under Ohio law. Because she was a woman, she did not have the right to vote and was not counted as a citizen when ratios were determined for the number of representatives to serve in the state general assembly. Because of her race, she was also subject to more discriminatory laws. In 1805, the position of black Ohioans was tenuous at best. Ohio was part of the Northwest Territory, a region of almost 250,000 square miles that Congress took under its control in 1780 and later carved into states. The Northwest Ordinance of 1787 outlawed slavery in the territory, meaning that anyone who moved there chose to live in a free state. But that didn't mean that blacks were treated equally under the law. Only white males received the right to vote from Ohio's constitutional convention in 1802, although a resolution to grant black men suffrage failed by only one vote. Additional laws passed within the first five years of Ohio's existence made it less than hospitable to blacks. The General Assembly of 1803 required that a registry of all free black and mulatto residents be established in each county. These people had to document their freedom with their county clerk of courts and pay twelve and a half cents to receive a certificate of freedom. This had to be done within two years of moving to Ohio. Whites were forbidden to hire blacks unless they produced these certificates. The fine for hiring someone without a certificate was the same as that for harboring or aiding escaped slaves—up to $1,000.

More laws regulating blacks and mulattos were passed in 1807. Newcomers were required to post a $500 bond with the county clerk of courts within 20 days of their arrival. They were not allowed to remain as residents unless they did this. The bond was supposed to guarantee the person's good behavior and provide for them if they became indigent. Many blacks would not have been able to afford the bond. Anyone who helped a person avoid the bond could be fined up to $100. That same act prohibited blacks and mulattos from testifying against whites in legal matters. The underlying assumption was that blacks were incompetent and untrustworthy.[10] With their equal acceptance of Middleton, the Believers seemed to refute such assumptions.

Blacks entered Ohio either on their own or, as Middleton did, with their previous owners. Several of the early western converts came from states where slavery was legal; a few had owned slaves. People who moved to Ohio consciously chose to live in an anti-slavery state, which was another reason the Believers chose Ohio as their new headquarters. They believed that all people were loved by God and had an equal right to salvation. McNemar and Worley had lived amidst slavery in Kentucky and had rejected it. McNemar's wife, Jennie, a native Kentuckian, inherited a slave when her father died. He willed her several pieces of furniture, a horse, seven head of cattle, and "one Negro wench named Seely."[11] The woman was later freed. The moral evil of signing over a human being as a piece of property could not have been lost on the young pastor. In some cases, freed blacks continued working for their former owners. Middleton's former owner may have been one of the whites attending those first Shaker meetings in Warren County. But the fact that she is listed as the second western convert shows she was acting on her own rather than following her employer into the faith.

No one seemed to try to dissuade Middleton from converting, but that wasn't true in most cases. Many New Lights adamantly opposed the Believers as they struggled to hold on to their own members. Conversions threatened friendships and family ties. When farmer David Spinning expressed interest in the missionaries' ideas, his extended family reacted negatively. His wife, parents, and most of his siblings thought converting was foolish. His father threatened to disinherit him, and eventually did so. Yet Spinning continued to be drawn to the Believers. He came to believe that a celibate life of striving for purity was the right path. In addition to his family's objections, Spinning struggled with the opposition of many of his New Light friends. He agonized over what to do:

> But Oh, the sacrafice began to appear tremendous! To loose my good name, and the good feelings and union of the great body of my New Light brethren, felt exceeding weighty; it felt like severing ties, that had for years been very strong with many near and dear friends. But still that which was nearer home felt heavier and that which was nearest felt heaviest of all. It appeared to me quite probable that an entire separation of my family would take place.[12]

Spinning followed his conscience and joined the Shakers that spring. He continued talking with his family, and they reconciled with him and later converted.

As other New Lights struggled with their futures, the missionaries focused on McNemar. They realized he was the key to establishing a Shaker community in Warren County. He was influential in his own congregation and in other New Light churches in Ohio and Kentucky. McNemar also had family ties to some founding families of Lebanon. He was related by marriage to Francis Dunlavy, a framer of the Ohio constitution and a common pleas court judge. Dunlavy, in turn, was closely associated with the Corwin family, who built one of the first homes in Lebanon and soon became politically and socially prominent. Young Shaker communities typically faced severe public opposition. The missionaries may have reasoned that McNemar's connections could buffer a new settlement in Warren County.

McNemar was clearly receptive to the Believers but wanted proof that they had the answers he had sought for years. At the age of 35, he was a devoted husband and father, awaiting the birth of his seventh child. The prospect of giving up a normal family life clearly troubled him. The difficult birth of his son, Richard Junior, on April 12, may have contributed to his decision to accept the celibate faith.[13] Years later, he reflected on his decision:

I very soon got to believe that Christ was in them [Shakers] and I knew that in me—that is, in my flesh—the Devil had a seat.... The contract into which I entered with the Shakers was to barter the Devil that was in me for Christ...to make this exchange had been my labor and study for many years and now, forsooth, I had a fair offer, but the terms were rather tighter than I had generally contemplated.[14]

A series of mystic occurrences finally convinced McNemar to convert. The first concerned a healing. Youngs and Meacham were talking with McNemar at his cabin one day when his young son, James, burst in, screaming hysterically. The child had periodically suffered such episodes since having a close encounter with a snake as a toddler. McNemar proposed a deal. If the missionaries could cure his son, he would become a Shaker. Although Shakers believed in divine healing, they weren't accustomed to producing it on demand, and were disconcerted. Jennie McNemar suggested that everyone pray. As the adults prayed, James relaxed and wandered outside to play. He ceased having hysterics after that and McNemar attributed the change to the Believers' prayer. Shortly after that incident, McNemar had a vision. While walking in his garden, he saw a feminine arm reach out of the sky as though it were beckoning to him. He took this as a visitation from Ann Lee and vowed, "I will follow thee ever."[15] He and Jennie converted on April 24, bringing their children into the fold.

> The contract into which I entered with the Shakers was to barter the Devil that was in me for Christ...to make this exchange had been my labor and study for many years.

McNemar's decision fulfilled the missionaries' hopes. Others from the Turtle Creek congregation and region began converting. The first formal Shaker meeting was held at the home of David Hill near the Turtle Creek Church on May 23. Meacham spoke about the sect's fundamental beliefs, and outlined the economy, behavior, and dress. He stressed the importance of unity among all Believers in every aspect of life.

The first religious lyrics attributed to the Shakers were also sung that day. Prior to that service, Believers hummed to sacred tunes or sang in "unknown tongues," which seemed to be random or singsong collections of syllables. The music, like the dancing, was thought to be a divine gift to praise God. No musical instruments accompanied the singing.[16] The simple first song began with a couplet: "With him in praise we'll advance/And join the virgins in the dance."[17] Issachar Bates, who with McNemar became a prolific composer for the United Society, probably wrote the words. Both had written songs before converting. Bates had penned a song in honor of a friend who was killed in an accident. McNemar had written religious songs for several years. He eventually was credited with writing more songs than any other Believer. The two men's musical abilities fostered a love of song in the frontier communities.

Bates also taught converts how to dance and "be exercised" in the Shaker manner. The world, as the Believers referred to all non-Shakers, ridiculed dancing as merely a physical release for the celibate members. Believers countered that they found ample scriptural support for the practice. They frequently cited two passages in support of dancing. One, Jeremiah 31:13, obviously influenced Bates' first lyric: "Then shall the virgin rejoice in the dance, both young men and old together: for I will turn their mourning into joy and will comfort them, and make them rejoice from their sorrow." In addition to sanctioning dancing, the passage could also be interpreted as an affirmation that the Believers could guide converts to sure salvation. The second passage was Psalm 149:3, in which the psalmist urged the faithful: "Let them praise His name in the dance: let them sing praises unto Him with timbrel and harp." It would take decades, however, for the Shakers to allow musical instruments at services.

> There are people in this place, who if they were permitted, would as willingly open our veins, as they would eat bread when hungry...

The missionaries began to feel at home in Turtle Creek. They called themselves the Old Believers; the new converts were known as the Young Believers. "We have found a number of people here that feel near and dear," the missionaries wrote to the central ministry at New York in early June. "They begin to feel more and more like Brethren and Sisters."[18] They acknowledged their adversaries but noted that many people chose to listen to the prophecy of a New Light named Kitchel, who had died the previous February near Turtle Creek. He was a religious man who was respected in the area. On his deathbed, he predicted the coming of missionaries who would preach against impurity. The Believers with their message of celibacy seemed to fulfill Kitchel's words. People were looking for "something extraordinary" to happen that summer and some of them found it in the creation of the Shaker settlement.

But even as the missionaries sought permission to form a settlement, they acknowledged the strong opposition they still faced. Celibacy and communalism raised the suspicions of many Turtle Creek neighbors. Death threats had been made more than once. "There are people in this place, who if they were permitted, would as willingly open our veins, as they would eat bread when hungry," the missionaries wrote to Wright.[19] Rumors circulated of a mob forming to drive them from the region, but the opposition was not yet organized enough to act. These attitudes did not surprise the missionaries. In the East, opponents had spread rumors about the Believers since the late 1770s, when Ann Lee and a small group of followers from England first settled in New York State. Once converts committed to Shakerism, family relationships changed drastically. Husbands and wives severed marital ties and lived as celibate brothers and sisters in Christ. Children were usually raised together in one dwelling called the Children's Order. Parents might see their children, but they were to treat all children in the community equally. This was difficult for many, and impossible for some, to accept. The separation of families was one of the most controversial aspects of Shakerism. In the early years, most of the attacks against the Turtle Creek settlement resulted from domestic disputes among relatives who were Believers and those who were vehemently anti-Shaker. Celibacy was often alleged to be a cover for promiscuity. Although several members at Turtle Creek left the sect over the years to marry, there is no evidence that sexual immorality was widespread. Most Believers took the vow of celibacy seriously and struggled to keep it.

They also struggled with lawsuits over the communal holding of property. When a Believer signed the church covenant, he pledged any property he owned to the joint interest (economy) of the community. Shaker villages were divided into spiritual families. Each family lived together in a large dwelling and worked together. The money they earned provided for their needs; anything extra went to the community as a whole. Many converts, including Worley and McNemar, donated their land to the community or received nominal payment for it. Relatives who felt they should have the property often filed suit against the United Society. A second type of lawsuit came from apostates, members who decided to leave the sect. They sought to recover property or to receive additional compensation for it. During the 107 years that the Warren County community existed, the Believers won the majority of the lawsuits.

The sect's theology also angered some opponents. Assertions that Christ had made a second appearance on earth in the person of Ann Lee shocked many Christians. They often misinterpreted Lee's statements about the second appearing. During a religious experience in an English jail in 1766, Lee believed that Christ blessed her with His spirit and made her a conduit for God's message. She took on the role of a mother, teaching her children through loving example. She believed that each person had the potential to become one with God in spirit. As the Believers began to venerate Lee and tell of miracles attributed to her, some people felt she was treated as a god. Her sex doubtlessly played a part in the public's disapproval. After all, this woman defied her husband, spoke publicly and with authority about her religious convictions, and gathered followers into a new sect that challenged conventional society.

Her followers also challenged authority by claiming that they received divine revelations that superseded church doctrine. Even some New Lights, who were open to revelations and stressed the individual's importance, felt the Believers went too far. John Thompson, pastor of a New Light congregation at Beaver Creek in nearby Montgomery County, severely criticized McNemar, his former associate. Thompson had witnessed the manifestations at some of McNemar's earlier revival meetings in Kentucky, and later attended services with the Shakers at Turtle Creek. He spoke out against the Believers' ways, calling them wolves dressed in sheep's clothing, and trying futilely to stop conversions in southwestern Ohio.[20] Ironically, the nucleus of his Beaver Creek church became a Shaker community.

Believers expected considerable opposition but remained optimistic. The members, now numbering about 45, were heartened by the world's presence at their public meetings. On some days, 200 spectators watched the services. As attendance grew, services were frequently held outside. A dancing platform was built between the McNemars' two cabins. When arsonists destroyed the platform in September 1805, determined converts immediately rebuilt it. The central ministry was encouraged by the converts' zeal, and by their appealing, economically viable location. Meacham described the Miami country, as the missionaries called southwestern Ohio, in pastoral terms:

> *The face of the Country both here and in Kentucky is in the main very beautiful, being neither mountainous and broken, nor yet a dead level, tho in many places it is entirely flat. As for the depth and richness of soil, it far exceeds any country we ever saw before. It is heavily timbered, but when it is cleared off, the land is free from stone, and is therefore easy to till, and brings forth in great abundance.... The Country is natural to grass and affords a plenty of milk and butter.[21]*

His enthusiasm blossomed as the countryside greened. After receiving favorable reports from the missionaries, Lucy Wright sent three other prominent Shakers to Warren County that summer. One of the men, David Darrow, would become the elder of the settlement and later of the entire

western region. His arrival confirmed that the Believers were serious about prospects in the West. A farmer and family man, Darrow had joined the sect in New York State while Ann Lee was still alive. At age 55, he was a vital link between the Old Believers (easterners) and Young Believers (westerners).
As the first (chief) elder of the central ministry's primary family, Darrow was important in the church hierarchy. Benjamin Youngs described him as "an angel sent from God–His dispositions are kind, agreeable, and full of benevolence, void of superstition, patient under tribulation, easy to be entreated, a wise councillor, a leader, a protector, a Father."[22] Such a respected leader would be needed to support converts in the face of sometimes violent opposition.

The central ministry chose its early missionaries and leaders carefully. Each had a special talent or connection to the church hierarchy. John Meacham, 35, was a son of Father Joseph Meacham, who had worked closely with Ann Lee. The elder Meacham was one of the first American converts to Shakerism, joining the sect in 1780 and bringing along his young family. He eventually became the primary leader for Shaker men, as Lee was for the women. After Lee's death in 1784, Meacham named Lucy Wright as the female leader. Believers addressed them as "beloved Parents." Meacham was dead by the time his son headed to Ohio, but John still enjoyed a close relationship with Wright.

Benjamin Youngs, at 30 the youngest of the missionaries, was a member of an old Connecticut family, which joined the Watervliet, New York, Shaker community in 1794. An intelligent theologian and writer, Youngs became the primary author of *The Testimony of Christ's Second Appearing*, one of the Believers' most important theological works. This book, written at Turtle Creek, became known as the Shaker "bible" to the outside world.

Issachar Bates, 47, was a former Baptist minister who converted in 1801. As a young man, he served in the Revolution and came to abhor war. Like McNemar, he was married and had a large family. Bates became well known as a songwriter and speaker. Always passionate, Bates often led New Believers in singing and dancing.[23]

Bates, Youngs, Meacham, Darrow, McNemar, and Worley were at the heart of the western spread of Shakerism. Although they shared a faith that strove for perfect unity, their personal writings reveal six distinctive, occasionally contentious personalities that sometimes led to conflict. But in the early years in the Miami country, they came together to spread Ann Lee's teachings under Lucy Wright's watchful eye. It was this group of men who would write the theology and mold the western communities for the next 20 years.

Wright had many decisions to make. The most expensive one had to do with land. Worley and McNemar gave their farms to the United Society. But more land was needed to establish a settlement. Bates walked to New Lebanon, New York, in late summer of 1805 to give Wright a progress report and seek more money. Wright was encouraged by his description of crowded public meetings in Warren County and strong pockets of interest elsewhere in Ohio and Kentucky, and agreed to continue the venture. She sent him back to Turtle Creek that fall with $1,640 and "a good treasure of gospel love."[24] Plans were made to send more brothers as well as sisters west in the spring. Wright was eager to provide women missionaries since women were to be instructed by other females, and to confess their sins to an eldress.

Housing was another immediate concern. One year after the missionaries' arrival, the easterners all lived with the Worleys. That made a total of 15 children and adults living in a 18x20-foot house. The Worleys also entertained a growing number of visitors who were inquiring about the sect. Meacham and Darrow intimated that more financial help and manpower would be needed to develop the settlement. "As the situation of the young believers in these parts now is, we do not feel it right to require any contribution from them of time or money," they wrote, "for most of them are yet living in cabins and unsettled, and being waked up to a sense of their loss have as much as they can do to get along with their own business."[25] It was difficult for converts to give up traditional family life and farms, and the missionaries didn't want to discourage them with additional demands.

———————————————— ◡ ————————————————

T he first communal dwelling was carefully planned. "At first, a proposal was made to build small and cheap for the present; but neither our judgment or feeling would admit of it on any consideration," they wrote, echoing the commitment to quality for which Shakers became famous. "We have therefore concluded...to build a frame house 30x40 feet, two story, with a straight roof and two stacks of chimneys."[26] Modest by New Lebanon standards, the dwelling formed the nucleus of the future Union Village. With carpenters charging $1.34 a day, the easterners tried to economize by doing much of the work themselves when they were not proselytizing. The work was time consuming and tedious. They made 1,200 shingles of black walnut, cut thousands of clapboards of white oak, and forged hardware on site. They conscientiously reported their expenses to the central ministry. The largest amount—$2,265—had naturally gone to purchase land. They also recorded spending $260 on essentials including three milk cows, grain, food, tools, cloth, feathers for bedding, and two saddles. Missionaries' expenses

for three months of travel in Kentucky and Ohio totaled $18.[27] Darrow and Meacham also wrote of spiritual matters. They asked Wright to send a history of the United Society for the converts. While revival fever still inspired many, the Old Believers knew that more specific information would be needed.

Malcolm and Peggy Worley's house

In May 1806, morale and spirituality improved at Turtle Creek with the arrival of three brothers and six sisters. Leading the women was Eldress Ruth Farrington, 42, who had served with Darrow as co-leader of the First Family at New Lebanon. Apart from the central ministry, Darrow and Farrington were the most well known people in the United Society. Moving both of them to Warren County was an emphatic notice that the ministry believed the future was in the West. The women's arrival had a remarkable effect. They were treated almost as saints, and emotional converts were inspired by their mere presence. Meacham and Darrow described the first service that the women attended:

> *The chief part of the Believers in this place were together and about 200*
> *spectators of the World were also present. The young Believers, especially*
> *the females, when their eyes met the Sisters coming in at the door, were*
> *very deeply affected, being filled with joy and wonder. Some fell flat on the*
> *floor, others shouted or cryed out and the greater part were immediately*
> *in tears. The spectators stood with their eyes fastened on them, while their*
> *countenances testified of the feeling of their hearts, that they were much*
> *affected at the appearance of the Sisters and at the solemnity of the whole*

*scene. One of the brethren informs us that he observed that the tears were...
from the eyes of some of our most hardhearted and bitter opposers.*[28]

The dramatic reaction of the westerners validated Wright's decision to send
the sisters. No matter how enthusiastic they were about their new faith, the
women converts must have mourned for the loss of their identities as wives,
mothers, and even daughters. Eastern sisters quite literally provided a hand to
hold during the grieving process. Many denominations talked about giving up
the old Adam and old Eve, or becoming a new creation. Shakerism demanded
that rebirth in a physical, as well as spiritual, sense. For the group assembled
that Sunday morning, the sisters seemed to embody Shaker virtue. The
westerners were putting the sisters on a pedestal before they got to know each
other. That raised unrealistic expectations among the crowd and put a burden
on the sisters.

Many women held positions of authority within Union Village, but the
primary leadership was decidedly male. That may seem curious in
a church founded by a charismatic woman, devoted to the inherent
spiritual worth of both sexes, and led by another determined woman. The male
leadership did not just happen; it was carefully planned. Practicality seemed
to be the impetus. Some of the early women leaders in the West were not as
educated as the men. Although Ann Lee had been illiterate and depended on
male Believers to write and to handle business matters, both men and women
now needed to be literate to preach and teach on the frontier. The Shakers
were about to share many radical ideas. They may have reasoned that making
women highly visible as authority figures would further alienate traditionalists
or distract converts from other spiritual issues. Wright had experienced
persecution herself and knew that the westerners were sure to face it as well.
Perhaps she felt that the sisters would have enough to bear on the frontier.
Wright knew each of the first elders and eldresses personally and it is logical to
assume that her knowledge guided the decisions that she and the others in the
central ministry made.

The eastern women had many burdens to bear in the early years in Ohio.
At first they were overwhelmed by the welcome and the converts' neediness.
They struggled to adjust to what was for them an exhausting, almost primitive,
lifestyle. All of the women had been ill since leaving New York and were almost
overcome by their new roles. Coming from established, comfortable homes

back East, Turtle Creek truly was the frontier to them. They moved into the 18x20 frame house while the larger dwelling was being completed. The little house was drafty and leaky; its one window already broken. The women filled cracks with sticks of wood and carried on. Meals for 20 to 30 people a day were prepared in a fireplace in a small smokehouse that had been converted into a kitchen. Cooking equipment was scarce, as was nutritious food. They found several of the brothers, particularly Darrow, "quite weak and feeble" from the meager frontier diet. The brothers' clothes were also becoming tattered and the women set about mending. To the women's chagrin, laundry was done outdoors, "only a shelter of bushes over us." Ironing was done in their cramped, hot living quarters. "We used to think that we knew what hardship was, and truly we did," they wrote to their sisters at New Lebanon, "but we knew nothing about it to what we know now."[29]

They wrote separately to Wright, describing their new home and responsibilities. Homesickness and weariness permeates the letter. But they vowed to stay in the West for at least five years, and wrote optimistically of the conversions they witnessed. They asked Wright to remember them:

> *For we are sensible that no one knows how it feels to go out of the Church where there is so much order and go into such a distant land where there is so much evil and so little good but those that have experienced it. But we do not feel discouraged, for we are sensible that good is increasing and evil decreasing, and it is all the comfort that we have to see the gospel increasing and souls acoming into the work of God having the gifts and power of God.*[30]

The women described the physical manifestations they witnessed at Turtle Creek: "powerful gifts of shaking, turning, leaping. And some of these when they get unreconciled, they have what they call the jerks so powerful that they are thankful to come down and seek their relation again." The Young Believers' spiritual needs were as great as the mundane:

> *Mother, we have not had one day of rest since we left New Lebanon, but we have our hands and hearts full continually either in things spiritual or temporal. And Sabbath day we have long heavy meetings, and when we are not in public meeting we are in private labors continually. And we tend a meeting with [converts] every week in the afternoon and sometimes evening meetings, and we have a great many young Believers that comes to see us of necessity, especially them that comes from a distance for they have need to be with us in order to gather strength. And we have them to cook for and*

*wait on continually. And our work in temporal things comes very hard upon
us indeed, and our circumstance is so that we do not see that we can gather
any helps from the young Believers at present.*[31]

The brothers recognized the women's sacrifices and contributions. "What
could we have done without them? Truly nothing," Youngs wrote.[32] By
assuming the domestic work, the women made the enclave a welcoming place
for potential converts. They demonstrated the communal life that Believers
shared. Their participation in religious life provided a role model that the local
women had been seeking. The previous autumn, Jennie McNemar had asked
some of the eastern women to come west to help spread the Gospel. She was
certain they possessed the spiritual purity she longed to achieve: "As yet we
can only see in part and are entangled with many fetters, while you enjoy the
full liberty of the King's Daughters. I hope you will remember us as little babes
just beginning to learn of Christ."[33] Women were needed to teach and support
each other in the Shaker tradition, and to embody the female spirit of God,
known as Holy Mother Wisdom.

Praise was also lavished on Worley's contributions. He had already made
a mission trip to Chillicothe, Ohio, and was eager to do more. Meacham and
Darrow enthusiastically compared him to Noah, Moses, and John the Baptist.
"Malcolm has received us at all times as the angels of God with fear and
trembling," they wrote to Wright, "[he] has ever counted it his privilege and
glory to share with us in all our tribulation and reproaches."[34] They clearly felt
the westerners had the potential to spread the faith.

Wright looked for such signs of unity. It would take a committed group
to establish successful communities so far away from the central ministry.
Although Darrow seemed well received at Turtle Creek, he had not been the
only man recommended for the top position. Before his arrival, the missionaries
suggested another eastern brother, Daniel Mosley, for first elder. Darrow may
have been perceived as difficult or demanding. In their letter to Wright, the
sisters wrote of being pleasantly surprised with Darrow's personality: "We found
Elder David much easier than we expected, for he has got the gift of wisdom
and charity that we feel thankful for."[35] Darrow would need those attributes to
successfully lead Old and Young Believers. His office also put Richard McNemar
in a new position. Since the Kentucky Revival, he had led Presbyterians into
the New Lights, and then New Lights into the Shakers. He was a leader and a
decision-maker. Now he would be subservient to Darrow.

Perhaps Wright was thinking of these personalities when she wrote to the
sisters and brothers that October. She affirmed that all must accept Darrow

as "your first Elder Councilor & Protector there in that distant Land." She admonished them to work together and to be wary of pride:

> *I am Sensible you have diversity of Gifts, but by the same Spirit: I desire you may build up & strengthen each other in the Gift of God—You may consider you could not be so complete if you was all a Head, or an Arm, or a Foot—therefore Labour to bring your gifts into Subjection to the work of God that you are called to in that Land.*[36]

Wright wrote a separate letter to the sisters who had written so poignantly of their experiences in the mission field.

"I remember you," she said, "and feel that you have taken up your cross so far in a greater measure cheerfully for the Gospel sake—therefore you must not seek now to please yourselves but to please God that has called you to that work...good is increasing and evil decreasing. I think you have great reason to take courage and press on for the prise..."[37]

Taking notice of their living conditions, Wright wrote that the rugged living might make them healthier. Her tone of concern throughout the letter, however, softened the brusqueness of the comment. She assured them that she was praying for them, and asking all Believers to pray for them. She acknowledged the rigors of their environment and the frailties of her own advancing age, but urged them to keep the faith:

> *I do not feel anxious though I never should see your faces any more in the body but I feel anxious that you may find a gift of God where you are sent and if you do you will honour your privilege and calling which will be a fine compensation for any trouble and sorrow. I think you have been very particular in writing. Some times you make me weep, sometimes smile but you never will cause me to repent in sending you there if you are faithful.*[38]

She signed the letter to the entire group "from your Parent in the Gospel," as she usually did, but she signed the letter to the women "from your friend and Parent in the Gospel." She was acknowledging a special bond between them, but she wasn't letting them forget their mission.

As the women settled into their new lives, McNemar and Youngs set off for another mission trip, this time to Kentucky. While the core Warren County settlement was being established, missionaries continued to travel. Sisters began to accompany the men on mission trips. Temporal and spiritual expansions were well underway, shaping the foundation of a new community.

THE
TESTIMONY
OF
CHRIST'S
SECOND APPEARING

CONTAINING

A GENERAL STATEMENT OF ALL THINGS
PERTAINING TO THE FAITH AND PRACTICE OF
THE CHURCH OF GOD
IN THIS LATTER-DAY

PUBLISHED IN UNION.
BY ORDER OF THE MINISTRY

Now is come salvation, and

⑀ Chapter Two ⑀
Sowing the Faith—
Publishing and Parenting

Not long after its initial organizing, the Turtle Creek Believers began one of the United Society's most prolific eras of proselytizing and publishing. The settlement, after 1808 being officially called Union Village, struggled through its hardships and parented several communities in Ohio, Kentucky, and Indiana. Members also published a number of important theological works that attracted converts, and fueled arguments and legal action by Shaker opponents.

This period, 1805 to 1823, was both exciting and trying for Old and Young Believers, as they called themselves. They continued to be attacked by New Light ministers, as well as other Christians, who preached that Shakerism was built on delusion. This public debate drew crowds of up to 300 people to the Believers' Sunday meetings. An estimated 1,000 people attended one service in the summer of 1806. Some experienced a dramatic

Left: *The Testimony of Christ's Second Appearing*, written at Turtle Creek in 1808, is considered a classic of Shaker thought.

Top: Shaker villages of the West: 1. Union Village, Ohio; 2. Whitewater, Ohio; 3. Watervliet, Ohio; 4. North Union, Ohio; 5. Pleasant Hill, Kentucky; 6. South Union, Kentucky; 7. West Union, Indiana   *page* 39

change of heart and converted. "One man not far from here who but a few months ago, testified, & gave out word that if any of the Shakers came to his house, to delude & draw away any of his family, he would shoot them with his rifle, has lately confessed his sins & set out in the Gospel, & his wife has set out with him," David Darrow wrote to Lucy Wright.[1] Little more than a year after gathering their first converts, the Believers numbered 260. The number is impressive, considering the opposition they faced and the radical personal changes the group required.

Darrow and the other easterners continuously adjusted to new circumstances. Contrasted with the order and conformity of New Lebanon, the westerners were considered unsophisticated and unorganized by the leaders.[2] They were encouraged by the converts' enthusiasm and hard work as they studied Shakerism, but at times the easterners felt overwhelmed. Writing to her sisters in New Lebanon, Rachel Johnson told of twice-weekly public meetings "when the young sisters are under exercise. Sometimes they get us into their arms and make us hardly fit to be seen. It is so hot and so many people here that the sisters make use of white muslin looseback gowns, sometimes white jackets on weekday meetings."[3]

The physical demands of frontier life continued, but a few improvements were made. While there were still huge amounts of laundry to do, some of the work was now done in a shed. Kitchen chores commanded much of the sisters' time. Three or four sittings were held at each meal to accommodate everyone. A benefit of this arrangement was that the Old and Young Believers mingled at the table, with Darrow and Eldress Ruth Farrington dining elbow to elbow with the converts.

Living arrangements were improving too, but were still rugged by New Lebanon standards. The leaking cabin had been abandoned for the new, partially completed dwelling. "The first of our house is finished, white oak floors without planing, to two lofts, four smoky fireplaces on each loft," Johnson wrote. "Our garret we have for a lodging room with seven beds chiefly on the floor. There is neither door nor partition upon the loft. We have some blankets hung up between the brethren's beds and ours."[4] Despite the hardships, Johnson wrote that she did not feel discouraged, but truly needed.

This sense of service to a greater purpose motivated many Believers and helped them overcome personal obstacles. When convert David Spinning agreed to accompany Richard McNemar on a missionary trip to Adams

County, Ohio, and to Kentucky that first summer, he left behind a corn crop that needed tending and "a sorrowful woman, disconsolate and alone with one child."[5] He wrote that he shared in his wife's sadness and discomfort, but had to follow his conscience. Spinning's conversion was a lasting one; he remained a Shaker for the rest of his life. Idealized conversions, where a sudden epiphany is followed by an effortless transformation, generally did not last. Many of the later apostates had joined in a spirit of spiritual camaraderie or in an attempt to escape the world. Like Spinning, the permanent converts struggled and continued to nurture their faith. Their writings frequently address the subject. As an elderly man, Union Village Elder Oliver Hampton wrote skeptically of members who claimed they never struggled. "I have heard some say

> When convert David Spinning agreed to accompany Richard McNemar on a missionary trip to Adams County, Ohio, and to Kentucky that first summer, he left behind a corn crop that needed tending and "a sorrowful woman, disconsolate and alone with one child."

they never felt any cross in doing right. I am a little different," he admitted. "For instance, I never took one step yet in the upward path of progress, that was not attended with an agonizing sacrifice of some selfish, darling idol."[6] Sacrifice, he wrote, strengthened faith. The degree to which members believed that statement often determined whether they remained Shakers.

In an autobiographical sketch written later in life, Spinning explained the hardships of the early years and why he persisted:

> *I have been particular in detailing some few things, out of many that took place in those days that tryed men's souls and tryed their faith, whether it was grounded in the truth and the power of God, or whether they believed this was the right way because somebody else said it was. I did not set out on conditions. My sense of my obligations to obey truth...to do the will of God when clearly made known to me in my own understanding, is such that nothing can release or [exonerate] me from continuing to obey.[7]*

Spinning's devotion to his new faith was repeated many times among the Young Believers, but more converts and potential converts needed additional guidance. In August 1806, Darrow and the other eastern brothers asked Wright to allow them to publish a book explaining Shakerism. Darrow wrote that they felt a strong "gift"—or calling—to publish such a book. In fact, they were already writing a rough draft. The proposal made to Wright is one of the most passionate letters written from Ohio at that time. Darrow stressed the urgency of publishing soon to save indecisive souls.

> *Thousands of those who have see a great light coming on the earth, and have felt its rays, are now perishing for the want of knowledge, & are prevented from coming even to the sound Gospel, by reason of incredible heaps of false & ungodly teachers who turn the truth of the Gospel into reports of lasciviousness to blind the minds of the simple—And when it is so that any of them come to a hearing, by that time their prejudices are so strongly rooted, & their sence so darkened by false & ungrounded reports, that it is not the work of an hour nor a day to remove the stumbling blocks of the way even of the truly honest & seeking soul. It appears to us that thousands of precious & sincere souls are losing their former light & going to destruction for the want of nothing but a fair statement of naked truth respecting the testimony of the Gospel.[8]*

Darrow admitted that the Old Believers were almost overwhelmed with ministering to the Turtle Creek people and widening the mission field without taking on the additional task of writing and publishing a book. But he argued that the book would be a tremendous help in instructing newcomers and reaching many people whom the missionaries would never be able to visit. He did not want the revival to be confined to one region. "Must the work of God stop here?" he asked. "Shall an understanding of what God is doing in this last & greatest dispensation of his goodness be confined to the testimony of a few children, & the work of God lie so much hid from the world till there is no more light on the earth?"[9] He challenged the central ministry to expand the mission field.

Benjamin Youngs had been writing the first draft, struggling with how to arrange all the material. He is generally acknowledged as the principal author, although Darrow and John Meacham signed the first edition of the book as well. Up to this point, the most extensive publication about the Shakers was *A Concise Statement of the Principles of the Only True Church*, published by Father Joseph Meacham in 1790. It had set down the basic tenants of the faith and established the framework of a communal economy. Darrow and Youngs wanted the new book to recount the background of the Shakers, explain their religious beliefs, and expound on their scriptural justification for those beliefs. Most significantly, Youngs wanted to explain Ann Lee's central role in the sect.[10]

Rumors had circulated about Lee since she had begun preaching in England in the 1760s. Tales followed her to America. At various times, opponents charged that her mandate of celibacy was a cover for promiscuity, that the shaking and dancing in services was an expression of carnality triggered by drunkenness, and that the Shakers worshipped Lee as a god. The missionaries were keenly aware of these charges and eager to refute them by telling Lee's story. "As far as the sound of the Gospel is gone, it is also gone, and established [by the world] that the foundation of our faith is built on the fables of a drunken old woman, and the world has nothing to the contrary to believe," they wrote.[11] The missionaries felt converts needed to understand Lee's importance to truly embrace the faith.

Darrow recommended that the book be presented to the world by four of the converts: McNemar, Malcolm Worley, John Dunlavy (McNemar's brother-in-law and another former New Light minister), and Matthew Houston, a promising Kentucky convert. This strategy would allow people well known in their respective communities to present the newcomers' teachings. The plan also seems to have counted on the fact that new converts to a cause are often its most zealous propagandists.

Although Darrow and the others formally asked Wright's permission to publish, they clearly expected the book to become a reality. The challenging tone of their proposal and their enthusiasm evidently persuaded Wright, although she feared the new community might be sorely persecuted for its views. Having undergone physical and legal persecution themselves in New England, the eastern leaders were aware of how violent opponents could become. In addition to the arson at McNemar's cabin the first summer, agitators had cropped the ears of Shakers' horses and hurled rocks through the windows of their homes.[12] Wright knew of these events and realized that more opposition would arise. But in a response to Darrow, written in the fall of 1806, she agreed to have the book published. "Now I feel satisfied the time is come & the gift is in you & with you to accomplish this work," she wrote. Wright pledged her support and that of the entire church to the publication. She hoped to live to see the project finished, and added a final prophetic note to the westerners: "It will not be unexpected to me if the wicked should write against the circulation of such books.... I hope and trust you will consider well, & not get anything printed but what you are willing to live by & die by."[13]

As Youngs continued working on the book, McNemar was writing *The Kentucky Revival*, the first major religious work to be published by the western

Believers. It began a rich tradition of writing and publishing in Ohio, and later in Kentucky. McNemar's book chronicled the history of the late revival movement, and recounted what he had experienced at the camp meetings. He argued that the revival paved the way for Shakerism in the West, and that those who had really experienced a spiritual change would naturally join the Believers, who had discovered the true path to salvation. First printed in 1807 in Cincinnati, the book was reprinted several times in the nineteenth century.

McNemar's book intensified opposition from the New Lights. Youngs' book, published in Lebanon in 1808, increased the furor, just as Wright had predicted. Called *The Testimony of Christ's Second Appearing*, the book was circulated first to the Believers and those in the mission fields. After a few years, the book—and sometimes incorrect assumptions about it—circulated among the general public, where Shaker adversaries predictably attacked it. A common criticism was that Shakers had supplanted the Bible as the word of God with the *Testimony*. Opponents derogatorily called the book the Shaker bible. Despite the

Travel trunk found at Union Village

public's misconceptions about the *Testimony*, Believers used it extensively to teach and reinforce their faith. Three more editions were published by the middle of the 19th century.

While *The Kentucky Revival* was more narrowly focused and slim at 131 pages, the *Testimony* took on a larger task in over 600 pages. Youngs explained the sect's early history; discoursed on theology; defended its teachings as the only way to salvation; and counseled the Believers on how to conduct their lives and remain faithful. As planned, great emphasis was placed on Lee's role in the church. She was portrayed as the female completion of the Christ spirit. The authors reasoned that Jesus, by himself, could not achieve God's goals any more than Adam had been able to achieve a new race without Eve. It seemed logical to them that a spiritual Adam and Eve were needed to lead the church. Lee had been freed of her carnal nature by Christ to become a truly spiritual maternal figure who could help others achieve purity and salvation. A father figure was also needed, resulting in joint male-female leadership in the church. In the same way that Lee and Joseph Meacham cared for the entire membership, each family elder and eldress took on a parental role to support his or her "children," the members.[14]

B elievers at Turtle Creek were convinced that the *Testimony's* message was absolutely vital to gaining converts. It was also a bold strategy that reinforced how deeply committed they were to Shakerism. Asking average people—farmers and tradesmen—to accept celibacy and give up private property was a huge sacrifice. Asking those same people to accept Lee as the second coming of Christ was an intellectual challenge for which they often were not prepared. Faith had to bridge the gap. While Shaker missionaries were not deceptive about Lee, they at first emphasized other aspects of the faith. Gradually, they taught the converts more about Lee as part of their induction into the sect. Publication of the *Testimony* publicly accorded her the prominence that the Believers had long given her.

Missionary efforts in the West began even before the *Testimony*. From the time that Bates, Meacham, and Youngs chose Turtle Creek as their base in 1805, outreach efforts were underway. During that first summer in Warren County, the easterners enlisted their new brethren to carry out mission work. As more sisters moved to Ohio from the East, pairs of women began to accompany the men on some of the trips. The most intensive period of mission work lasted until 1826. Turtle Creek Believers succeeded in establishing five more major Shaker communities in Ohio and Kentucky. Three other fledging villages were established, but gradually disbanded to be absorbed into the larger settlements. In the 1850s, land was purchased in Clinton County, Ohio, in hopes of starting a new village, but plans were eventually abandoned. Near the end of the century, leaders unsuccessfully tried to establish colonies in Georgia.

Earliest proselytizing occurred in areas where McNemar had a following. Christians there sought fulfillment of the changes that began in the Kentucky revival. In late June 1805, Benjamin Youngs and David Spinning visited a settlement on Eagle Creek in Adams County, Ohio, where John Dunlavy had a congregation about 60 miles east of Cincinnati. Eagle Creek, close to present-day West Union, became a frequent stop for the missionaries as they traveled from Warren County to Kentucky. McNemar and Issachar Bates also visited the people there in July. Dunlavy converted by the end of the month, bringing several of his members into the sect. By autumn, Youngs and John Meacham visited Straight Creek, Ohio, (present-day Georgetown in nearby Brown County) and preached to potential converts there. Small communities of Believers developed at both sites. Union Village leaders planned to purchase 1,000 acres halfway between Eagle and Straight creeks to establish a larger village. But five years later, many converts had left the sect and those who stayed had difficulty adapting. "They unwisely run wild at their meetings for want of a guide," a missionary complained after one visit.[15] By 1811, when the combined communities totaled only 150 people, leaders decided to move some members to Warren County, and others to new communities that were being developed at Busro, Indiana, and Pleasant Hill, Kentucky.[16]

Kentuckians quickly contacted the Shakers, who responded immediately. In a letter written in the spring of 1806 to residents in Mercer and Shelby counties, Kentucky, the Ohio leaders spoke of salvation in comfortably familiar terms. "The blessed Jesus" is identified as the Saviour and the Son of God. The assertion that He had already reappeared and was about to separate the righteous from the unrighteous must have been startling. Lee was not mentioned as the second appearing, but a strong warning was given to embrace celibacy. Like Jesus, Believers were to resist temptation and remain pure.[17]

The Ohioans first visited several farmers near Shawnee Run in Mercer County, Kentucky, in 1805. Believers began to meet regularly the following year, and farmer Elisha Thomas donated 140 acres to begin a settlement. In 1807, a delegation from Mercer County visited Turtle Creek, seeking support and spiritual instruction. The first stone building was erected near Shawnee Run at the community called Pleasant Hill in 1809. In 1814, Believers there signed a covenant. John Meacham became the first elder of the new community.[18]

Pleasant Hill is best known in Shaker history as the birthplace of *The Manifesto*, published by Elder John Dunlavy in 1818. His book examined Shaker belief and life in depth and explained in detail the rationale and implementation of Believers' communal economy. *The Manifesto* joined the *Testimony* and two other eastern books as the major Shaker works of the early nineteenth century. The third was *Testimonies of the Life, Character, Revelations and Doctrines of Our Ever Blessed Mother Ann Lee, and the Elders with Her*, which gave personal testimonies from people who had known Lee or been affected by her. It was published in 1816. The central ministry at New Lebanon appeared concerned that the newer western communities were publishing more than they were. Feeling that the westerners were asserting too much autonomy, the ministry became more involved with their projects. Easterners edited a second edition of the *Testimony*, which appeared in 1810. Wright attempted to be more involved in the publication of Dunlavy's *Manifesto* as well.[19] Logically, the central ministry would want to be fully informed and in agreement with any publication that purported to express Shaker theology. But future events would confirm the westerners' desire for more independence and the central ministry's determination to quell those desires. Two easterners published a fourth major book, *A Summary View of the Millennial Church*, in 1823. It expanded on topics discussed in the other three books, and established a set of 12 principles for which all Shakers were to strive.[20] Perhaps, on some level, *A Summary View* also balanced the publishing rivalry between East and West for a time.

> In making Union Village the bishopric, or headquarters, for all of the western settlements, the central ministry set the stage for an inevitable power struggle.

In making Union Village the bishopric, or headquarters, for all of the western settlements, the central ministry set the stage for an inevitable power struggle. While distance necessitated regional leaders on the frontier, the new settlements' loyalties would only be as strong as those of their elders and eldresses. The first elder and eldress of Union Village, who were the primary leaders for the entire West, were very loyal to their New Lebanon parents. Darrow showed his allegiance by choosing a name for the Turtle Creek settlement that linked it to New York. The public had taken to calling the community Shakertown, a practice that displeased the members. Darrow wanted to call the village West Union, in deference to the settlement's geographical location from its parent, but another Ohio town in Adams County had already taken that name, so Union Village was chosen. "The word union is precious and has a spiritual signification," Darrow noted in his recommendation to the central ministry, "so we think it the most beautiful [name]."[21] Union—consistent agreement and action—was a central concept of the United Society, and of the creation of frontier villages. Most of the new western communities then began to be named according to their location from Union Village.

Darrow and Farrington became the central ministry's voice on the frontier during the period. They conveyed and enforced New Lebanon's rules. They consulted the central ministry on a wide variety of matters, ranging from dealing with critics to establishing uniform clothing styles. They had authority to make routine decisions, but they were to seek New Lebanon's guidance on weighty issues. Their decisions could be altered, expanded, or countermanded by Lucy Wright. Action on theological questions and issues that affected the entire Society was the prerogative of New Lebanon. The central ministry gave its full approval to the expanding mission field.

A second Kentucky community began at about the same time as Pleasant Hill. Gaspar Springs, in Logan County, southwest of Bowling Green, had been the site of McNemar's first revival meetings in late 1800. The community began with a large land bequest from prosperous landowner Jesse McComb, and grew from there with Union Village's help and encouragement. McNemar, Bates, and Matthew Houston led missionary efforts. A meetinghouse was built in 1810 and the community was christened South Union. Benjamin Youngs became first elder in 1811. Union Village provided much needed material and spiritual aid over the years, particularly around 1813, when more than 50 brethren at Gaspar Springs perished from fever and influenza.[22]

Union Village trustees sent over $400 worth of supplies to South Union in 1819. Following the example of generosity that New Lebanon had shown them, trustees hoped the spirit of giving would be continued by South Union. "We teach them the way to be good is to do good—is not that right?" Ruth Farrington wrote to a New Lebanon friend. Her note also conveyed a sense of the enormity of the missionaries' task in the West: "I love all Mother's good obedient children wherever I have visited them in this part of the vineyard— and the vineyard is middling large thee may depend, so that it would weary thee stoutly to inspect every part of it and pull out all the evil weeds that are growing in it."[23]

Back in Ohio, the Montgomery County hamlet of Beaver Creek became the next Shaker community. Bates and Benjamin Youngs first visited the area in May 1805. McNemar soon visited as well, and added his persuasive preaching to theirs. By fall, a handful of Beaver Creek landowners had broken with John Thompson, the New Light pastor who opposed the Shakers. The landowners accepted the Shaker faith, and in March 1806, a Shaker order was established at the site, southeast of Dayton. Union Village leaders visited Beaver Creek frequently over the next few years. In 1810, they sent 27 men to help build a log meetinghouse. The community became increasingly self-sufficient over the next eight years with the addition of a gristmill, tannery, coopers' shop, woolen mill, and woodenware industry. Shakers there signed a covenant in

December 1818, and the village was rechristened Watervliet, after the New York settlement. Bates became lead elder there in 1824.[24]

The most troubled of all the early settlements was West Union at Busro Creek, Indiana. The Believers' experiences there demonstrated that they were willing to risk everything, including death, to bring their faith to the West. Fever, natural disasters, and impending war plagued the community from its conception. Believers endured many hardships and deaths because of their determination to establish a settlement on the banks of the Wabash River in Knox County. Bates, McNemar, and Youngs nearly died during a mission trip there in January 1808. The men, each equipped with a blanket and five days of provisions, set off on foot for the Indiana territory. The 235-mile trek took them through trackless wilderness and over bridgeless streams. Five days turned into 16, and they ran out of food. They survived by sharing a turkey caress found at a fox's den. They melted snow for drinking water and fashioned crude beds of brush on the snow. A squatter and his wife fed them venison, bear meat, and cornbread, and another settler treated their frostbitten feet. A camp of Miami Indians allowed them to partially dry their clothes at their fires. They arrived at Busro exhausted but heartened to find the people "steadfast in their faith to the gospel work."[25]

This zeal drew the Believers to Busro despite the fact that the area was prone to fever and malaria, and that a war between the United States and the Indians was imminent. At one service with a large group of people, "white, yellow, & black, the mighty power of God was there," wrote missionary Constant Mosely, who kept a diary of one Indiana trip in 1808. Familiar manifestations occurred: jerks, barking, dancing—"the whole multitude were in motion."[26]

At another service, the local people built fires to repel disease-carrying mosquitoes, and the missionaries preached from the dooryard. Blacks and whites alike accepted the Shaker message. At least one interracial couple was among the Busro converts.[27] No Indian converts were noted but because of the Shakers' hospitality, members of various tribes frequently visited. Back in Ohio, the Shakers actively courted a group of Shawnee Indians, including the rising young warrior, Tecumseh, to the dismay of many of their neighbors. Believers' reputations as pacifists and as friends of Indians followed them to Indiana and raised questions about their loyalty to the whites' government. Skirmishes between Indians and settlers still occurred, and war talk was in the air. That may have prompted Bates to remark that it would take "the wisest man on earth" to lead Busro.[28] Shakers believed that they were not to participate in worldly affairs such as politics and imperialism; their mission was a higher, spiritual calling. Their air of neutrality often irked their opponents, including those at Busro.

Believers finally decided to proceed with the settlement because of the converts' enthusiasm, cheap land, abundant waterpower, and the promise of protection and religious freedom from General William Henry Harrison, governor of the Indiana territory. Bates soon came to believe that the Shakers needed as much protection from whites as from Indians. Harrison promised both. A formidable Indian fighter, he was a lieutenant by 19, and captain in charge of Ft. Washington (later Cincinnati) by 24. By the time the West Union Shakers were dealing regularly with him in 1811, Harrison was 38 and had been governor of the territory for a decade. He was committed to protecting settlers and pushing the boundaries of the frontier westward. He guarded the Shakers' religious freedom, but he was no bureaucrat. Harrison was always a solider first and he was prepared for war.

Despite all obstacles, West Union Shakers proceeded with the settlement. In 1811, members of the struggling Eagle and Straight Creek communities, as well as some Believers from Red Bank, Kentucky, joined the community. Soon after the Believers began breaking ground and building cabins, skirmishes broke out nearby between Indians and soldiers until the settlers were so frightened they couldn't sleep at night. New rumors circulated that Believers were actually encouraging Indians to go to war against the whites. When several Indians appeared in Busro in June 1811, requesting that the Shaker smiths repair hoes and other agricultural tools for them, suspicions of collaboration were further aroused. Believers went to Harrison for counsel.

The general refused to allow Believers to repair most of the tools, and he accused the Indians of planning to use many of the items in war. He did allow Believers to provide food for the Indians. Bates wrote sympathetically of the Indians' circumstances. When the Indians found the majority of the tools not repaired, they were "much grieved at the white people's jealousy...these hungry creatures were about us nearly three weeks, singing and dancing to the Great Spirit...all peaceable...and never, to our knowledge, took the value of one cucumber without leave," Bates wrote.[29] In contrast, the militia helped itself to what it needed, both from the Shakers and other settlers. Some of the whites threatened to kill Believers if they refused to fight against the Indians, Bates added. Harrison soon ordered the Indians out of the area and sent a party of soldiers to escort them out of the Shaker settlement to prevent pilfering, but this, Bates scoffed, "was like setting the dog to watch the butter—for they did more mischief in one night than the Indians had done all summer."[30]

The Believers' next encounter with a group of Indians, the Potawatomis, demonstrated their belief in non-violence and their continual bad luck in Indiana. Samuel Swan McClelland, a West Union member, explained what happened that fall in his diary (*Memorandum of Remarkable Events*). One fine September day, Indians stole four of the Shakers' best wagon horses. James Brownfield, a wagon driver; Abraham Jones, a black man who was an Indian translator, and Robbins, a hired man, set out on fresh horses to recover the stolen ones. On the third day out, the Shakers caught up with the Indians. They admitted they had no guns and would not fight, but demanded that the horses be returned. The Indians refused and started loading their guns. The Shakers took off on their horses and outran the Indians for eight miles until their horses slowed down in a muddy swamp.

The Potawatomis got close enough to fire their rifles. The Shakers jumped off their horses, and ran for their lives, leaving behind the three fresh horses, saddles, blankets, overcoats and provisions. By the time they got out of the swamp, their hats and shoes were gone, and by the time they hiked through shoulder-high brush and briers to get back to West Union, they were "pretty well-famished and almost naked."[31] And out six horses.

As the men straggled back into Busro, the first returnee reported that he thought the Indians had shot one of his companions. By the time the other two arrived, unwounded, "the loss of the horses felt very small to me," Bates wrote to Union Village. He was thankful that the Believers had not been pressured into fighting, and

William Henry Harrison

reflected philosophically that the incident had at least "cooled the prejudice of the world concerning our friendship with the Indians."[32] He also stressed that the theft was the act of a particular group of individuals, and not indicative of Indians in general. Bates, like most of the western Believers, still hoped for converts among them.

The incident also had an economic effect on the Shakers. The loss of the horses and supplies, valued at $500, burdened the struggling settlement. Two deadly outbreaks of fever, a string of unexpected earthquakes, and crop failures also weakened the community. Civil unrest and hunger finally drove them temporarily out of Indiana in 1812. "It was impossible to keep the Gospel between two such fires," David Darrow wrote, "for if [Shakers] escaped the tomahawk, they must battle with famine for the Army would without all doubt...devour all their living and if [Shakers] should get any money for it there was none [grain] to be bought in all the territory."[33]

> The Believers stood out because of their old fashion clothing and King James English, still favoring yea, nay, thee, and thou...

Members moved to Union Village, Pleasant Hill, and South Union until the War of 1812 ended. They returned to West Union in 1814 to face more hardships. Fever was a constant threat. Several people succumbed to it over the years, including Eldress Ruth Darrow, David's daughter. Frequent flooding of the Wabash and low-lying areas contributed to the unhealthy environment, noted a worldly visitor in 1816. At the time, approximately 200 people lived here in four families, occupying 10 log structures. The Believers stood out because of their old-fashioned clothing and King James English, still favoring yea, nay, thee, and thou, the traveler noted. He was skeptical of Believers' celibacy and dancing, but supported their right to practice their religion. He indicated that the Believers were generally accepted by their neighbors, "In their dealings they are esteemed as very honest and exemplary. Until within a few months they entertained travelers without any compensation; but the influx has become so great that they have found it necessary to depart from that practice."[34] Tolerance from their neighbors encouraged the settlement to continue when common sense would have dictated otherwise.

The next western settlement took place in a much more peaceful setting. In 1822, a small community was gathered at Warrensville, Ohio, near Cleveland. Ralph Russell, a Warrensville farmer, had visited Union Village in 1821 to learn about the Shaker faith. He was extremely impressed with the Believers, and converted. While at Turtle Creek, he had a vision showing him where to build in his own community: "I saw a strong clear ray of light proceeding from the northwest in a perfectly straight horizontal line until it reached a spot near my log cabin. Then it arose in a strong, erect column and became a beautiful tree."[35] That spot, according to the vision, was where the Center House should be built. Returning home, Russell shared his enthusiastic faith and vision with friends and family.

McNemar, Elder Richard W. Pelham, and James Hodge, accepted Russell's invitation to visit Warrensville to preach, and to teach converts. In addition to land which members donated, Union Village trustees purchased acreage to enlarge the settlement, now called North Union. The Center House was built according to Russell's vision. At the start, the majority of the converts were from the large Russell family, but others eventually joined as well and the settlement began to build an economy based on light manufacturing and millwork.

The last major Shaker village established in Ohio was Whitewater (White Water), west of Cincinnati in Hamilton County. A Methodist revival in the community in 1823 left some of the devout hungering for a new way. One young woman, Miriam Agnew, traveled to Union Village to join the Shakers that spring and entreated elders to send missionaries back to her family and friends. Pelham headed to Whitewater and soon gathered the nucleus of a new community, including Agnew's husband and brother. The Whitewater community was small and poor. Union Village elders decided to move another group to Whitewater that same year from Darby Plains in Union County, Ohio. The Darby community had been meeting since a New Light revival in 1818. In 1820, after meetings with McNemar and Union Village's Calvin Morrell, the Darby group joined the Shakers. Union Village continued to support Darby Plains, and in 1823 sent members to help build a meetinghouse. Union Village continued to nurture the struggling colony for several more years.[36]

The extent and success of the western missionary efforts is impressive. Within the first few years, seven settlements were planted. The rapid growth paralleled that of the eastern Shaker communities that developed around Watervliet, New York, in the late eighteenth century. In both cases, the development can be linked to the missionaries' zeal and to people who were seeking more spiritual assurance. The western converts believed the Shakers offered truth and comfort. Whether they would continue to believe that remained to be seen.

"The little flock...are now all together."

—David Darrow and
John Meacham, 1806

Top: Poultry house at Union Village
Right: Union Village Schoolhouse

❧ Chapter Three ❧
Building The Community

While mission work flourished on the frontier, forces at home shaped Union Village's identity from 1805 to 1810. The most important was David Darrow's strong leadership. Darrow inspired the followers to work harder than they ever had worked before, and to accept a demanding faith and lifestyle. His people proved to be independent-minded and innovative from the start, ignoring the world's gossip about them while they sought converts. Soon the Believers created a united

membership and developed a self-sufficient operation in rural Warren County. They added more buildings to their growing village, educated area children, set up craftsmen's shops, farmed the countryside, built sawmills, and tended to one another's spiritual needs.

Uniting new members proved to be the most crucial achievement for the settlement's future. The task was not easy. Becoming a full member of the United Society of Believers required accepting a radical faith, transforming family relationships, and merging into an altruistic communal society. The desire to take the first step, along with the support of the eastern brethren, somewhat eased the second part of the process. But it was Darrow who was chiefly responsible for creating a cohesive, self-sufficient community.

Unity at the temporal level began with the most visible, ubiquitous aspect of life—personal appearance. Far from being trivial, adherence to a dress code established identity. It distanced the world, and connected newcomers, who began to dress alike regardless of their previous social class. Clothing also demonstrated

Cobbler's Table

how communal living affected daily life. Like their rural neighbors, the Believers wore homemade clothing of linen and wool, which they produced. But the quality and quantity of their clothing was much better. One homemaker, sewing linens and clothing for a larger family, in addition to her innumerable other tasks, could not match the productivity of Shaker tailors and seamstresses. At Union Village, an entire shop was soon devoted to clothing production. Brothers and sisters who worked there had the freedom to concentrate on textiles and sewing. They learned styles and techniques from their eastern counterparts, and then trained younger members so that skills were passed along. As a result, clothes were better made and produced more easily in larger quantities.

Most of the early western converts were of modest means and the homespun clothing they brought with them into the community fit in with what other Believers wore. As their old clothes wore out, they received new ones made for them in the tailors' shop. Members' initials were embroidered in each article of their clothing. Ann Lee's emphasis on unity and moderation resulted in an understated, functional wardrobe. Members had some choice in fabrics and colors but could not choose garments that were not readily accessible to everyone. No one was to look finer than another.[1]

Both male and female fashions echoed society's post-colonial trend away from excess and affectation, and toward utilitarian clothing. In place of knee breeches and long, full coats, men wore long trousers and shorter jackets. Still, the men's clothing apparently wasn't completely up to date (McNemar specifically took note of the "old-fashioned" appearance of the first eastern missionaries). By 1806, the brothers wore white linen shirts, blue waistcoats (in homage to the missionaries), gray coats, and khaki trousers. The women were a bit more progressive. Their dresses featured a more modern silhouette: slimmer skirts, three-quarter length sleeves, and collarless necklines. The dresses were easier to work in than more old-fashioned, voluminous gowns, and safer with no long sleeves or full skirts to accidentally drag into the kitchen fire. Dresses were usually black or blue. To protect their dresses, the sisters wore blue and white striped smocks as well as blue and white checked aprons. Around their shoulders they wore a black silk kerchief. (A bit later, the sisters made their own silk.) Their hair was neatly gathered under a simple bonnet, made of a pasteboard foundation covered with silk. Men wore broad-brimmed hats of wool or fur, depending on the season. Cloaks and overcoats (called surtouts) were woolen. Children's clothing was similar to the adults', although some other muted colors, such as a soft red left over from dying rug material, might also be used. Each person had a relatively substantial wardrobe of work clothes, travel clothes, and Sabbath best. The style of their clothing was not radically different from their neighbors but the quality, and the impact of seeing masses of people dressed almost identically, attracted attention. Some envied the Shakers' apparent wealth while others saw their "uniform" as another sign of a brainwashed cult.

Another item that set the Believers apart was shoes. At the beginning of the nineteenth century, most children and many adults in rural areas did not have shoes. They were a luxury for the wealthy and a necessity for adult males doing rigorous outdoor work. At Union Village, however, a group of tanners and cobblers provided shoes for everyone. These craftsmen, recruited or trained from the membership, operated their own shops where they worked most of the day. Their shoes were simple but better than those worn by many local farmers. Calfskin shoes were secured with laces of cotton or leather. The heels of women's shoes were made of wood, and covered with leather. Soles were covered with leather and the uppers were made of cloth.[2]

In addition to appearance, Darrow unified members' daily routines.

Members breakfasted at 6 a.m., dined at noon, and supped at 6 p.m. year round. They rose at 4 a.m., sang and prayed silently together at 4:30 a.m., then did chores before breakfast. Daily work was divided by sex, much as in secular society. Women performed most of the indoor tasks, and men did the majority of the outside work. Each person stripped his bed in the morning to air the linens, and then sisters came in to make the beds while other sisters prepared breakfast. Each sister was assigned to look after a particular brother: making his bed, mending his clothing, delivering clean laundry. Brothers fed livestock and milked, although sisters often gathered the eggs. Evenings were similarly organized although Darrow fretted that he could not get the schedule down to the minute. Evening worship gatherings, or meetings, began at 8 p.m. and ended at various times. Afterwards, people retreated to the tiring rooms (bedrooms), which were shared by at least two members. There they rested, talked, knelt for evening prayer, and went to bed. Darrow worried about people having too much unstructured free time in the evenings and wished for shops where they could occupy their free time. "If we should make them set up until 10 o'clock in the evening, they would either be in mischief among them that are to work, or they would be sleeping and slugging in their rooms and that would bring loss upon their souls," he wrote.[3]

> Daily work was divided by sex, much as in secular society. Women performed most of the indoor tasks, and men did the majority of the outside work.

The strict supervision of Believers' time had both practical and spiritual motives. Ann Lee had admonished the first members to avoid sloth: "The Devil tempts others, but an idle person tempts the Devil. When you are at work, doing your duty as a gift to God, the Devil can have no power over you, because there is no room for temptation."[4] Take away time to sin and fewer offenses were possible, especially for converts who might have been more easily tempted to revert to worldly ways. The dedication to productive use of time reflected the motto "hands to work and hearts to God." Time was a precious gift from God to be used productively. Slugging (being lazy) was an unappreciative waste of this gift that ultimately led to corruption. Physical labor was required of all adults, even the elders and eldresses. Pauses for rest and worship were built into each day. The goal was to allow everyone to contribute to the general good without overworking.

s the new community evolved, more land was added to the original
160-acre holdings of Richard McNemar and Malcolm Worley. Many of
their neighbors were happy to sell and move away from the Believers.
Knowing the easterners were eager to buy, some landowners demanded—and
received—twelve dollars an acre for land that otherwise sold for three dollars.[5]
By 1830, Union Village had amassed a number of sturdy buildings on 4,500
acres. Raw construction materials were plentiful in the Miami Valley. Native
walnut, oak, and cherry were frequently used in construction. Large brick
structures began to be built in 1819 when the village had the manpower to
make and fire its own bricks. Believers proved to be excellent town planners,
selecting logical sites for shops, dwellings, and the meetinghouse. As their
needs changed over the years, they constructed new buildings, changed the
function of older structures, or moved existing buildings by mounting them
upon rollers. Oxen and horses pulled them to other sites. As the buildings'
purposes changed, so did the names.

The first dwelling built for the easterners in 1806 became known as the
South House. That August, Peter Pease noted in the church journal that a
smith's shop had been built for Daniel Moseley, a few rods north of the elder's
dwelling. Several more smithies were added over the next few years to produce
hardware, nails, latches and hinges, horseshoes, wagon fittings, iron railings,
wrought-iron building numbers, and iron-plated heating and cooking stoves.
A simple sawmill, powered by oxen, was built as one of the first construction
projects. In 1807 a dam was built on Dick's Creek (later called Shaker Creek) to
allow for a more efficient water-powered sawmill. By that fall, workers finished
the second story of the South House.[6] The village was beginning to take shape
and become self-sufficient.

A cemetery was started in April 1807, when Prudence Farrington, one
of the original eastern sisters, died. She had been in Ohio not quite a year.
The church record does not list the cause of Farrington's death but one sister
recorded finding another woman suffering from "a violent dysentery, high
fever, and inflammation of the stomach and many bad symptoms."[7] That sister
survived but the death and illnesses were harsh reminders that the hardships
of the frontier were much more than inconveniences. A large group attended
Farrington's funeral, according to Pease, but he gave no other details of the first
Shaker funeral in the West.[8] Typically, Believers' funerals were simple services
that focused on the soul's immortality. A procession of members escorted a
plain pine casket to the burying ground where prayers and songs were offered.

Sometimes—particularly in the western communities—songs were composed in honor of the deceased. Shakers believed the soul could remain actively involved in the lives of the living, and there are many accounts of divine spirits attending funeral services. Grave markers, when used, were small slabs containing the deceased's initials, age, and date of death. Cedar trees marked some later graves at Union Village. A circa-1807 drawing of the village shows the cemetery located north of the site of a planned meetinghouse. A small drawing of a grave features what appears to be a plant growing and the caption "Prudence's Grave."[9]

That year, the Warren County board of commissioners opened a public road that ran north and south through the village. The county road was a reminder that the world would constantly travel through the community. As autonomous as the village became, it was always a part of the larger society. Also in 1807, two new families and dwellings were established. The Square House Family was in charge of the first sawmill, a tannery, and a fulling mill, used to clean wool with heavy fuller's earth. The Grist Mill Family operated the gristmill, a linseed oil mill, and another sawmill that was added in 1808.

Work on the meetinghouse began in the winter of 1808; the first church meeting was held there on December 24, 1809. In 1810, the brothers hauled huge cherry logs to a site opposite the new meetinghouse, and built another dwelling called the Center House. This was home to the "more progressed" Believers. A Shaker historian wrote that the dwelling was to serve as a "Center of Union to which all the other prospective Families were to look both for Instruction, in absence of the ministry, and examples in faithfulness in all good order, purity, love, and sympathy at all times."[10]

Some dwellings featured the exterior twin doors for men and women that were common to eastern Shaker architecture. All of the dwellings featured separate staircases leading to the brothers' and sisters' respective retiring rooms. Each room was bordered with utilitarian pegboards, first called clothespins due to their primary use. To prevent fires, kitchens were in the rear of the dwellings and detached from the living quarters.[11] Fire was always a threat. Pease's journal notes that a barn belonging to the elders' family was nearly consumed by fire on November 29, 1807, and that Worley's log kitchen was destroyed by fire the following January. Some of the many fires at the village over the years proved to be arsons.

A burst of construction during the first five years allowed most of the Believers to move into the village and limit their dealings with the world. Creation of a school in 1808 further solidified the community. John Woods was the first teacher for the boys, who attended school during the winter. Malinda Watts taught the first summer session for the girls. Each term lasted four months, an organization borrowed from the world's schools. Early schools in the New England colonies had offered separate sessions for boys and girls, and the pattern was followed when Midwest states began establishing schools. Few girls attended in the late 1700s and early 1800s in the United States. They were not forbidden from most schools but were not encouraged to attend, either. Parents decided the matter. The major difference in Shaker education was that Believers advocated that all children go to school.[12] If males and females had equal value to God, they should be treated equally in all things, including education.

Studies focused on three areas: academics, religious and moral instruction, and vocational skills taught through apprenticeships in the village. Books were scarce. Children learned to read from the New Testament and Webster's spelling book. Lessons were similar to those taught in the world's schools. The use of the Bible as text was not unprecedented. Colonial students frequently learned to read from the Bible, and literacy was often advocated as a means of spreading religion. Practical skills were stressed in the Shaker classroom; lessons were limited to spelling, grammar, reading, writing, arithmetic, and occasionally a little geography. Science was at first ignored in the curriculum because Shakers believed it contradicted Biblical teachings. They were not alone. Other Christian denominations shared this attitude.[13]

Despite limitations in the curriculum, Union Village children received a better education than many of their contemporaries. The Northwest Ordinance of 1785 established the idea of public schools, but implementation took decades. Lebanon, the county seat, did not have a public school system until 1830 and did not have a public school building until 1847. Public schools were segregated. Not until 1854 did a school for black children open in Lebanon. There was no racial segregation at Union Village. Another important distinction was the cost of education. While schooling was free to Believers' children, it was not until the mid-nineteenth century that all public schools in Ohio were free to students. The earliest schools, in the East and West, had been subscription schools where parents paid a fee to a teacher who set up school on his own.[14]

L earning was not limited to children. Women attended night school by 1828. Believers wanted to be literate enough to read and write about spiritual matters, and to communicate with one another. Evening classes focused on spelling, followed by an emphasis in reading and writing, and thirdly, in arithmetic and grammar. McNemar compiled a grammar textbook that was printed at Union Village and used throughout the West to educate adults and children. The cover of the eleven-page booklet bears an appropriately pragmatic saying: "He that would learn without good grammar rules is like a tradesman working without tools."[15] The structure and ideals of Shaker society led to a more progressive view of basic education. While evening education classes for males were offered in the world by the 1820s,

Child's Chair

night school for females did not become widespread until about the middle of the century.[16] Where the Believers were weakest, by secular standards, was in their attitude toward higher education. Although young men—and some young women—in the United States had begun to attend colleges and universities, Believers strongly discouraged their own from furthering their education. They believed the knowledge of God was far superior to any secular knowledge. Sending a Believer away to college would conflict with uniformity in a cohesive community. They did, however, hire outsiders to train members in special skills, including medicine and dentistry.

The communal society also provided other benefits. New Lebanon's financial backing gave the Believers a head start over what individual farmers or businessmen could accomplish on their own. Consolidating expenses and labor led to prosperity—and to suspicion and jealousy among some of Union Village's neighbors, who already gossiped about the Believers' lifestyle. One of the most controversial Shaker practices was raising all the children together in one family. A Children's Order was established at Turtle Creek in 1809. Several sisters were assigned to this order to care for youngsters who entered the community with their parents or as orphans. No one minded Believers caring for unwanted children but many people objected to the separation of parent and child. Parents, who assumed new roles as brothers and sisters in Christ, concentrated on their spiritual lives and their assigned jobs. The children focused on their chores, schoolwork, and religious training. Because they were all children of God, no preference was to be given to biological relationships. Lofty in concept, the principle proved difficult to enforce.

Many of the mob attacks and some of the defections that occurred at Union Village in its early years were over the custody or welfare of a child. Each time, the public concerns over treatment of children at the village proved groundless. The children were strictly disciplined, as were most children of that period. And Believers did use the fear of Hell to convince children to behave. But there is no evidence that the children were disciplined any more harshly than their worldly counterparts. Union Village's future was in its children, and in many cases they were probably better cared for and better educated than those in the world. At the very least, they learned to read and write, and acquired at least one vocation as they worked beside adults. Whether they ultimately chose the security of life at the village or returned to the world, the children had the skills to make their way in life. But that held little comfort for some parents and children who deeply missed their family ties. When girls were 14 and boys were 16, they left the Children's Order and were placed with one of the other families. When they reached adulthood, they had three options: become full members and sign the church covenant; remain in the community but not sign the covenant, or leave Union Village entirely.

Organizing members into families and orders was often controversial, but central to Shaker life. Joseph Meacham had developed the system at New Lebanon in the late 1700s. In accord with God's dual male and female nature, an elder and an eldress—Darrow and Farrington in this case— led each bishopric. The pair was also first in the ministry at Union Village; each had a second person to support and assist them. Each family also had their own elder and eldress to supervise members' spiritual welfare and personal conduct. Open confession of sin was an important tenet of faith, and part of the job of an elder or eldress was to hear confession from a Believer of the same sex, and to give spiritual guidance. The need for educated women as well as men was inherent in the hierarchy. Eldresses had to be literate and familiar with theology to fulfill their roles properly. Good writing and math skills were also necessary for the deaconesses, the women who took care of the temporal needs of the other women in their respective families. One or two trustees controlled the entire village's finances and commerce with the world, but each family had its own deacons and deaconesses to supervise their respective affairs. Similarly, each family had its own dwelling, barns, and shops. Shops were sometimes all male or all female. In some cases, the men and women worked cooperatively, but usually on separate tasks. Families also bartered with one another within the village for goods and services.[17]

Members were assigned to families according to their spiritual progress and seniority. At Union Village, the senior family, called the Church or Center family, was the original group of easterners. Other families were obedient to the Church family. Families lived in different orders, based on their spiritual progress. The Gathering Order was composed of people who wanted to become Believers. As the village was being formed, these people at first lived outside the community, but as more dwellings were built, they moved into the village. Members of the Gathering Order retained their property and maintained more traditional family relationships while they were instructed in the faith. After this apprenticeship of sorts, they progressed into a Junior Order. There they exchanged their biological families for spiritual families, and generally donated their time and services to the community, although they might retain personal property. Members who joined the most advanced group, the Senior Order, were those who dedicated all their time, talents, and property to the community by signing the covenant.[18]

> Members were assigned to families according to their spiritual progress and seniority. At Union Village, the senior family, called the Church or Center family, was the original group of easterners. Other families were obedient to the Church family.

This structure provided order within the community and gave both sides time to consider membership. Members who signed the covenant gave up all rights to property for themselves and their heirs. Their property merged into the village's holdings, called the joint interest. Many Shaker adversaries were outside family members who felt cheated out of their inheritance. Members who left the United Society were given some remittance in cash or goods commensurate with what they had brought into the community, but that didn't always satisfy their relatives.[19] Leaders tried to ensure that all prospective members were independent souls—not enslaved, not indentured, and not involved in domestic disputes. Still, custody questions led to some ugly confrontations. "Caty Reubert's child stolen from the place of worship today by a wicked man," Pease noted tersely of one early incident.[20] Husbands generally had jurisdiction over their wives and children in that era. However, the Believers considered a wife's custody rights as valid as a husband's, particularly if the woman wanted to become a Shaker.

Later, the Believers took even more precautions against domestic disputes by having prospective members complete an "Investigator's Application." Very pointed questions were asked, including: If separated from your wife or husband, is separation legal? Is anybody dependent on you for support? Can you liquidate all your debts? Do you use tobacco? Do you use intoxicating liquors? In moderation or excess?[21] At one point, members were required to sign a type of loyalty oath where they promised not to create anarchy in the community. The agreement also stated that if members did decide to leave, they would do so peacefully and with advance notice enough so that they could be compensated for wealth they had brought into the community. They also pledged never to seek claims or additional compensation from the United Society.[22]

Despite the precautions, Believers were unable to avoid problems and lawsuits. They were also unable to stop the rumors circulated by opponents. Believers kept extensive records, published frequently, and opened their villages to the public in part to try to quell rumors. They often painted an overly positive picture of their lives, but they did not mask their beliefs, even when they created public hostility.

Top: The Shakers' relationship with Tecumseh, the Shawnee warrior, led to problems.
Right: Corner cupboards like this one were only found in Union Village and Pleasant Hill, Kentucky.

ॐ Chapter Four ॐ
Defending The Community

When Union Village grew between 1805 and 1810, so did the opposition to it. The believers' efforts to reach people outside mainstream society, and their insistence on reshaping biological families into spiritual families, alienated many of their neighbors. These angry and frightened opponents turned to violence to oust the Shakers.

In 1807, the Believers began a relationship with a group of Shawnee Indians that resulted in "endless trouble."[1] Believers had been interested in Indians since the Mohegans befriended Ann Lee during her first winter in Niskeyuna in 1776. The Mohegans were fierce warriors who had battled other Indians and Europeans, yet they treated the small band of Shakers graciously. The Indians gave them food and showed them how to grow sweet corn and harvest maple syrup. From the Mohegans, the Believers learned how to dry seeds, make herbal medicines, and weave baskets, all of which became staples of their later industries.[2] When the Believers heard of a religious revival among

the Shawnee Indians in Darke County, Ohio, about 75 miles northwest of Warren County, they hoped it might be similar to the Kentucky revival. They hurried to befriend the Shawnee.

Since the Treaty of Greenville ended open warfare between whites and members of the Miami Confederation in 1795, the Shawnee had lived quietly in the Miami Valley. By 1805, one young warrior, named Tekamthi (Tecumseh), was developing into a leader among his people. His younger brother, Lalawethika, often accompanied him. After a dissipated youth, Lalawethika began to have trances in which the Great Spirit spoke to him. Because of his dreams and visions, Lalawethika became known as the Prophet. Tecumseh encouraged his brother's new spirituality. Like the Shakers, the Shawnees believed in a deity who created life, and in an afterlife.[3] By the time the Believers met the Shawnee band, other Indians who had had known white missionaries had exposed the Prophet to additional Christian ideas. Two of those concepts, confession and Hell, were fundamental to Shaker theology. Both groups also believed in divine revelation. Not all of the Shawnees approved of the Prophet's religious revival, so in 1806 he moved his followers from a larger settlement at Wapakoneta, Ohio, southwest to Greenville to form a new village. The village was built about three miles south of the ruins of Fort Greenville, near a large prairie. The Indians planted corn at the edge of the prairie, and built 57 small houses and a large council house, 150 by 34 feet.[4]

Darrow, McNemar, and Benjamin Youngs set out to visit Greenville in March 1807. They knew that other Christian missions to the Indians had been largely unsuccessful but reasoned that the time and approach had not been right in those instances. McNemar, who wrote a detailed account of the visits between the Believers and Shawnees, noted that many had questioned "whether God would not convert the heathen in some way different from what had hitherto been laid out by man: probably move them by his Spirit to flow to the Church as soon as she was prepared to receive and instruct them."[5] The Believers disregarded growing political and territorial tensions between the U.S. government and the Indians to focus on spiritual and charitable concerns.

When the three missionaries arrived at Greenville after a six-day trip, they greeted a group of men standing near a tent, and asked if they were friendly. One of the men who spoke English assured them that they were all brothers. While Tecumseh and the Prophet were at a sugar camp where maple syrup was being processed about four miles away, the Shakers began asking the group about their beliefs. They learned that the Prophet conversed with God in dreams and then passed along divine instructions. Eventually, the Indians consented to take the visitors to the sugar camp. There they found between 30 and 40 Indians, including George Blue Jacket. He was the son of the famous Chief Blue Jacket who had led the Indian coalition against General Anthony Wayne at the Battle of Fallen Timbers in 1794. George spoke excellent English, and was very protective of the Prophet. He told them the Prophet was ill and could not see them. It soon became apparent that the Indians feared the visitors would mock the Prophet's beliefs, "that

> The Believers didn't understand a word—Blue Jacket said he could not translate the message adequately—but they were impressed with his sincerity and his listeners' attentiveness.

ministers of the white people, would not believe what he said, but counted it foolish and laughed at it, therefore [the Prophet] could not talk."[6]

The missionaries, who often had been mocked for their beliefs and style of worship, assured Blue Jacket that they were not like the other white ministers. He asked if they believed people could know God in their hearts without going to school and learning to read. The Believers affirmed the idea, adding that such knowledge was the best type. They waited while he went into a tent where the Prophet rested. After an hour, the Prophet emerged and gathered a circle of about 30 people. He spoke for half an hour. The Believers didn't understand a word— Blue Jacket said he could not translate the message adequately—but they were impressed with his sincerity and his listeners' attentiveness. The translator tried to summarize the Prophet's story. The Prophet had previously been a doctor but was very sinful. All that changed two years earlier when he received a vision while tending the sick at Attawa [Ottawa]:

> *...he appeared to be travelling along a road, and came to where it forked— the right hand...led to happiness...the left to misery.... He saw vast crowds going swift along the left hand road, and great multitudes in each of the houses, under different degrees of judgment and misery.... At the last house their torment appeared inexpressible; under which he heard them scream, cry pitiful, and roar like the falls of a river. He was afterwards taken along the right hand way, which was all interspersed with flowers of delicious smell, and showed a house at the end of it where was everything beautiful, sweet and pleasant....[7]*

This very Anglicized vision of Heaven and Hell encouraged the men to question the Prophet further. McNemar recorded some of the conversation:

Q. *Do you believe that all mankind are going away from the Good Spirit by wicked works?*

A. *Yes; that is what we believe. And the prophet feels great pity for all.*

Q. *Do you believe that the Great Spirit once made himself known to the world, by a man that was called Christ?*

A. *Yes, we believe it, and the Good Spirit has showed our prophet what has been in many generations, and he says he wants to talk with some white people about these things.*

Q. *What sins does your prophet speak most against?*

A. *Witchcraft, poisoning people, fighting, murdering, drinking whisky, and beating their wives because they will not have children. All such as will not leave off these go to Eternity—he knows all bad people that commit fornication, and can tell it all from seven years old.*[8]

The Shawnee faithful were to confess their sins to the Prophet and four chiefs. They had learned about confession from some Wyandot Indians who had converted to Roman Catholicism at Detroit. Then the Indians questioned the whites about their own sect. The Indians "rejoiced" to learn that some whites did not drink alcohol. McNemar, Darrow, and Youngs were encouraged by the Shawnees' willingness to talk with them. They seemed intent on that first visit to learn about the Indians' beliefs and practices rather than to proselytize. The Believers were also concerned about their physical well-being, and asked if they had enough provisions. The Shawnees told them that food was scarce due to the numbers of Indians visiting Greenville. "The only meal we saw them eat was a turkey divided among thirty or forty," McNemar noted. "And the only relief we could afford them was ten dollars for the purpose of buying corn."[9]

As the visitors prepared to leave the sugar camp that evening, they witnessed a memorable scene, dramatically recalled by McNemar. Under a full moon, a solitary speaker stood up and solemnly addressed his people, his remarks punctuated by loud affirmations from the crowd. "On this occasion," McNemar wrote, "our feelings were like Jacob's when he cried out, 'How dreadful is this place! Surely the Lord is in this place!' And the world knows it not."[10] The men spent the night at the village. They awoke to a morning service of thanksgiving that lasted nearly an hour. As the main speaker addressed the community from the southeast corner of the village, the Indians, still in their individual homes, responded at the appropriate intervals. Once again, the Believers were moved by the simplicity and sincerity of the service:

> *We felt as if we were among the tribes of Israel, on their march to Canaan.*
> *Their simplicity and unaffected zeal for the increase of the work of the Good*
> *Spirit—their ardent desires for the salvation of their unbelieving kindred,*
> *with that of all mankind—their willingness to undergo hunger, fatigue, hard*
> *labor and sufferings, for the sake of those who came to learn the way of*
> *righteousness—and the high expectations they had, of multitudes flocking down*
> *to hear the prophet the ensuing summer...were considerations truly affecting.*[11]

They invited three or four of the Indians to visit them at Union Village. In June, 20 Shawnee arrived at Turtle Creek, setting off shock waves in Warren County. They camped in the woods near the meetinghouse for four days. Each evening, the Shawnee held a worship service in the camp. On Sunday, they attended the Believers' meeting and "behaved with order and decorum." They were cordially received by the Believers and responded accordingly. However, rumors flew throughout the county. McNemar and Peter Pease went into Lebanon with a dozen of their visitors to sell furs, attracting the attention of many citizens. Memories of past bloodshed and hatred were still fresh in the minds of many Ohioans, and territorial disputes in Indiana were far from settled. Some people claimed that the Indians were moving to Union Village. Others said the Shawnee had been insulted by a Believer, and were ready to seek retribution against all whites. The most dangerous rumor was that the Shakers encouraged the Indians to go to war or, at least, try to regain lost land. Ignoring public sentiment, the brethren loaded 27 Shawnee horses with provisions to be taken back to Greenville to feed hungry families.[12]

When the central ministry learned of the Shawnee mission and the public reaction to it, they advised the Believers to proceed carefully. Based on McNemar's observations, the ministry concluded that "God is doing a great & marvelous work among them & that their prophet & elder has the revelation of God & may be able to lead and protect them in their own order & nation by receiving a small measure of counsel from some of the Believers."[13] The Shakers were to offer guidance but to allow the Prophet to instruct and minister to his people as he saw fit. If God were really revealing divine truths to him, the Shawnees would indeed be led to salvation.

Such advice was politically and culturally astute. Relationships between the numerous Indian nations and whites in the West were not uniformly harmonious. As settlers spread across the frontier, various Indian groups struggled to maintain their lands and autonomy. Conflict with each other as well as with whites was always possible. By 1807, Tecumseh was becoming recognized as an emerging leader who might not be content simply living in his brother's religious community. Residents' reactions as the Shakers and Shawnees rode down the streets of Lebanon demonstrated the fear and, in some cases, the hostility many whites felt about Indians as a group. That a group of 20 Shawnee visited Union Village instead of the expected three or four indicated that the Indians were apprehensive about visiting a white community as well. Culturally, the central ministry was advising a strategy similar to that which the missionaries used when they arrived at Turtle Creek in 1805, i.e., work with the new group's established leader. Look for similarities between the two groups and build on those commonalities. Offer support but don't push. Respect the intelligence and sensibilities of potential converts. Then, introduce the unique concepts that will be the most difficult for them to accept.

> "We are threatened with being put to the sword's point for showing charity to the poor Indians."

Surprisingly, that July the central ministry gave Darrow and other elders permission to reveal their beliefs about Ann Lee and explain the need for celibacy. In retrospect, it seems the Believers expected the Indians to absorb too much too quickly. These central concepts were difficult for people from a Christian background to grasp so they would be understandably difficult for another culture to accept. The central ministry did advise Darrow to wait until the Indians came to them to provide more doctrine:

> *If they should come to visit you & make inquiries [about] what the Gospel has done for you, we believe it to be your duty and what God requires of you to open the way of God & inform they that Christ has made his second appearance into this world.... Let them understand what the Gospel teacheth you and how it teacheth you to take up your cross against all fleshly and carnal desires & to live soberly, righteously, and godly in this present evil world.[14]*

The ministry advised Darrow to allow the Young Believers, who were just learning to witness in the Shaker way, to talk with the Indians. No rationale for this is given in the letter. The ministry was very clear, however, about one point: the missionaries were not to try to persuade the Shawnees to join the Turtle

Creek community. "By no means gather them, for they are Indians & will remain so…[they] must be saved in their own order and nation," the ministry instructed. The ministry noted that their remarks were based on what the Shakers had told them and they would "leave the matter with you to act as you can answer to God in relation to them." Eastern leaders often made that type of statement in the early days. It may have meant they trusted the judgment of Darrow and the other elders and realized that such decisions needed to be made close to home. Or perhaps it signified that they believed the westerners ultimately would act autonomously, despite what New Lebanon advised.

In August, McNemar returned to Greenville, accompanied by Issachar Bates. Once again, they seemed more intent on learning about the Shawnees' religion than trying to convert them. McNemar wrote that the Believers had little conversation with the Indians, indicating that they did not share their beliefs about Lee and celibacy. Rather they enjoyed another worship service. The Prophet delivered a long talk, then the crowd gathered and sang and shouted so loudly that they reportedly could be heard two miles away. McNemar, a budding songwriter at the time, praised their spirit and perfect musical harmony. "But all this," he wrote, "appeared far inferior to that solemn fear of God, hatred of sin, and that peace, love, and harmony which they manifested among each other."[15]

Fifty Shawnees returned the visit at the end of August, to the dismay of the Believers' neighbors. "We are threatened with being put to the sword's point for showing charity to the poor Indians," Pease said.[16] Some people thought the Believers and Shawnees were brewing a traitorous scheme. The Shawnees professed their peaceful intentions, and told the Believers that the only reason they would fight was if the whites went to war against them. If that happened, the whites "would be destroyed by a day of judgment, …not one soul would be left on the face of the earth."[17] Upon that ominous note, the Shawnee left Union Village.

McNemar clearly felt more comfortable with the Shawnees than with some of his worldly neighbors. The Indians had been interested in the Shakers' beliefs, viewed their religious services respectfully, and graciously shared their own worship. That was more than some of the Believers' neighbors were willing to do. McNemar declared, "in point of real light and understanding, as well as behavior, they shame the Christian world."[18] For their part, the Shawnees were disappointed when they realized that the Believers were not more respected by other whites.

When they first met, Tecumseh had proudly shown the missionaries letters of friendship from Ohio Governor Edward Tiffin and military leaders. When he discovered that many whites ridiculed the Believers—whom he considered part of the white, Christian culture—he used the knowledge to question whites' trustworthiness. If white people had crucified Jesus Christ and now mocked the Shakers, how could the Shawnees trust their word, he asked William Henry Harrison, governor of the Indiana territory.[19]

Political ramifications were not the missionaries' primary concern, however. They wanted to spread the Gospel and save souls. Ann Lee claimed to have received the Christ spirit in a dingy English jail. Why couldn't the Indians receive the divine spirit under the broad Ohio skies? Political realities interrupted this utopian picture, however. McNemar later conceded that the friendship between the Believers and Shawnees probably contributed to a mob uprising at Union Village and caused problems for the West Union Believers. The Indiana Shakers did not aid the Indians in any way without Harrison's permission. The Believers' mission trips to the Indians stopped as the War of 1812 heated up, but they continued to welcome sincere believers of any race.

As a tool to attract new members and explain the sect's beliefs, McNemar wrote *A Concise Answer To The General Inquiry, Who, Or What Are The Shakers* in 1808. Reprinted at Union Village in 1823 and 1825, the 150-line poem refutes common criticisms of the sect and outlines its basic principles in simple couplets, one of McNemar's favorite formats. He noted in the 1825 edition that the poem was prompted by an application from a person in Georgia who was interested in learning more about the sect. McNemar presented Believers as holy, honest, and peaceful:

> *No secret lust do we conceal,*
> *But open plainly all we feel;*
> *We ever stand in open view,*
> *And can hide nothing that we do...*
> *Our confidence no man can crush,*
> *Or put a Shaker to the blush...*
> *Against the flesh we all unite,*
> *And bear our cross by day and night;*
> *For virgin purity we hold,*
> *More precious than Peruvian gold...*

Tho' we renounce all fleshly lust,
We give each heir their portion just;
With which they're free to go away,
If with us they choose not to stay...
Bloodshed and carnage we abhor,
And therefore cease from learning war.
In civil courts we hold no seat,
Nor great ones with high title greet...

He also addressed opponents' claims that the Believers forced members to work and prevented them from leaving the community:

We're all industrious young and old,
But lying tongues have often told,
That Shakers are in bondage held,
And their hand labor is compelled;
But truth must say that nothing binds,
But living faith and willing minds...

Their worship services were depicted as joyous, and reference was made to the role of women:

We meet on every Sabbath day,
And unto God our homage pay;
In silent prayer sometimes we kneel,
Or sing, or speak, just as we feel;
And as salvation we possess,
Our joy and gladness to express,
We dance, each like a living spark,
As David danced before the ark...
We have a blessed Mother too;
Though human wisdom cannot scan,
How woman here can help the man;
Yet by the woman in her lot,
The way of God is plainly taught.[20]

Yet the Believers' way was still not plain to everyone. Misconceptions and rumors continued to circulate throughout the countryside. As the members began to prosper, a story started that vast amounts of cash were kept in the village. On a Saturday night in August 1808, a band of burglars acted on those rumors. Bates had just returned from New Lebanon with cash for land purchases. Late that night, thieves entered the elders' house and ransacked the downstairs rooms. The noise awakened members who were understandably intimidated. Knowing the Believers were non-violent, the intruders boldly entered the building. But they didn't count on McNemar's resolve. He had been asleep in the garret of the dwelling when he heard the commotion below. He ran to the third floor landing where he saw the burglars, quickly picked up a heavy chair and hurled it down the stairs, scattering the culprits, who fled for their lives. McNemar immediately sat down and wrote a song about the incident. He sang it at the Sabbath meeting the next morning.[21]

Not all attacks could be treated so lightly. Some of the worst came from apostates, including an infamous mob uprising that occurred in August 1810. At the heart of the conflict was a dispute within the James Smith family. Smith and his daughter-in-law, Polly Smith, had left the Believers. Smith's son, James Jr., had remained in the sect and kept his children there. The grandfather and mother wanted the children to live with them. Other apostates seized upon the custody issue to polarize public opinion against the Believers.

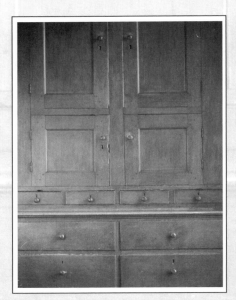

Detail of trustees' desk from Union Village. The desk contains a secret drawer that could have held cash or confidential correspondence.

Youngs chronicled the event in detail in a pamphlet entitled *Transactions of the Ohio Mob, Called in the Public Papers 'An Expedition Against The Shakers,'* published August 31 at Union Village. Youngs maintained that the Believers continued their daily routine as though nothing unusual was happening during the uprising. Worldly affairs, he implied, could not disrupt the work of God. Yet the attention to detail and the speed of publication indicate that the members were deeply disturbed by the incident and eager to present their side of the story. Opponents portrayed the Believers as "a poisonous nest, and enemies to the cause of American liberty," Youngs wrote. In June, accusations against them were published in *The Western Star*, a weekly newspaper published in Lebanon. Reports charged that adults in Union Village were living promiscuously, that children and "underlings" were being beaten, that Darrow was a corrupt tyrant who, with the other elders, "live sumptuously on the labors of others," and that children in the village were not being educated.[22] The controversy was played out in the local papers where court depositions of lawsuits against the community were routinely published. McNemar responded in a rebuttal article published in *The Western Star*, and challenged Smith to prove the allegations.

———————————————— ∽ ————————————————

Rumors swirled through Warren County all summer. Smith Sr. was said to be recruiting fellow Revolutionary veterans to help rout the Believers. Troops allegedly were being mustered in Kentucky to liberate the children, and the Light Horse Cavalry from neighboring Springboro, Ohio, was headed to Turtle Creek to keep the peace. As the heat mounted, so did emotions and rumors. McNemar was to be tarred and feathered, the easterners banished, and the converts returned to their former denominations and lifestyles. The frequent leaks of information and extensive rumors and threats indicate that the apostates may have hoped to intimidate the Shakers into leaving Warren County. The Believers took the threats very seriously. Easterners had faced mobs armed with clubs and whips, particularly in Massachusetts, in the early days. They recalled Ann Lee's stoic faith during persecution, and prepared for the mob as she had by continuing to preach and to live their faith. On the Sunday before the mob gathered, an opponent came to the Sabbath meeting to announce that all the opponents would be there Monday with violence on their minds.

Spectators began to assemble at Union Village early on the morning of August 27. Youngs estimated that between 1,500 and 2,000 people from the world had gathered by 1 p.m. A Cincinnati newspaper later published a second-hand account of the incident that estimated the crowd, including the militia, at around 1,000.[23] Five hundred armed peacekeeping troops arrived. Several prominent citizens intervened to ensure that the Shakers were not attacked. Warren County Sheriff T. McCray, state's attorney Joshua Collett, Revolutionary War General William Schenck, community leader Matthias Corwin, and First Circuit Judge Francis Dunlavy were present to promote peace.

Of all the officials present that day, Dunlavy was one of the most sympathetic to the Believers' desire for religious freedom. He knew from personal experience what it was like to hold unpopular views. When Dunlavy helped write the Ohio constitution in 1802, he labored long and unsuccessfully to obtain the vote for non-white men. He was also somewhat of a religious rebel who caused "mortification" for his staunchly Presbyterian family by defecting to the Baptists. His brother, John, later outdid him by becoming one of the key Shaker leaders in the West.[24]

The public officials faced an "undisciplined multitude...armed with guns—some with poles, or sticks, on which were fixed bayonets; and others with staves, and hatchets, and knives, and clubs. The exhibition presented a scene of horror," Youngs wrote.[25]

Twelve of the anti-Shaker faction presented their demands. Three of them concerned grandparents, including Smith, getting custody of their grandchildren, or—in one case—simply seeing a grandchild. The fourth demand was that the Believers stop dancing at worship services and stop proselytizing. The Shakers immediately responded to the custody issues, contending that such decisions were in the hands of the parents, although the grandparents were free to see the children. There was no immediate response to the fourth demand, but both sides agreed to meet in one hour to discuss the situation. The committee of 12 vowed violence unless all demands were met. Tension grew on both sides.

The elders, accompanied by Dunlavy, Corwin, and Schenck, met in an upper room of the elders' dwelling. After the Believers discussed the situation, Dunlavy and Schenck spoke with a committee leader about the "illegality and consequences" of mob action. Villagers proved resolute. As rowdy protesters shouted threats, the elders reiterated that they would not hand over the children against their parents' wishes. They also refused to abandon their faith or their land. Their adamant response summarized the position they would defend for the next 100 years:

> *Respecting our faith, which we held in the gospel, we esteemed it dearer than our lives, and therefore meant to maintain it, whatever we might suffer as the consequence. And as to our leaving the country, we were on our own possessions which we had purchased with money obtained by our own honest industry. It was our endeavor not to owe any man anything; we had not a cent of any man's money; we enjoyed our own peaceable possessions in a free country, and were entitled to those liberties (including the liberty of our consciences) which the laws of our country granted us.*[26]

Protesters crowded around the elders' dwelling, children's dwelling, schoolhouse, and meetinghouse. It was a chaotic scene:

*...there was a vast and promiscuous concourse of armed men and
spectators, some disputing, some inquiring, others railing out against, and
endeavoring to scatter falsehood, and urging the propriety of banishing
us out of the country by violence. Women of the baser sort, who were in
fellowship with the riot, had placed themselves within sight of the buildings,
on the edge of the woods, waiting to see the destructions of the Shakers;
others, of the same cast, were taking an active part in urging on parties of
the mob to take away, by force, children of their connections...*[27]

As the afternoon wore on, the mob's charges grew more fantastic. One
brother, Amos Valentine, was suddenly accused of murdering a young Shaker
boy who the apostates claimed was missing. Valentine, who had recently been
named one of the first deacons in Ohio, was immediately placed under guard
as the Believers sent for the boy, who was staying at another house two miles
away. The safe arrival of the boy did little to calm the protesters. Judge Dunlavy
commanded the mob to release Valentine and to disperse. The man holding
Valentine was armed with a pistol and a sword. He refused Dunlavy's order at
first, but later acquiesced while the crowd cursed the judge.

Another committee was formed to enter the elders' dwelling to discover if
people were being held against their will. One of the first to be questioned was
a sister, Betsey Seward, who said she wanted to remain because the Believers
treated her far better than her own family ever had. Prudence Morrell said
she would rather have her head chopped off than leave the community. Caty
Reubart and Jennie McNemar were among other women questioned in the
house. All said they wanted to stay with their new spiritual family.[28]

After thoroughly searching the dwelling for hostages and finding none,
the committee relaxed slightly. They cooled down with large mugs of cold
coffee provided by the Believers. They next interviewed members in the New
Believers' dwelling and were again reassured that all the inhabitants were there
by choice. Then they decided to examine the school.

*When they went into the school, they found Testaments plenty...They looked
at the children's writings, which they acknowledged far surpassed their
expectations...When they asked [the children], First—have you enough to
eat? they answered, Yea! yea! yea! as much as we want, ran all through the
school. Second—are you whipped more than you deserve? They answered,
Nay! nay! nay! all through; and many said, Not whipped at all. Third—do
you want to go from these people? If you do, continued they, fear not, we
will protect you. Nay! nay! nay! ran all through the school. They were*

then wished [by the Shakers] to hear the children read, but they would not,
declaring themselves fully satisfied.[29]

Unable to find anything improper at Union Village, the mob finally
dispersed. Youngs does not mention if the grandparents saw the children in
question, but no children left the village that day. Youngs emphasized that not
the entire crowd was anti-Shaker. He and the elders had no desire to alienate
themselves, for their mission was to minister to the world. The crowd could
contain potential converts. Economically, the Believers also needed to be a part
of the community. They were largely self-sufficient but they wanted outside
markets for their products.

Youngs wrote that the Believers acted as normally as possible throughout
the day. They performed their regular tasks, ate dinner, and spoke with
many visitors: "They answered those mildly who spoke to them, whether
peaceably, or in a taunt. Such [of the crowd] as wished to enter the rooms from
the noise and clamor, did so, and spent their time in conversation."[30] They
turned the ordeal into an opportunity to witness about their faith, an action
that must have infuriated their enemies.

Not all of the brethren were able to remain as calm as Youngs suggested that
day. Stories handed down by later Believers reveal more emotional reactions
to the event. Some members wanted to fight back against the mob. "Richard
McNemar found it necessary to go among the younger members and insist on
non-resistance, for there was an indication among them to act in self-defense,
and some of the Shakers were struck with whips and knocked down," wrote
a Shaker historian. However, a contemporary newspaper account reported,
"no acts of violence were committed either on the persons, or property of the
Shakers."[31] Whether or not anyone was physically attacked that day, the assault
on the village had one clear result: it brought the Believers closer together
against their detractors.

The conflict continued to be played out in the pages of *The Western Star*
that fall.

In depositions printed that September, Shaker opponent Thomas Freeman
appealed to the legal system to control members. He argued that since they had
removed themselves from society, they felt no obligation to follow the world's
rules. He also claimed that the Believers' real goal was to obtain converts'
money and possessions. He distanced himself from the unruly mob of August

by appealing to the law for support. "There is, I believe, no way to regulate the Shakers, or make regular or good members of society of them but by the law; and to make them conform to the rules of the community it is always best to apply to the law," he wrote. "Neither force of arms nor force of argument answers any purpose so long as their moneymaking scheme persists...."[32] Freeman argued that Shaker leaders had no incentive to conform while they profited from their communal economy. He compared Darrow's influence over the Believers to that of the Roman Catholic pope, a move calculated to prejudice the largely Protestant community. While Darrow held the Believers enthralled, Freeman said, they would not be swayed:

> *One might as well sing psalms to a dead horse...as to reform their errors. But make a law that will make them conform to the rules of well regulated society, or for every infraction thereof pay a stipulated sum, and I will engage that before they will part with their money, Elder David will absolve them, and let them all free from their faith and from their testimony and set them all at liberty to join the world, for the consideration of what cash they will by that time have in bank.[33]*

While Freeman's attack focused on legal issues, Smith's accusations centered on the Believers' relationship with the Shawnees. James Smith claimed that McNemar had told the Indians to ignore the Bible when other white missionaries came to them with it. He wrote that according to McNemar's "shakerified" story:

> *...that book is good for nothing now; it was once good but bad men changed it, and made it bad; but the great spirit hath now revealed to Indians what he had to the Shakers, and now they were brothers. This is just what the Shakers tell their proselytes when they get them fully into their testimony; that the bible is good for nothing now, it was once good; but they are come with a new revelation, and a new dispensation; and that the bible is of no more use than an old almanac.[34]*

Smith twisted the sect's beliefs to antagonize other Christians. In the *Testimony*, Youngs wrote that Christians had misinterpreted and corrupted the Bible's true message over the centuries. He also vehemently criticized other denominations but he didn't claim that the Bible was obsolete. Divine revelations to Believers had resulted in a more accurate interpretation of the Scriptures, according to Youngs, and future revelations could still reveal more of God's true plan for humanity. The Shakers believed that the Scriptures were a work in progress. Simply implying that the Bible was incomplete was heresy to most traditional Christians. Smith further inflamed opponents by claiming that the Shakers were collaborating with the Shawnees. He alleged that members frequently gave large amounts of provisions to the Indians and pledged them to secrecy about those gifts. He claimed that elders gave the Shawnees $25 specifically designated to buy ammunition in Lebanon. The implication was that the ammunition was to be used against the whites.[35]

The depositions did increase hard feelings against the Believers among some people but they also resulted in two front-page newspaper articles supporting them. One article, reprinted from a Cincinnati newspaper "by request," pleaded for religious tolerance and questioned the legality of the mob's actions at Union Village. The writer, who signed only the name "Justice" to the article, defended the Believers as decent, hardworking, and law-abiding. He raised the possibility that the armed protestors were actually infringing "upon the constitution of the state and chartered rights of the people by wishing to enforce their precept with the sword."[36] The writer cautioned opponents to refrain from another attack, which was rumored for November or December. At that time, the Believers were to be "torn up root and branch" from southwestern Ohio. Justice advised the rabble-rousers to reconsider their plans and respect Believers' freedom of religion.

Another anonymous, pro-Shaker article was reprinted from New York and Philadelphia newspapers. Apparently, the Warren County war over religious tolerance made national news. The story praised the sect for its honesty, charity, and industry. The unnamed writer claimed that James Smith's accusations were filled with "absurdities." A variety of Shakers' virtues were listed:

> They do not allow of corporeal punishment, or the use of ardent spirits, only as a medicine. They carefully abstain from political affairs, not even voting at elections, but submitting quietly to the laws of the land. They are remarkable for their veracity, and their word may be relied on with perfect safety.... They are a model of neatness, economy; ingenuity; temperance, and industry, for any people or nation of earth.... Their charity to strangers is exemplary; and, on the whole, an acquaintance with them furnishes nothing to laugh at, little to despise, somewhat to pity, and much to commend and admire.[37]

The anonymous nature of the positive articles suggest that they were written by someone within the United Society, such as McNemar, or by a public person who was familiar with the law but could not or would not publicly support the Shakers, such as Francis Dunlavy. Both positive and negative articles had powerful impacts. Although another group of protestors visited Union Village at the end of December that year, they were quickly dispersed without incident, indicating that the pleas for nonviolent, lawful assembly were being heeded. More importantly, the articles influenced how the public viewed Union Village and how its inhabitants viewed themselves. By appealing to the law, Freeman and Justice each tried to prove that their points were rational and worthwhile. But emotionalism was also part of each writer's strategy. Freeman caricatured Shakers as gullible dupes; Justice romanticized them as noble innocents. The people of Union Village began to be stereotyped—positively and negatively—as the public debate over tolerance and community standards continued in the press.

Membership in any group fosters stereotyping almost by definition. This promotes unity within the group; however, individuals become obscured by the group stereotype, and some group characteristics become exaggerated. The Believers began to take on a public persona before they had completely defined themselves as members of a new communal group. This sparked a noticeable increase in apostates and custody cases as the unsure members began to question such a stringent lifetime commitment. But it also strengthened the resolve of the firmly committed converts who now identified more closely with the eastern Believers.

The battle of the pens continued. Smith published an anti-Shaker booklet the following year, and McNemar promptly responded with another pamphlet. The debate strained the Believers' energy and diverted their purpose. They wanted to focus on their prime mission: spreading the Gospel, and living in harmony. Their opponents were equally determined to stop them, and they were about to get some help.

Top: Looking north on Dayton-Cincinnati Pike (State Route 741) from Union Village. The road crossed through the village, bringing Shakers in daily contact with the world.

Right: A large jar, signed "Stephen" on the bottom, is thought to be the work of Union Village potter Stephen Eastin. In keeping with the ideal of a selfless society, craftsmen were discouraged from signing their work, although a few like Eastin apparently did.

❧ Chapter Five ❧
Times of War— Battling Enemies Within and Without

For a peace-loving people, the Believers fought many battles. During their second decade at Turtle Creek, they battled the state legislature, their neighbors, a deadly fever, the militia, and Satan. While achieving an uneasy truce with their respective foes, the Believers managed to produce a self-sustaining, growing community  through resolve and hard work.

In 1811, local opposition spread to the state level when the Ohio legislature passed a law to protect women abandoned by husbands who joined the United Society. Lawmakers named the Shakers as the reason for the act. A man who left his wife to join the Believers—or any sect that required celibacy—violated the marriage covenant and was subject to legal action under the law. He lost authority over his children, who were placed in the custody of the mother or a guardian. Money and property controlled by the husband went directly to the wife and the children. That provision was intended to prevent a man from signing over his property to the community's joint interest and possibly leaving his family destitute. Officials attempted to balance the law. Anyone who tried to "entice or persuade" a man or a woman to join such a sect could be fined up to $500, a large sum on the frontier. But anyone giving a "public sermon, exhortation or address" that advocated joining a celibate sect was not to be penalized.[1] This concession to freedom of speech and religion saved the Believers from being arrested every Sunday at their public meetings but made proselytizing a riskier endeavor. The fine line between advocating and persuading would be difficult to determine in court. Still, the law was a victory for opponents like Thomas Freeman, who believed that legal sanctions should be used to pressure the sect to leave. Like the so-called black laws of 1803 and 1807, the legislation aimed to make Ohio less welcoming to a minority group. Both also seemed to be selectively enforced.

The Shaker law was typical for the time in its assumption that men decided whether the family would convert, and that often the wives and children were unwilling to do so. Union Village records note that many times women sought admission with their children, sometimes seeking sanctuary from a husband. Foreseeing domestic conflict, Ann Lee originally counseled wives not to convert until they persuaded their husbands to do so. Yet that did not always happen, and Shakers gained a reputation for breaking up families. They certainly disliked turning away perspective members, especially those that seemed in need. They were rare in that time for thinking that mothers should have as much control as fathers over their children's custody and future.

At the time, women and children were still considered property by much of society. Men who felt that way either sought to control or protect them. The notion that a woman could not survive without her husband was not so much an insult to women but an acknowledgement of how nineteenth-century society operated. Outside of domestic work, few jobs existed for women, particularly on the frontier. Single women typically lived with family members, helping with domestic tasks to earn their keep. Women who left or lost their husbands often faced a bleak future. Those without families could literally find themselves out on the streets. Charitable institutions were rare; Believers were one of the first groups to take in homeless people. The Believers were willing to face a husband's anger for sheltering his wife. Wives who voluntarily left their marriage could expect little sympathy from society. Husbands usually held the power, as in the case of Frederick

Pobst, who published a run-away wife notice in an early issue of *The Western Star*. Pobst forbade anyone in the community "upon their peril to harbor or trust her [his wife] on my account, as I will not pay any of her contracts from this date." An addendum to the notice states, "My house is open at all times to receive her whenever she sees proper to return to me in peace."[2] Such notices were frequently published in frontier newspapers along with rewards for the return of wayward indentured servants and stolen livestock. It was not uncommon for desperate, homeless people to turn to prostitution or suicide. The 1811 law sought to prevent these tragedies at the cost of religious choice.

Concerns about families caused much of the early hostility towards the Believers in Warren County. James McBride, a young businessman from the nearby city of Hamilton, expressed concerns that were aired many times during Union Village's first few decades.

> *I have known several instances of women leaving their husbands and children and going to the Shakers; and of husbands leaving their wives wretched widows, to shift for themselves in the wide world, and attaching themselves to the Shakers.... One woman whom I knew survived the separation but a few months, I believe principally from the unnatural and unheard-of conduct of her husband—wretched, unnatural man.*[3]

McBride decided to attend a meeting at Union Village that July to observe the Believers. The excursion did little to change his opinion of their religious practices, but he did provide one of the more detailed portraits of the community in 1811. He was pleased by the neatness and order of the fields and gardens that "appeared to be cultivated with great care and considerable taste." He was surprised by the size and solidness of the meetinghouse. Visitors approached the frame building through a beautiful, enclosed lawn, walking up neat gravel paths to enter dual gates that led to two separate entrances on the west side. Inside, the meeting space was "handsomely plastered" and sparsely furnished—just four or five rows of wooden benches for visitors.

McBride's account of visiting the village shows how much building progress Believers had made in six years. Had he visited during the week, he likely would have been welcomed by a trustee or deacon at the village office and invited on a tour of the village. In the neatly tended gardens, he would have found an array of plants for the table and for medicinal purposes. Those gardens grew into the packaged seed and medicinal herb businesses that familiarized the public with the Believers and secured their place in the local economy. All of their food was produced in the village. They harvested sugar from their maple trees, and brewed hot beverages from the spicebush and sassafras root they grew. Their dairy herds produced cream and milk to make butter and cheese in the village's creamery. As the population and food demands grew, horsepower was used to turn the huge churns.

Workhorses and cattle grazed in the pastures. Merino sheep—the first in Warren County—were added in 1812, and in 1816 Poland-China hogs, developed by the Shakers, became a staple of their economy. McBride would also have found fields of wheat, oats, corn, rye, flax, and hay. New apple orchards and vineyards dotted the grounds. Agriculture was the first and foremost business of the Shakers, but it would be soon be joined by the manufacture of woodenware, brooms, bonnets, and boxes.

Had school been in session, McBride would have found students studying reading, spelling, manners, and elocution at a time when public schooling was rare in the region. In 1811, a total of 110 students were enrolled.[4]

McBride did attend the worship service that Sunday and witnessed the practices that separated the Believers from their neighbors:

> *After sitting some time silent, they [Believers] all rose at once, as by general consent and commenced singing a tune, in which each one joined, and sang so loud that it made my very ears tingle...if noise could crack the ceiling of the house, this would have long since been fractured, although it is the strongest frame building I have ever seen—perhaps the strongest of the kind ever erected. In their singing, I could not discover that they sang any particular hymn or song, as I could not distinguish any words, but merely a humming sound.[5]*

After about an hour of such singing, an elderly man, perhaps Darrow, rose to speak about Shaker beliefs. McBride concluded that the speaker was clever and knew how to lead his listeners to the intended conclusion. Dancing came next. First, the brothers removed their coats, and then six men and six women lined up on opposite sides of the meeting room, and:

> *commenced singing a lively air of a tune, on which the whole assembly joined in a dance, but without running any regular figures, or the men and women intermingling together, each dancing on the space which they occupied, keeping exact time to the music, and, at each turn of the tune, turning half round and facing their next rank...some of them would jump up, clap their hands, whirl round on their toes or heels, like a top, cutting all kinds of extraordinary capers, and sometimes the whole assembly shouted so loud that I thought...they would bring the house about our ears.[6]*

The dancing lasted nearly two hours. The singing reminded McBride of "brisk lively airs" similar to those played at country-dances. One dancer, a girl of 10 or 12, captured his attention. "She looked so pleasant and kept capering about amongst them during the whole time," McBride wrote. " I conjectured that some of the old pious dances had brought her there to pay her devotions to her Maker, but that on setting off in the dance with the music, she had fancied herself in a ball room."[7]

If the adult dancing seemed rehearsed, it was because the Believers practiced during weekday meetings. Dancing and singing not only praised God, they sustained and inspired members, and reinforced unity. These forms of worship continued to evolve during the nineteenth century, with the dancing becoming more choreographed and sedate, and words and hand gestures added to songs. Weekday meetings were a way to relax and renew spiritual relationships after a long day of work. Farming, gardening, planning and constructing buildings, and simply taking care of the daily needs of a "family" of hundreds kept

Old Meetinghouse

members purposefully busy, but often separated them from their peers. Union meetings, held one to four times a week, were designed to provide social interaction between men and women in a structured yet informal atmosphere. Socializing between the sexes was otherwise discouraged; men and women even dined separately. At union meetings, however, they sat in their respective rows, facing each other. They conversed on spiritual issues, village matters, or news of the day—as long as the subject was not too provocative.[8]

While controversy continued outside the village, Believers reached a milestone on January 15, 1812, when they signed the first formal covenant at Turtle Creek. Peter Pease, John Wallace, and Nathan Sharp were consecrated as the first trustees the next day. Darrow and Farrington continued as first elder and eldress. They, along with Solomon King and Hortense Goodrich, the second elder and eldress, lived in the second story of the meetinghouse. This quartet was called the Church Family. Some Young Believers joined Old Believers in the newly finished new center dwelling to form the First Family of the community. Like the Shakers who signed the first written covenant at New Lebanon in 1795, the Turtle Creek people waited seven years to take the final step. Darrow and Farrington had been among the original signers in New York. Those Believers had not signed a covenant until they were convinced that their religious community was pleasing to God, and that there was no debt or claims on donated property.[9] The Ohio Believers seemed to take the same precautions. A Shaker writer noted that the United Society's covenant had been published in the world several times and had been tested in various courts, where it generally had been upheld. He emphasized the total commitment of body and soul that the document represented: "a total surrender of him or herself, together with all they possess—money or temporalities—and a consecration—dedication and devotion of all their strength, ability and faculties to the service of God in obedience to the ministry Elders and deacons of the Society, and to any and all other purposes and objects of Charity which the Gospel may require."[10]

> Like the Shakers who signed the first written covenant at New Lebanon in 1795, the Turtle Creek people waited seven years to take the final step.

Believers considered the covenant a legal and spiritual document. Every facet of their lives and work reflected their religious beliefs. The profits of their labor were used to spread their faith, care adequately and equally for their members, and provide charity to the needy. Subjugating their individual desires for the good of the whole community was supposed to bring individual fulfillment. It was a selfless approach to life that proved fulfilling for many and a challenge for others.

As the Union Village Believers grew into a more cohesive group, they often waited for word from Indiana, where several of their members, including Issachar Bates, had gone to help the struggling community. In response to the persistent rumors of Indians joining British troops, more American soldiers gathered along the Wabash River and used civilian facilities. In September 1811, a company of light horsemen and two companies of riflemen camped near West Union. Bates, who still recalled with horror the bombardment and fires of the Battle of Bunker Hill during the American Revolution, bemoaned the approaching conflict:

> *The (military) contractor made use of our shop in the dooryard for a storehouse, and had a slaughter yard back of it. There it was drums and fifes—blood and whiskey—alas ! alas! There they staid waiting for the other troops to come on. They had their washing, baking, and some lodging, and all their forage for their horses among us—tho' they paid for it, and behave civil towards the Believers, yet, alas! alas!*[11]

Ironically, the first death at West Union was due to malaria, not battle. Bates, stricken by the deadly fever in August 1812, became critically ill. John Dunlavy left Pleasant Hill, where he was the lead elder, to assist Bates and the Indiana Believers. He contracted the fever and died on September 16. Bates recovered, but fevers continued to plague the settlement.[12]

As they struggled with illness, the Believers also prepared for the consequences of war. Older members, including Bates and Darrow, had served in the Revolution before their conversion. But the younger men had never been subject to a military draft. Militia service became another source of friction between the Believers and the world. On June 2, 1812, McNemar met in Dayton with Ohio Governor R.J. Meigs, who had announced that a draft might be necessary. Union Village took the lead in presenting the Society's pacifistic views to the government. Having been taught to turn the other cheek, they could not contemplate raising arms against anyone. McNemar asked for an exemption from military service and an exemption from paying militia fines for all brothers. In his personal notes on the issue, McNemar wrote that the law stated that a man must be free to serve in the military, "free both in relation to God and man, under no restraints or legal obligation— here the law will afford me the privilege of a plea for exemption, if I can show I am devoted to any such religious service in the ministry and support of the Gospel." He further reasoned that the government could not confiscate his property for refusing to serve "because beyond my wearing clothes, I profess nothing to which I have either personal claim or demand."[13]

Meigs was not swayed by such arguments. No exemption was granted. Union Village men escaped the draft in 1812, but several of their West Union brothers were called up that fall. They refused to serve and were heavily fined. An officer, who was sympathetic to the Believers, interceded on their behalf with William Henry Harrison, who was by then a brigadier general. The men were assigned to do hospital work in place of a fine or service. Shortly after this, the Believers relocated to Union Village and the Kentucky settlements to escape the war and the fever that had plagued the community.[14]

The people who moved to Union Village brought with them stories of the war, and—unwittingly—the fever. Believers were soon fighting another kind of battle. Church records for Christmas Eve, 1812, noted: "Distressing fevers prevail among the Burseron [Busro] people, especially among the children—36 sick in the children's order." Several members died before New Year's Day, and the deaths continued into 1813. Like all Shaker communities, Union Village had its own infirmary and nurses, most of whom had only informal training. The Shakers typically provided primary care to members, using purchased medicines as well as herbal remedies, but outside physicians could also be called in, especially in cases involving children. A common treatment for fever was tea brewed from dried sage leaves, a plant that was widely grown at Union Village. Other native plants commonly used to treat fevers include dogwood bark, spicebush, sumac, and lemon balm.[15] Fevers were common and dangerous illnesses during this era, and recovery seemed to depend as much on the patient's constitution as on medical care.

Between December 1812 and April 1813, 160 people fell ill with fever. Several died. Darrow was especially stricken by the deaths that March of "three of our beautiful young people." His narrative of the death of one young man, Jethro Dennis, demonstrates the closeness Believers shared:

> *The fever was of that nature and so powerful, that, in a few days, it would take the flesh nearly off their bones, and bring them very low.... On Sabbath [March 21], Jethro sang very beautiful for the assembly and on the morning of the 29th, he departed this life...In Jethro's sufferings his mind was bent on going home. They [nurses] asked him if he was not at home? He said, this was a good home, but it was not his home. A little before his departure, he told Sister if she would only open the gate and give him his liberty, he would be gone instantly.[16]*

Darrow questioned why such good people, and such young people, had to suffer so much. They had unselfishly served the sick and needy of West Union, and now their only reward seemed to be suffering and death. "How shall we account of these things?" Darrow asked his elders at New Lebanon. "The work of God has been great in this country and must increase." He found an answer in a vision he experienced while praying on the evening after Jethro's funeral:

> *Mother [Ann Lee] came here in the meetinghouse. I immediately kneeled down close to her feet with a full heart, and wept both with sorrow and thankfulness. I could not refrain taking hold of Mother; she also kneeled down. She appeared sorrowful and very heavenly and pure indeed. She spake many good, strengthening words to me. I said, surely I will remember them and open them to the Brethren and Sisters, but they would go from me and I could not keep them correctly. But the gift I kept and intend to keep it.[17]*

Another young person, Patsy Dragoo, died the next morning. Strengthened by Lee's spirit, Darrow was determined to share the gift of faith and hope with his flock. "The gift had an extraordinary affect upon the people," Darrow wrote. "The spirit of God moved thru the people and their crys were so great that they were plainly heard and felt across the road to the house where the sick were so that Sister Rachel and those among the sick partook of the gift." Twenty-seven people "miraculously" recovered. One more young woman, Clarissa Sharp, died. "We had to let her go," Darrow noted. "Her case was singular. Before she was taken, she was told in vision that she must go soon... she died after five days of illness, singing with those who were caring for her."[18]

As Believers cared for the sick and grieved for the dead, they also faced two groups that attempted to remove members from the village. "Mob at the West Section; trying to take a woman away against her will" was the terse entry in the May 12, 1813, church record. Apparently, the attempt was unsuccessful. No other mention is made of the woman. A more detailed account is given of a December 16 incident, when "a violent mob" arrived at the Center House to reclaim the four children of James Bedle, an apostate. According to the Shakers, Bedle had given custody of his children to Peter Pease, but now wanted them back. Bedle's wife was still a member of the sect, living in the village. This group was not turned away so easily. "The house doors being closed and barred, they took a battering ram and broke a door in two; they then rushed in and committed considerable violence and abuse; but failed in getting the children," the church diarist wrote.[19]

Bedle had gone to a court referee to prove that his children were being abused at Union Village. He was unable to prove this, but the referee recommended that Pease hand over the children in the interest of peace. The next morning, Bedle appeared at the village, and "dragged off his 2 youngest children, much against their wills. They went off screaming and holloring. The mother and the 2 oldest children have fled to some other quarter to avoid violence and enjoy their own faith."[20] Several mentions are made in the church records of Shaker communities sending members to other villages to prevent disapproving relatives from forcibly removing them.

Some children and adults were eager to leave Union Village. For them, the quest for perfection and the regimented routine were simply overwhelming. Children of parents who separated over their faith often wanted to rejoin the parent who was in the world. Darrow held a special meeting for parents and minor children where he lectured them about appropriate behavior and loyalty. "It had a good and great effect and cast out many evil spirits," Darrow wrote. "They were told they need not think to run away...for they [parents] should hold them and govern them...and they should be obedient to the faith, principles, and orders of the Church.... There is nothing promised to rebellious Children, but Eternal Punishment."[21]

The amount of influence parents had over children varied. Biological ties were to be diminished as children and adults grew into one family of Believers. Yet Darrow appealed to the biological parents to try to hold on to the young people. He clearly saw Union Village's future slipping away. By 1815, over half the children of covenant-signing adults had left the community, either with another relative or on their own. Of 83 children, 46 departed by year's end.

Traditionally, girls decided at age 14 and boys at 16 whether to remain in the community, or go to the world. Darrow increased the age of decision to 18 and 21 respectively in an extraordinary attempt to retain the youth. On Christmas Day, 1815, parents signed an agreement stating that their children were "lawfully bound and obligated to...remain and continue under the care direction and government of the church, and faithfully to serve and obey those who are over them in the Lord..."[22] The agreement also addressed a financial concern. Any assets the youth possessed or inherited up to those ages were also to remain under church control.

Parents signed a second document that tried to guarantee the children's obedience and protect the community's assets the next summer. Children who obeyed their parents—and church officials—would receive a sum of money upon reaching maturity, and be invited to become covenant members of the church. Children who disobeyed forfeited their inheritance: $150 for young women and $300 for young men. Elders also hoped that the plan would quiet critics who claimed that the Believers cheated members and their heirs of their legal inheritance.

But the plan drew criticism from within the Union Village leadership. McNemar claimed the proposal had several weaknesses. He questioned the legitimacy of the document, noting that it seemed more Biblical than legal, and that allotting different sums for men and women was inconsistent with the church's principle of equality. Although church leaders obviously hoped that the young people who signed the covenant would donate their inheritance to the joint interest, a different custom evolved. Those who stayed and received the money were allowed to keep a portion—often half—for themselves. They spent it on books, clothes, and other incidentals, which McNemar believed set them apart from other members and threatened unity.[23] Such desperate measures are a clear indication that persuading young people to adopt the faith was a difficult task. Many of the young people undoubtedly left to pursue personal family lives. Spiritually, the Believers' doctrine might not have been fulfilling. At least one of Worley's sons and one of McNemar's had left by 1816. Some of the older boys may have left to pursue their own fortunes or even to serve in the military. By 1813, more young Ohioans were being asked to fight the British, while Believers actively defended the principle of conscientious objection.

> Some children and adults were eager to leave Union Village. For them, the quest for perfection and the regimented routine were simply overwhelming.

Fear of the British and the Indians gripped the Miami Valley. The Believers were closely watched by their neighbors because of their relationships with several of the key figures. Their old friends Tecumseh and the Prophet had joined the British, hoping that an English victory might preserve more Indian lands and independence. William Henry Harrison, who had protected them at West Union, defeated the Prophet at Tippecanoe, Indiana, in 1811, but Tecumseh still threatened the region. The fighting was close enough to southwest Ohio to put citizens on alert. Lebanon was the gathering place for militia from Warren, Butler, Hamilton, and Clermont counties. Volunteers were promised $16 for joining, and 160 acres and three months wages if they served for five years. But despite a swell of patriotism, not enough men enrolled, resulting in a draft.[24]

Seven brothers were drafted for military service in September 1813. When they refused to report for duty, seven more were drafted. Still more brothers would be drafted if those men did not report, Darrow informed New Lebanon. If all refused to serve, they would be fined until they were without money. The first draft occurred while most of the elders were visiting in Kentucky and there was some confusion at the village on how to respond. Finally, the draftees went to Lebanon to turn themselves over to the military so that other brothers would not be persecuted. They told the authorities their faith would not permit them to carry weapons or shed blood. They enrolled on the militia list, but when they were ordered to take up guns for parade practice, they pulled out their Bibles instead and began reading. When the militia set off for active duty, the brothers refused to march. A guard was assigned to make them march to Dayton where the Warren County troops camped for a few days, waiting for the arrival of the rest of their regiment. The field officers were ready to send the Believers home, but the commanding officer, a colonel, could not release them without facing disciplinary action himself. When the time finally came to leave, the colonel did not force the Believers to accompany the troops. They were free to find their way home. Darrow complained that the troops "were so unkind that...they left the poor Brethren on the ground without any guard to protect them."[25] Obviously, the brothers feared retaliation by citizens who might consider them traitors.

They did return to Union Village safely, but their military obligation was not yet over. The colonel informed them that he was bound to take them back into the army. They were given three options: desert their country, take their chances with bounty hunters, or believe his assurances that they would be treated humanely if they surrendered to him. They consented to the third option, and on October 1, the colonel arrived alone at Union Village to collect the seven men. In the officer's presence, the elders read their own orders to the brothers. In part, the instructions read:

Preach the word; be constant in season, out of season. Be an example to all men. Go forth as lambs in the midst of wolves—be wise as serpents— harmless as doves—do violence to no man—render not evil for evil but overcome evil with good. Do good to them that hate you, pray for them that despitefully use you.[26]

"We told him (the colonel) that in a true sense we considered every true follower of Christ a Preacher of the Gospel as there was Diversities of Gifts... and according to a free government such disciples ought to be free from military duty," Darrow wrote. "He appeared under some mortification and was silent on the subject, a guard of twelve men soon came on, orders came to march, the Brethren slung their packs and marched off, the Colonel walked by their side through our street."[27] In Lebanon, the Believers were housed together, apart from the regular soldiers. Another brother brought the men food and supplies so they would not have to use military provisions.

A few weeks later, the pacifists were in Sandusky, near Lake Erie, with their regiment. They sent word back to Union Village that "all the officers and soldiers are very kind to them—but the tender mercies of the wicked are cruel when compared with Zion," Ruth Farrington wrote to the central ministry. "They say the world's people have full confidence in them that they will maintain their faith and integrity."[28] And they did. The men refused to perform military duty, or to care for the sick and wounded. They would do nothing to contribute to the war. After six weeks, the officers in charge used the men's back wages to hire substitutes for them. The seven were allowed to return home. With Admiral Oliver Hazard Perry's defeat of the British Navy at Lake Erie that fall and the death of Tecumseh during a battle with Harrison's troops in southern Canada, the need for militia diminished. No more Believers were drafted during the war.

They were not the only residents of the region who resisted the draft, but they were one of the most united and resolute groups. Both Warren and Clark County, just to the north, had sizeable Quaker populations. Like the Believers, the Friends were enjoined not to fight or serve as medics. There is evidence, however, that some Friends found a less confrontational way to cope with the militia. Records for the Springfield Friends Meeting, held in Clark County, state: "1812–1814—Complaints were made to the Monthly Meeting for paying muster fines, army service, waggoning for the army."[29]

The Believers' dedication to their pacifist ideals benefited them in three ways, according to one military scholar. First, some of the world respected them for not wavering. Secondly, their actions helped develop and publicize a rationale for Shaker pacifism. Lastly, it encouraged more efforts among all Believers to be exempted from muster fines and military service.[30]

While McNemar worked on formulating a defense for pacifism, Bates put his feelings into song. His hymn, "Rights of Conscience," appeared in *Millennial Praises*, the first Shaker hymnal published in 1813. Bates and McNemar contributed heavily to the book, but it was Bates who focused on pacifism. His hymn praised George Washington's fight for religious freedom, but reminded the world that the Believers' ultimate duty was to obey God's command to live purely and peaceably. He rebuked those who sought to force Believers to fight for earthly causes:

> *Carnal swords are laid aside,*
> *Every fleshly lust deny'd*
> *Each one seeks his neighbor's good,*
> *No more shed each other's blood…*
> *Liberty is but a sound,*
> *If the conscience still is bound;*
> *Could you but her reigns controul,*
> *You would creed-bind every soul.*[31]

Despite the conflict over military service, western Believers prospered. In the fall of 1813 Darrow wrote that Believers had escaped the severe drought that was troubling much of Ohio and Kentucky. In his recent trip to Kentucky, he noted, "it appears that the Believers have been more blessed with Dews and rains from heaven than other people. At Gaspar, we found among the Believers in their fields, 160 acres of noble corn growing and other crops very good. At Pleasant Hill, their corn was very good…. At Watervliet, all their crops is right good so we hope all the Believers will make out middling well for bread to eat." Crops also flourished at Union Village.[32]

After harvest, in November, the community held a special children's service of thanksgiving. "Father [Darrow] spoke to them, then the Brothers and Sisters sang a song composed just for that purpose…then they [the children] paced in order and labored, big and little—some little things three or four years old, their little heads all went up and down together," wrote Farrington. "It was a beautiful sight to see. There was exactly 100 of them."[33] Children were included in worship as much as their age and understanding would allow. Like the adults, they were expected to confess when they did wrong and make amends.

The children also participated in the "war-time" revival of 1815. This war referred to the battle Michael and his angels waged against the great red dragon (Satan) in Chapter 12 of Revelation. When life went well and crops flourished, the Believers felt God was blessing them for their faithfulness. When disease and disaster struck, they reasoned that Satan was persecuting them. No pacifists against the Devil, they wholeheartedly fought sin. "War-time," declared the church record that winter. "A meeting with much noise. An extraordinary time of power and zeal in meetings." Services were filled "with many displays of muscular exercise, such as stamping, shaking, vociferating and shouting, besides the usual exercises of dancing, marching, singing, etc."[34]

The Believers might not be able to influence the military and the legislature as they wished, but they could lash out at Satan. An immediate effect was felt in the church. "The most extraordinary event that has taken place here of late is the mighty power of God on the people like a mighty rushing wind," Darrow and Farrington reported to New Lebanon. "Great numbers speaking with other tongues at once—all kind of exercises—moaning and moving against the flesh and Devil like the sound of many waters." Manifestations spread until they were taking place in dwellings as well as the meetinghouse. The buildings would "rumble for hours together by day as well as by night. Indeed there never has been the likes in this country before and we are thankful for it, for it makes hell tremble and wicked spirits has to flee."[35] The revival eventually spread to Watervliet (Ohio) and West Union. Bates, who was back in Indiana, described people stamping their feet so hard that their heels and ankles turned black and blue. "Think what the serpents head must feel/ Beneath a black and bruised heel/ His hope of life is small indeed/ Among the blessed woman's seed," he wrote.[36] The "warring" lasted several months.

Battle of a more secular nature was still needed to address the question of military service. The issue resurfaced in 1817 when Shaker opponents petitioned the legislature to either force Believers to serve in the military or pay fines. The petition, circulated throughout Ohio, galvanized Union Village leaders. Darrow noted that he had put up with lies, slander, and hatred for years, but he could not ignore the petition. "We believed the time was come for civil rulers to know that this [society] is the very Christians and [will] be no longer imposed upon by the tongue of common...slander," he wrote to New Lebanon.[37] McNemar, who had been following the military issue in the East as well as in Kentucky, immediately began to work on a reply to the petition. The Believers' response was signed by 123 members, and carried to the Ohio capitol in Columbus by McNemar and Calvin Morrell in December 1817.

Legislators invited the men to explain their faith during a session. They were momentarily intimidated by the request but called for spiritual guidance. The next day when McNemar rose to speak in the legislature, "the Scriptures rolled in like thunder and lightning, sufficient to prove every point of doctrine they requested to know," Darrow wrote. "All fear of man was taken away and they felt the place was surrounded by the heavenly host. And it was true, for several here [Union Village], at that very instant saw in vision the Angels of God gathering around that place."[38]

Legislators listened politely, and several men spoke with McNemar and Morrell after the session but their request for military exemption died in committee. Instead of granting their request, Ohio enacted a new militia law, based on the opposition petition, on January 27, 1818. In part, the law stated:

> ...in collecting fines assessed by the provisions of this act, all stewards, managers, agents, trustees or elders of any connected or associated society, whose property is all vested in common stock, shall be bound for each and every member thereof, who is liable to do military duty, and the common stock, goods, chattels, lands and tenement, of all or any body or bodies so connected or associated, shall be held liable and bound for the payment of any fines assessed by the provisions of this act.[39]

The wording was aimed directly at the Shakers, and it refuted McNemar's assertion that individual members had no personal property and therefore could not be forced to pay militia fines. If the individual could not pay, the United Society would, according to the law.

This was more than a financial issue for Believers. They never sought tax exemptions as some religious groups did, and they paid their taxes willingly. They resisted the militia fine because it violated their religious rights, and they knew the money would be used to further war. McNemar soon drafted a rejoinder to the new measure. The law, he wrote, would "deprive us of our rights and privileges, and compel us to abandon that manner of life which we conscientiously believe to be the most acceptable to God and beneficial to mankind."[40] New York brethren had cited the Declaration of Independence and the United States Constitution in opposing militia laws. McNemar now cited the Northwest Ordinance of 1787. He focused on three relevant points: no one should be persecuted because of religion; no law was to be enacted that interfered with any previous legitimate contracts, such as the United Society's covenant; and no one should be deprived of their property without their consent.[41]

The strongest point was the religious argument. Believers then did not call themselves pacifists. They wanted religious liberty, or the rights of conscience. Their religion taught them not to bear arms or perform any duties that supported war. McNemar argued that this right was inherent in the ordinance that stated that "no person demeaning himself in a peaceable and orderly manner shall ever be molested on account of his mode of worship or religious sentiments..." This became the "premier right" of inhabitants of the Northwest

Territory.[42] McNemar equated molestation with forced military service. Believers continued to seek exemption as the state legislature refused to drop the militia law. Darrow vowed to pursue the matter:

> *The brethren here have paid no fines for several years, and the militia officers know of no way that they could collect it and this made them very angry. Now they have framed mischief by a Law. So they think they have us well fixed now but the matter has to be settled yet, between the Lamb and the Beast, for the Brethren are determined not to pay any fines.*[43]

Darrow told the central ministry that the law was obviously directed solely at the Believers because there were no other societies in Ohio that "support a joint interest...If they persecute us, let them do it with their eyes wide open and we will labor to bear it patiently for the Gospel's sake."[44] Decades later, as the storm gathered before the Civil War, the battle for the rights of conscience continued.

> "A third class (or rather those of a riper travel) are looking for a continual increase, not only in spiritual things, but in temporal also—they are looking for a new heaven, and a new earth…"
>
> —Rufus Bishop to
> David Darrow, 1817

Top: West Brick Dwelling
Right: Old school bell at Otterbein-Lebanon

🌀 Chapter Six 🌀
Creating a New Heaven and Earth

nion Village reached its greatest population and started the industries that brought local acceptance and, eventually, national recognition, from about 1810 through 1825. Believers frequently had to adapt to circumstances in order to thrive, and as a result modified their worship, fashion, and commercial enterprises.

Change began first in the way the Believers worshipped. More structured dancing replaced the ecstatic shaking and spinning of earlier worship services. The quick dance, introduced in 1811, featured both singers and dancers, sometimes moving in a circle. The square order of exercise or laboring, as dancing was called, was introduced in 1812.

A conjectural modern drawing of the square dance, based on an original Shaker document, shows vocalists positioned in a central square in the meeting room, with worshippers moving around them, maintaining a square formation.[1] Marching, introduced in 1817, allowed even the most uncoordinated Believer to participate, resulting in more

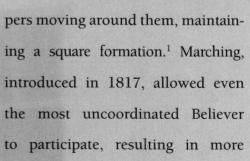

members being actively involved in worship. Darrow described a stirring march on a summer Sunday:

> *They all marched out into the street, Brethren and Sisters in a body together.*
> *They began their march with these words:*
> *March on—march on O ye little band,*
> *March on—march on to the heavenly land.*
> *For God will reward you with peace and pure Love*
> *And give you a place in His mansions above.*
>
> *The strong band of Singers went forward and lifted up their voices…. They*
> *marched down south to the crossroad below the South house, then wheeled*
> *about and came to the North house, strewing their garments in the way,*
> *as they did when Christ rode into Jerusalem; sounding all the way so they*
> *were heard for miles…. It truly was a pretty Gift as my eyes ever beheld.*
> *I suppose there were about 300 in the Street, full of Life and power, and*
> *sounded the Gospel all the way.*[2]

Such uninhibited worship strengthened the community's unity and individual faith. Large crowds of visitors sometimes inhibited the Believers' worship. One 1812 meeting found overflow attendance at both the private and public services. In the morning, the Union Village residents and Busro refugees filled the meetinghouse. "There not being many spectators, about three-quarters of them [Shakers] laboured. They were as thick as a lady's fingers," Darrow wrote. "In the afternoon so many of the world gathered we could not labor."[3]

While the dancing was still exotic to many visitors, the musical portions of the services began to sound more familiar to them. Encouraged by McNemar's and Bates' early lyric writing, more easterners were also writing hymns with words. Hymns and songs were frequently sung in services. Publication of the *Millennial Praises* hymnal in 1813 provided an opportunity for all Believers to learn the new songs and to sing more frequently in services. The hymnal contained "A Covenant Hymn," a McNemar composition that became a signature song of the United Society. Believers continued to be prolific songwriters throughout the nineteenth century. James and Vincy McNemar continued their father's legacy during the mid-century. Oliver Hampton wrote many songs later in the century. Any member could contribute a song, if it was deemed worthy. They collaborated with Believers in other communities as well, sometimes sending lyrics to which music was added. Believers exchanged songs and hymns in letters and during visits.[4] Periodically, songbooks and hymnals were published.

McNemar compiled and published *A Selection of Hymns and Poems* while living at Watervliet, Ohio, in 1833. Later, Hampton and Sanford Russell compiled a book of hymns and marches, entitled *The Musical Messenger*, published at Union Village. During a period of intense spiritualism in the1830s and 1840s, many songs were received as spirit gifts through divine revelation. Seasons of the year also inspired songs for special meetings, including the thanksgiving service held after the fall harvest, and the Christmas service.

Early Christmases at Union Village present a glimpse of how Christians of various denominations assimilated their customs into a common celebration. The Believers stayed true to their largely Protestant roots by observing the holiday simply with a special worship service. Ann Lee decreed in 1776 that Shakers should observe the day by emulating Jesus' example of charity and forgiveness. Members were to reconcile with anyone whom they had quarreled with or wronged. Clothing and provisions were gathered for the poor. Eastern Shakers began the observance by fasting on December 24. On Christmas Day, they held a special meeting where many imaginary spiritual gifts—robes of righteousness, cakes of love—were presented and used. Adults sat on the floor, as children would, to receive these gifts. Special dances and songs marked the observance, as well as some specific rituals. In one ceremony, the adults formed a "ring of love" and a young child was placed in the center of the circle to symbolize faith and purity. Sometimes cleaning rituals were performed. The cleansing was spiritual as members tried to banish sins of pride or envy, but at times physical cleaning also occurred, as the meetinghouse, communal rooms, and shops were thoroughly scrubbed.[5] Western Believers gradually adopted these customs over the first few decades on the frontier. Some traditions transcended any doctrine, such as the reuniting of absent loved ones. Several of Richard McNemar's poems from the era capture the excitement of families coming together for a special celebration. On his way home to Union Village from Pleasant Hill one Christmas, McNemar wrote: "Home to Ohio we are advancing/ Come little children let us be dancing/ Sweet love & union what can be better/ Where there is freedom nothing's the matter."[6]

On another Christmas at West Union, McNemar and the brethren were awakened with song at 3 a.m. The sleepers were invited to:

> On Christmas Day, they held a special meeting where many imaginary spiritual gifts—robes of righteousness, cakes of love—were presented and used. Adults sat on the floor, as children would, to receive these gifts.

Awake Awake arise and dress
And let us all each other bless
With ev'ry word we can express
That's full of love & Union
How lovely you do all appear
How glad we are to see you here
Since we have liv'd another year
Rejoice in sweet communion.[7]

"After this the time was principally spent in mirth till breakfast was ready," McNemar wrote. As the men sat down to breakfast, the women began to sing to them. Their song reflected the impending departure of the Shakers from West Union. Perhaps more importantly, the song resonates with the simple satisfaction of watching people enjoy a special meal together:

Now we with pleasure do attend
And wait upon our dearest friends
For while we are remaining here
We wish you all to have your share
Those of the village do be free
And with much pleasure drink your tea
And all who go to Pleasant Hill
We hope will eat & drink their fill
Those of South Union don't be slack
For no good thing you soon shall lack
So let us all quite merry be
While we each others faces see.[8]

The sisters' song also demonstrates that Believers (typically portrayed as extremely somber) laughed, sang, and enjoyed fellowship. Although they often seemed constrained while being observed by the public, their humanity as well as their message attracted individuals. In 1817, Darrow reported, "The world throng our public meetings abundantly." At one meeting, there were "about 112 sleighs in our streets at one time, besides horsemen and foot people. They hear the Truth and Believe but will not obey."[9] Missionaries from Union Village continued to travel throughout Ohio, Kentucky, and Indiana, and even into Pennsylvania, seeking converts. Many who heard the Believers' message did decide to join and "obey." Union Village's population peaked in 1818 with 634 members.[10] Based on public interest, the Shakers expected even more people to join. An estimated 2,000 visitors attended services on July 4, 1821. "We gave them such preaching as we had for them; they behaved well and went off peaceable," Darrow wrote.[11] While the Shakers still had vigorous opponents, they were becoming more accepted by the community, and spectators were usually well mannered. They often felt singled out by detractors, but hecklers were always a possibility at any type of public meeting. A newspaper notice of a Protestant revival meeting in 1825 near Lebanon indicated that troublemakers did not distinguish between denominations. Organizers requested that no "spirits, cider, or beer...be sold within one mile of the encampment...We are sorry to say, that we have been insulted, and our religious rights trampled under foot, on some former occasions."[12] Believers practiced their religious rights by continuing to welcome the world at Sunday meetings. They did not, however, socialize with the public, except to discuss their faith. Visitors entered the meetinghouse by separate doors; men and women sat apart from each other, and from Believers. After the service, a few select visitors might be invited to Sunday dinner at the Trustees' Office.

Even if the members had sat with the public, their distinctive appearance would have identified them. Conformity in appearance continued to be encouraged to prevent vanity, lessen envy, and promote unity. For decades, the Believers favored uniform hairstyles. Men wore short bangs across the forehead with longer hair in the back, and women covered their hair with caps. Clothes were a different matter. What began with light-hearted dialogue among the sisters about styles ultimately became a serious matter as Darrow sought to keep a cohesive community. In a long letter to Rachel Spencer, her New Lebanon friend, Ruth Farrington departed from her comments about missionary efforts on the frontier to discuss another topic: "Now good sister, I want to talk a heap more about our little affairs here. So I think to begin first on our new fashion of bonnets, as thou knowest that we old Shaker women are always after some new fashions."[13] Farrington described new sunbonnets that the Union Village women made from fabric remnants. The new bonnets were so popular that the women made one for the eldress of each western community and sent a half dozen to New Lebanon as gifts. Farrington also thanked Spencer for gifts of caps, gowns, cloaks, shoes, and aprons. Spencer in turn thanked Farrington for the sunbonnets and found them "quite pretty and...made very neat." The New Lebanon sisters might like the bonnets even better than their old style, "But as we have all got good silk bonnets made in uniform, we do not think it would be prudent to alter our fashions."[14] Practicality dictated other fashion choices as well. In answer to Farrington's question of whether New Lebanon sisters wore white gowns, Spencer replied that the women within the Church Order wore a light-blue striped costume for their Sabbath meetings. Sisters still outside the Church Order had begun wearing plain white gowns for convenience. Hours spent in hot meetinghouses and traveling either muddy or dusty roads resulted in extremely dirty garments. White dresses could be more easily boiled and whitened than colored ones. Very often, Shaker color choices were completely pragmatic, although sometimes they did have particular meaning.

Darrow did view clothing somewhat symbolically. It signified a new birth, weaning members from worldly ways and maintaining harmony in the young community. Changes in men's clothing began around 1811. Gray suits were gradually exchanged for an even more neutral color. Jackets and vests were redesigned to eliminate large double pleats, and plainer hooks and eyes replaced buttons. Clothes, which had once been fitted solely by the wearer's girth, now considered height as well, making for a neater fit and reducing the amount of fabric used. Added to men's jackets were a small, mandarin-style collar and a shoulder-length cape.[15] Tailoring was becoming an increasingly important job in the community. Rufus Bishop, the New Lebanon elder, was a tailor. Changes in clothing, particularly men's, came primarily from the central ministry there. Trying to keep up with the New York fashions exasperated Darrow. He informed Bishop in 1817 that the "truly holy" brothers at Union Village wanted to dress as the first missionaries had in 1805. "They say the outward dress that the first three Brethren appeared in...witnessed to them that they were the true followers of Christ and had forsaken the course and fashion of the world," Darrow wrote. But there were dissenters who wanted more contemporary fashions. "Some of them got high-crowned hats near like the world. For thee may depend that the flesh here is as hard to grapple with and, I think, worse than ever it was in the East," he confided to Bishop.[16]

Fashions did change that summer at the decree of Lucy Wright, who seemed to respond to the desire of her New York flock to update and simplify their clothes without looking like the world. In a letter to Darrow, Bishop mentioned the elimination of decorative buttons and buttonholes, a slight change in men's hats, and an increasingly economical use of fabric. Great coats were not cut as full, jackets were shorter, and trousers were trimmer.

Practicality again caused some of the changes. "Our color for Coats &c. was shifted merely out of necessity," Bishop wrote. "Indigo was scarce, and beside this, our cloth would crack and fade, but this was not all; we poor taylors had so far worn out our eyes that we felt unable to work so much blue."[17] Bishop reassured Darrow that New Lebanon was as committed as Union Village not to dress like the world. Darrow's response acknowledged Wright's authority to direct Believers in every aspect of life, affirmed that his only desire was to promote unity among all members, and revealed that the western converts still need to be treated a bit differently from the more established easterners. "The Believers here were chiefly raised in the woods, and accustomed to living in cabins and they are not able to this Day, neither in abilities or faculties, to keep up with old Believers in all things," he wrote. "Nor do we think it right in their unmortified state to fix them up and make them look as slick as those that have travelled deeper in the Gospel, lest we should build them up in Pride."[18] Darrow wanted Believers to feel they belonged to the larger group, and he wanted them to look alike in public meetings. "Changing the colors breaks the uniform, causing uneasiness, and throws the Believers into confusion," he maintained. If styles continued to change, the time and expense of trying to get all members "into uniform" would be prohibitive. He described his own clothing as worn, but functional:

> As to myself, I care not much what my clothing is...[if] I can only get it in union and everybody will be satisfied. I have a blue coat and a gray one that was sent to me from the Church that are decent coats yet. In warm weather for several years I have worn a thin butternut colored coat. All these please one well. For more than two winters I have worn a drab-colored surtout, strait before, and would have worn it longer, but it looked so bad, the Sisters took it away from me...[19]

Darrow pleaded for a simple consistency in dress, so that more important matters could be pursued.

His letter vividly describes western Shaker dress during the 1810s and 1820s, but more importantly it illustrates his leadership style. A pragmatic, frugal New Englander by birth, he wanted to avoid waste. At the same time, he realized that western differences had to be accommodated, and that fashion fostered an important sense of belonging. He also knew that his letter could be construed as a criticism of New Lebanon policy, but he felt he was the westerners' advocate.

During Darrow's time, western leaders sometimes seemed like awkward teenagers: alternately wanting to impress their elders, and to assert their independence. McNemar, for example, was eager to prove himself to the central ministry. He visited New Lebanon for the first time in 1811 and met Lucy Wright. She was so impressed with his understanding of Shaker precepts that she gave him a new name, Eleazar (Hebrew for "God has helped") Right. He consented to the change, provided he could change the spelling of the surname to Wright to emulate her. McNemar began to use the new name in his personal and theological writing.[20] McNemar undertook many positions of responsibility in the frontier communities, ranging from proselytizing to defending the Believers' legal rights. The central ministry sent him throughout the West in 1829 to persuade Believers to sign a new covenant. He visited the East for a second time that same year, and preached at the Canterbury, New Hampshire, and Harvard, Massachusetts, communities. McNemar actively sought to be influential in the United Society. Among his prolific correspondence with eastern leaders are many letters exchanged with Seth Wells, who was in charge of education for the sect. McNemar shared many of his views on education and theology with Wells over the year, writing as an eager pupil but always supporting his views forcefully. His *Kentucky Revival* was used as a textbook for a time in some eastern schools.

The West's impact on the United Society was undeniable, starting with Youngs' *Testimony* in 1808, and later with Dunlavy's *Manifesto*. Western Believers, however, still felt they had to prove themselves. In an 1812 letter to the central ministry, Darrow and Farrington protested rather peevishly that the westerners felt no jealousy towards the easterners:

> *But perhaps some of them [easterners] may boast a little, because they can sit daily at Mother's gates and wait at the posts of her doors. We'll let them; we shall not envy no one for that if they do suck those blessings immediately from Mother's breasts. We receive them by faith through the spirits and sometimes we get it pure from the fountainhead, but we are willing they should love as much as they can. We will love also for we do not intend that [we will always be] as far off as Ohio, but we mean to crawl closer than all that. That is if we can possibly get little enough and clever enough so as to find a little place in Mother's House when she comes to gather up her jewels—perhaps door-keepers. That will do right well.*[21]

The striking images of the westerners as less-favored children and lowly servants in a distant land suggest that they sometimes felt neglected and isolated. Both of those perceptions influenced the growing voice of independence emanating from frontier writers. The central ministry did not visit Union Village until the 1830s, a decision that may have been unwise. A stronger relationship with the East earlier might have prevented some of the regionalism that led to disharmony later.

Regardless of any hurt feelings, Union Village continued to build throughout its second decade to accommodate the growing population. A large frame dwelling and accompanying complex of barns and shops were built for the West family in 1813. A new meetinghouse, painted white, was completed in 1818. The old meetinghouse was moved to another location and later remodeled into a shop. The new structure was the centerpiece of the village. Everyone met there for Sunday worship and special meetings in an open 60x44-foot space. The first floor was simply furnished with movable wooden benches, and peg rails, which held coats and hats as well as several large lanterns. The second floor was divided into separate retiring rooms for the lead elders and eldresses. Eight-to 12-inch thick timbers framed the structure, which the Believers claimed was the strongest building in Ohio at that time. Brick chimneys rose from the ends of a gable roof. There were separate entrances for men and women, and for the ministry.[22]

A large brick dwelling was built north of the meetinghouse in 1819, and a family of 74 Believers headed by Malcolm Worley moved in just after New Year's, 1820. The quality of the building exemplified the workmanship that became synonymous with the Shakers. When the building was scheduled for demolition in 1965, local contractors purchased salvage from it before the Lebanon Fire Department burned it in a training exercise. After the interior burned, the shell of the building still stood and a bulldozer had to finish the job. "I have never seen such wood (used in construction)," one contractor told a local newspaper, "walnut, oak, and white pine, and even the basement steps made of walnut. There never again will be builders like the Shakers."[23]

Another house, the West Dwelling, was built of brick in 1819. The Square House, built for the original Mill Family, and a dwelling for the East Family, which included the Children's Order, were built the next year. A large brick dairy was constructed in 1821. The South Family moved into a new residence in early 1823. A large brick dwelling and kitchen for the North Family was completed that year. Another brick building, which became the Trustees' Office and Visitors' House, was started that fall. During this same period, numerous other buildings were constructed including the washhouse, cow barns, horse stables, sheep sheds, shops, and mills.[24]

Union Village was no longer a small settlement of easterners. The community rivaled several surrounding towns in population and commerce. In the 1820 census, Lebanon reported 1,079 residents, and Hamilton, the county seat of adjoining Butler County, was only a bit larger than Union Village with 660 residents. Hundreds joined the sect in the teens and began living quiet, productive lives. Those who chose to leave the Believers, however, did not always go quietly.

The Davis family affair, which led to a riot at Union Village on July 31, 1817, illustrates the opposition the sect still faced, as well as the consequences of accepting family members who disagreed about converting. Jonathan and Susannah Davis joined the Believers in 1805. When they signed the covenant in 1812, Mr. Davis pledged his 250 acres and all his personal property to the United Society. Eventually, the Davises and their children moved into the village. Mrs. Davis was sent to West Union for a time. When she returned to Union Village in 1813, she was ready to leave the sect. Mr. Davis left soon after, taking their daughter, Hulda, with him. Their son, Jonathan Jr., remained at Union Village. Mr. Davis later sued to recover losses for his farm. The Believers, who had already won a lawsuit instigated by apostate Robert Wilson for $250 back in 1811, again defended themselves in court. The Ohio Supreme Court finally decided the Davis suit in favor of the United Society in 1816.

Some Davis relatives retaliated. A cousin, John Davis, came to the village on July 31, 1817, to claim Jonathan Jr. The cousin, also an apostate, blamed the Believers for causing a rift in his marriage. Accounts of what happened that day vary. Another relative, William Davis, claimed that John Davis arrived at the village armed with a knife and club. After failing to collect Jonathan on his own, he returned with a mob armed with clubs and "loaded whips." Jonathan supposedly hid in the woods to escape his would-be liberators while mayhem ensued. Farrington and another eldress, Martha Sanford, were among those allegedly whipped by John Davis. According to another account, Jonathan was helping McNemar paint a dwelling when he saw

Hand-forged numbers dated a Union Village building

the mob approaching. He ran to the Mill family to hide until dark. McNemar remained up on the ladder where he had been painting, and preached to the mob for two hours until they dispersed peacefully, without the boy. Several brothers were arrested for keeping the boy from his cousin. McNemar and Samuel Rollins were formally charged with assault and battery. McNemar was later acquitted. Rollins was fined and returned to the village.[25]

The public was understandably confused about what happened at the village. Depositions against the Believers published in local newspapers after the riot led to more rumors. That fall, complaints by nine apostates were published. Most complaints involved compensation for land pledged to the United Society, separation of family members, and allegations of harsh treatment of children in the village. Darrow and McNemar were most often named in the depositions. Editor Abram Van Vleet abandoned objectivity when he published a note in the *The Western Star*, along with an apostate's complaint. The former Believer had struggled to bring home his son, who still lived at Union Village. Van Vleet wrote that the apostate had been "once under a satanic influence," but had escaped the sect's spell to locate his son and rescue him from the "perdition" he had been living in.[26]

As usual, neither corroborating witnesses nor evidence were produced to prove the various charges against the Believers. When someone wanted to leave the sect, other members tried hard to dissuade him or her. When someone did leave, he was usually given an open invitation to return. Asking to be re-admitted was called seeking a privilege. Prudence might have dictated a less open readmission policy, but the letters and church records from this period show that the Believers were passionately concerned about saving souls. Retaining the apostates' property was not the prime motivation. The church covenant had been upheld more than once in the civil courts, and the sect had structured its own system for compensating apostates. Shakers truly believed that their faith was the one sure path to salvation, and their tenacity in holding onto members appears to have been spiritually motivated. Each time opponents failed to discredit the Shakers in court, their opposition grew bitterer.

The blend of bitterness and tenacity led to the infamous Shaker Curse, and to mobs in 1819 and 1824. After the attacks in *The Western Star*, a Union Village brother received a vision in 1820 that Lebanon should be warned against persecuting the Shakers and that Dayton should be blessed for its comparatively kind treatment of the Watervliet settlement. Darrow dispatched McNemar and Francis Bedle to ride down the main streets of Lebanon one morning to pronounce woe on any who would persecute the Believers. In the afternoon, they rode through Dayton, pronouncing a blessing on all those who were kind to the Believers.[27] Several considerations may have motivated this unusual action. Revenge was not a Shaker practice, but Darrow may have reasoned that only a very dramatic public gesture could counteract the scurrilous items being printed in the local newspaper. The elders may have believed that they would lose potential converts—or be attacked by more violent mobs—if they did take not react strongly. After all, a newspaper publisher was a powerful person, but no match for the wrath of God.

Church records for the mobs of 1819 and 1824 are terse. The entries for the 1819 incident read:

Aug. 7. A mob at the South House today, of between 30 and 40 men; from in and about Middletown after a young woman named Phebe Johnson; whose Father had left her...in care of the Society, and who wished not to leave it. The mob failed in their design.

Aug. 9. Another mob make their appearance today; about 200 in number, on the same errand, with additional malice. The mob were quite wicked, some of them; Calvin Morrell was quite badly beaten by a wicked mobocrat. David Johnson, the young woman's father, came here today and disapproved of the riotous proceedings, but they appeared to care but little for him. They, however, failed finally in their object.

According to another account, Morrell was beaten almost to death by the mob. This was the second time that Morrell, an educated, prominent member, was targeted for mob violence. Opponents may have feared that his respectability would attract more converts. At any rate, Phebe told the mob she wanted to stay. Her mother, who had died, had been a Believer and had brought her children to Union Village, although her husband had not joined the sect. A younger brother was removed by the crowd, but escaped and returned to Union Village the next day.[28]

The 1824 mob was smaller and more easily managed, according to church records:

Sept. 7. This evening at 8 o'clock, a small mob of about 16 men came to the East House [the Children's Order] with one Francis Drake, to take away his daughter, Harriet R. D., a young woman, who did not chose to go. After making some disturbance in the family, the Church heard the alarm. The Brethren immediately repaired thither and took 10 of them prisoners without any harsh means, and brought them to the office—fed and lodged them comfortably till morning.

Sept. 8. This morning we discharge our prisoners, on their giving us their "Word & Honor!!" that they would do better hereafter.

Although church journals sometimes minimized the effects of these mobs, Union Village residents must have been disturbed by such vehement displays. As an old woman, Eliza Sharp recalled the aftermath of mob attacks that she lived through as a teenager. She recalled an incident where about 30 agitators waited until they knew the men were in the fields before storming one dwelling. The sisters inside barred the doors but the men broke through them, rushed into the house, and began breaking up the place. They tried to reach the upper floors of the dwelling, but the women filled the staircase, physically blocking their path. By the time the melee was over, the agitators numbered 300, Sharp wrote. Several of the brothers who had returned from the field were injured by the mob before a civil magistrate dispersed them. Nevertheless, tension lingered in the village. Opponents threatened to destroy the Believers' property and to burn down the village. According to Sharp, the brethren hid their clothing and furniture, and did not sleep for several nights as they guarded their homes.[29]

Occasionally, public officials threatened the Believers' property. In September 1819, the Warren County sheriff confiscated a horse from the Church family and a yoke of oxen from the West section for muster fines. Believers still refused to participate in militia musters or pay the subsequent fines. As a result, they lost livestock several times over the years.

One of the most stinging losses of this period was caused by one of their own: John Wallace, a trustee responsible for the community's financial health. Well-known in the county, Wallace had been mentioned in the anti-Shaker depositions published in 1817. He was accused of punishing a child harshly, and of defrauding converts of the full purchase price of their property. Neither accusation was proven, but Wallace's actions of 1818 were well documented. He left Union Village on February 12 to sell garden seeds in Hamilton and Springfield. He was scheduled to head next to Columbus but instead he rode into Cincinnati, went to a bank and borrowed $3,000 in the village's name. He left town with the money.[30] Wallace violated the Believers' trust, and made them debtors, something that church policy adamantly opposed. Despite that, the other trustees did not take legal action against Wallace. They simply started working to repay the money.

Two other losses were more permanent. Lucy Wright, who had supported the western Believers since the beginning, died on February 7, 1821, in Watervliet, New York. Union Village joined the United Society in mourning. Wright's death raised special concern in New York about the West's loyalty to her successor. Darrow and Farrington were considered—and called—Father and Mother by Believers throughout the frontier. Over a thousand members in Ohio, Kentucky, and Indiana followed their lead. Darrow reassured New Lebanon elders that spring of his love and obedience. He promised to treat the ministry as though Wright herself was still physically present.[31] The West's loyalty to the United Society and its central ministry had been publicly pledged in McNemar's book, *The Other Side of the Question. A Vindication of the Mother and the Elders*, published at Union Village in 1819. The book answered Shaker critics and demonstrated solidarity with eastern leaders.

Mortality was still on the central ministry's collective mind that summer. Darrow responded to their questions about his age and health in a letter. At 71, his sight and teeth were "middling good." Although his physical stamina was fading, his spirit was strong:

> *Yet I can go into a large assembly of Believers and fill them with life and power, so that they will be filled with the spirit and life of the Gospel. I have a large number of strong faithful Believers—Brethren and Sisters—here to support me, or I should not live...The Gospel is now planted here, that never can be shaken or removed, but will abide forever.[32]*

Darrow seemed to be assuring New Lebanon that the western societies could survive the loss of their first leaders. His assertion was soon tested. Farrington, who had stood beside him as lead eldress since 1806, became ill with dropsy in the fall of 1821. Her final illness was "borne with patience and Christian rectitude."[33] She died on October 28 at age 58. Her passing marked the end of a long partnership with Darrow, first at New Lebanon, then in Ohio. Rachel Johnson, who had been second in the ministry for the women, was elevated to the vacant position.

With hardships and losses, there was also success and camaraderie. When the church covenant was renewed in 1818, 259 members signed it. (That number did not reflect children and the Believers who had not taken the final step of membership.) It was a time of active growth. Members traveled fairly often between the western villages, sometimes assisting for a few days or for a few months at other communities. Union Village's residents included blacksmiths, masons, stonecutters, carpenters, tanners, fullers, clothiers, tailors, weavers, carders, spinners, cabinetmakers, and chair makers.[34] Most people knew how to do more than one job, and they were sent where their skills were needed. Jobs were sometimes shifted as well, because of the seasonal nature of the work or simply to provide variety.

Believers shared their talents, money, and provisions with other communities, just as the eastern settlements had done for them years earlier. Union Village sent sixteen barrels of oil, salt, sugar, pork, and flax to South Union in 1819, and later lent that community $2,000 to buy land.[35] Members also helped to construct most of the western communities. In the spring of 1825, several men spent four days in Watervliet, helping to build a meetinghouse. Although work was the most common reason for traveling, there was also time for fellowship. Ministries within the bishopric frequently visited each other. Those visits provided a change of pace in daily life. When some Pleasant Hill Believers visited in the fall of 1824, a large picnic was held in the woods for a "convivial notice of our...friends."[36]

Cooperation was also evident among the various families at Union Village. Members who had signed the covenant, giving their all to the joint interest, were particularly magnanimous, Darrow wrote. Those Believers, he told New Lebanon, were completely altruistic and single-minded in following their faith. Families frequently traded services and products. The Church family supplied the West section with brick for their new buildings one year, and did the West family's tanning and carding for them. In return, the West family gave the Church family 20 acres of wheat to harvest, and ten acres of grass to mow. Darrow praised his flock for their generosity:

> *And if there is any strife among them, it is to see who will be the most liberal and do the most good...The same faith and love exists between Believers here and at Watervliet that have come into Covenant relation in the Gospel. For instance, the Brethren at Watervliet by reason of sickness and other burdens were not able to sow their hay and grain. The Church here were forward in their work, so they sent them 14 Brethren who wrought one week and sowed their crops. Also, the Believers here learned that the Brethren at Watervliet had lost considerable of their meat, so that they were rather short. Well, the Church sent by the Brethren that went to help them, one barrel of meat and a quantity of sugar. We only mention this to show the faith of the Believers.*[37]

Union Village was increasingly "forward" in its agricultural and manufacturing efforts, and used commerce to forge better relations with the world. After the persecutions and the mobs had quieted down, the Believers decided to "forgive and forget," Oliver Hampton wrote. "By pursuing this plan and policy, it was not many years before we were left at peace in our possessions and indeed soon came to be highly respected and kindly patronized in many ways; especially in regard to finding ready sale for almost anything we chose to manufacture."[38]

By necessity and inclination, Union Village began as an agrarian community, and agriculture first brought it widespread respect. Shaker livestock soon was considered among the best in the county. The village is credited with introducing Merino sheep and thoroughbred cattle into Warren County, and for developing the Poland China hog.

Shaker loom

Their choice of Merino sheep proved that the Shakers were astute businessmen who wanted to make a profit. In 1812, when the animals were purchased by Union Village, Merinos were the craze of sheep producers across the country These Spanish sheep were valued for their fine wool, but import restrictions made the sheep difficult to obtain. Prices went as high as $2,500 for one full-blooded ram. The animals were thought to be the future of the American wool industry, and the Shakers wanted to offer their buyers the best, most profitable product.[39] Jeremiah Morrow, a Warren County native who was then a Congressman, was so impressed with the animals that he soon introduced them to his township, and the wool industry took off in the region. By the late teens, the Believers were manufacturing hats, blankets, and garments made from Merino and Saxon wool. Three thousand pounds of wool were carded in 1821. A young man from the nearby village of Monroe gave an unique endorsement for Shaker woolen goods: "I shall never forget a fine lamb wool hat that they made for me; it weighed about two pounds, and I frequently used it to take the edge off my teeth after I had eaten a sour apple, by biting the brim."[40]

Cattle also provided steady revenue. With their large farms and abundant resources, Believers led in introducing improved breeds of all kinds of farm animals. The Patton stock of English cattle was bred with the common cattle of the region to produce a superior animal. Longhorn cattle arrived about 1817, followed by shorthorns. The Shakers were also instrumental in importing thoroughbred Scottish shorthorns at mid-century and later exporting their Durham shorthorn cattle to England, selling $8,420 worth of blooded stock there in one year. Large dairy herds provided for the needs of the village, as well as surplus for the world. In one season, sisters produced 5,042 pounds of cheese.[41]

The Shakers' best-known agricultural achievement was developing the Poland China hog. Ironically, John Wallace, who later became an apostate, helped introduce the breed in 1816. A contemporary, Cephas Holloway, who had lived at Union Village since 1813, told the 1872 convention of the National Swine Breeders' Association how the breed developed. Holloway explained that Wallace had first seen the Big China breed during an 1816 trip to Philadelphia. Pleased with the breed's appearance, Wallace purchased one boar and three sows. At Union Village, the animals were crossed with the Russian breed, which was considered the best of its day. Their offspring was a superior swine that was first called the Warren County Hog. The name changed after Polish immigrant Asher Asher started buying stock from the Shakers. He resold the swine to a neighbor, who bragged that he had purchased the animal from Asher, the Polander. From that event, the breed soon became known as the Poland China hog. It thrived in the region's groves of nut-bearing trees and nutritious grasses. Hogs were bred for two main characteristics: size and ability to travel to market. The Poland Chinas were superior feeders and travelers, weighing up to 1,500 pounds at maturity. The breed was a mainstay of the economy until pork consumption was frowned upon by the central ministry in the 1840s.[42]

Meanwhile, furniture making also began at Union Village. Like most of the community's enterprises, residents began making furniture for themselves and then branched out to the world. Union Village's location was better for farming so it never became a large commercial furniture maker, as did New Lebanon. Their sales remained modest. Only a few pieces, primarily chairs, were sold to the public. In 1813, for example, sales included three chair frames for a grand total of $1.87, and a few sets of chairs for $5.25 per set. McNemar was one of the most prolific early furniture makers. Between 1812 and 1821, he made 1,463 chairs, as well as numerous wheels, reels, spools, and whirls for spinning. Most of these were used by the community. By 1820, a few Shaker chairs were being sold in Cincinnati. Frames were typically made of poplar or black walnut, harvested from the Shakers' property. Seats were first made of strips of woven wood, and of cornhusks. Later chairs featured woven tape seats. Some rocking chairs were made at Union Village, in addition to the more prevalent straight chairs. A large variety of furniture, including cabinets, beds, tables, stands, and built-in storage pieces, were also crafted for Believers' use.[43]

Whatever they made, they strove to make well. They believed they honored God by doing the best work they could. Humble tasks promoted humility. Handmade items were to be highly functional; ostentatious ornamentation was discouraged. But excesses occasionally crept into their products. As early as 1812, the New Lebanon ministry asked Darrow to "purge" superfluities and inflated prices throughout the bishopric. At issue were some baskets and knives being made at Pleasant Hill. Through the grapevine, the ministry had heard that the Kentucky community was making "very superfluous baskets—of diverse colors! which they sell to the world, to a great amount altho' they are worthless things." The ministry was also shocked that a Shaker-made knife had been sold at Pleasant Hill for the inflated price of $2.25. Such "Babylonish merchandize" was "an abomination in the sight of God."[44] Darrow was reminded that church rule forbade such practices. He was urged to speak out against these issues and make sure the western villages followed Gospel rule.

Pleasant Hill may have been swept away by optimism. As the Shakers entered the 1820s, a general feeling of progress prevailed. With confidence sometimes comes recklessness, and the central ministry might have been trying to prevent that with the publication of the Millennial Laws of 1821. These rules, some broad and others quite specific, governed Believers' relationships with each other and with the world. Lucy Wright had been pressed earlier to gather the United Society's unwritten precepts into a written code, but had resisted doing so. She may have feared that enforcement of the rules would become arbitrary and inflexible. She finally allowed Freegift Wells, an elder at

Watervliet, New York, to write down and categorize the rules, which were still not widely disseminated to the Believers. But six months after Wright's death,

the new ministry began to spread the laws among the communities.[45] There were now written regulations to guide and evaluate Believers. Ann Lee had believed that people could live in harmony and achieve a heavenly life on earth by following the Golden Rule. Publication of the Millennial Laws was in some ways a step backwards to the codified religion she had left behind in Manchester. The challenge for the next generation of Believers would be to keep the true spirit of Lee's faith, found in the prelude of the laws:

Cheese Strainer

The first & great command enjoined upon all Believers is, 'That we love the Lord our God with all our heart & with all our strength.'
And the second is like unto it, namely, That we love our Brethren and Sisters as ourselves.

Under the influence of the first we shall always be obedient to our Parents & Elders in the Gospel; and under the influence of the second we shall always do to others as we would wish others to do to us in like circumstances. On these two important points depend all the statues and ordinances contained in the following pages.[46]

Publications of another nature took place at Union Village during this period. Benjamin Youngs was called back to Warren County from South Union in 1823 to prepare a new edition of *The Testimony*. The village had obtained its own press by then, and McNemar set the type for the book. Since *The Testimony* was part theology and part history, the Believers saw nothing strange about updating it, and leaving it open to further revisions as history was made and more divine revelations were received. Youngs and McNemar wanted to publish the newest edition while Darrow was alive, and they succeeded. He must have been weakening visibly during his last months. There is no note of surprise in the characteristically brief mentions of his last days in the 1825 church records:

June 5. Father David Darrow is declining fast, so that it is expected he cannot last many weeks longer.

June 27. Father David deceased this morning, 20 minutes before 5. Elder Issachar and a number of the Watervliet people come down to attend the funeral.

June 28. The funeral was numerously attended at 2 o'clock p.m. The burial followed of course.

Five hundred members attended the funeral. Darrow was remembered as a direct link to Ann Lee, the parent of the western communities, and as a holy man. One speaker at the funeral suggested that Darrow could still lead and protect his people in the spirit realm. Shakers did not believe in the physical resurrection of the body but they strongly believed that the soul survived and could visit the living at will.

Local newspapers did not report on Darrow's death or funeral. It would take decades, but he would eventually be remembered in regional history books as "just in his dealings, firm in his convictions, wise in his understanding of human nature."[47] As years passed, Darrow's tenure was seen as a golden age of Shakerism in the West. Those views are reflected in many comments written about Union Village from the early to mid-20th century. It is clear that Union Village experienced its greatest growth during Darrow's time. Some of the most lasting Shaker theology was written then, and religious faith flourished. Darrow's leadership certainly contributed to those achievements. He weathered some of the most tumultuous conflicts between western Believers and the world, and helped the frontier communities survive. He has been ranked along with Joseph Meacham and Lucy Wright as the most influential Believers of the first quarter of the nineteenth century by a modern historian.[48]

After Darrow's death, the central ministry appeared uncertain of what to do next. As second elder at Union Village, easterner Solomon King would have been the logical successor. That was the pattern followed when Rachel Johnson became first eldress after Ruth Farrington's death. Yet that did not happen at Darrow's death. Speculation must have been strong about who the next leader would be, for in spite of equality of the sexes, Darrow had always been perceived as the primary leader of the bishopric, rather than Farrington or Johnson. The original three missionaries were now leading other communities. John Meacham had been called back East in 1818. Benjamin Youngs was at South Union. Issachar Bates was at West Union, and also spent time at Watervliet. McNemar seemed qualified for the position but was also valuable in other capacities throughout the West. Despite being trained in the Gospel as a young man and remaining a devoted Believer, Malcolm Worley never seemed to be considered for a higher position. McNemar and Worley reportedly had conflicts with Bates that may have removed all three from consideration.

David Darrow had asserted in 1821 that Union Village was so deeply established in the Gospel that nothing could ever shake it. At his funeral, a song written by McNemar was sung which repeated that theme:

The Gospel foundation is faithfully laid.
On Heaven's unchangeable plan.
An Order established to second and aid,
The Work which good Father began.
These pleasing reflections may comfort us all,
And strengthen our Ministry's hands.
Assured that no part of the Building need fall,
So long as the foundation stands.[49]

The foundation was about to be tested.

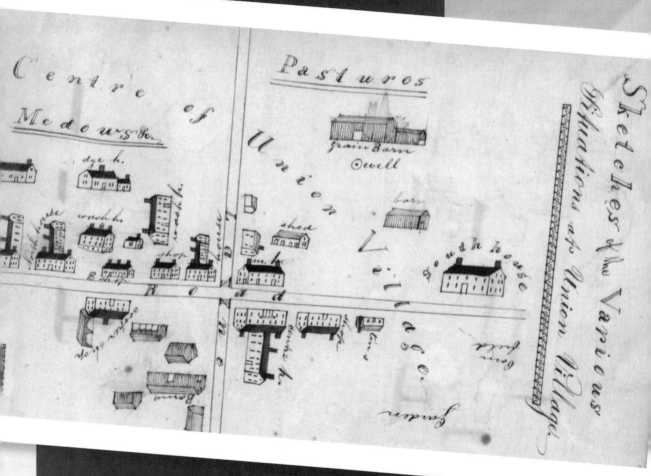

Top: Isaac N. Youngs, a member of the United Society's central ministry, toured Union Village for the first time in the summer of 1834. As he visited the various families in the village, he sketched each "lot," or section. It was his way of taking a picture of the community back home to New Lebanon, New York. This drawing and the ones on the following pages are copies made from Youngs' originals in 1835 by another Shaker, George Kendall. **Right:** Detail of Marble Hall

✺ Chapter Seven ✺
Fault Lines—
Life After Darrow

The five years following David Darrow's death were critical for Union Village. While the Believers built up industries that helped make Shaker a household name, they found some satisfaction in being tolerated by the world. But inside the village, members were often anything but tolerant of one another and confident of the future. Uncertainty and disharmony in leadership strained their daily and spiritual lives.

Believers realized that the future of the entire western move-

ment was at stake, not just that of Union Village. North Union and Whitewater, young and struggling, were in need of considerable financial and spiritual aid. West Union, which had struggled since its inception, was beginning its final decline. A leadership crisis loomed at Pleasant Hill, where the lead eldress was eventually removed from the community. Solomon King and Rachel Johnson led Union Village with little experience or authority to oversee a large bishopric spread over three states. Darrow had been a link between New and Old Believers, and had the confidence of the central ministry behind him. There was no one exactly like him to take his place, and no clear agreement about how his successor should be chosen.

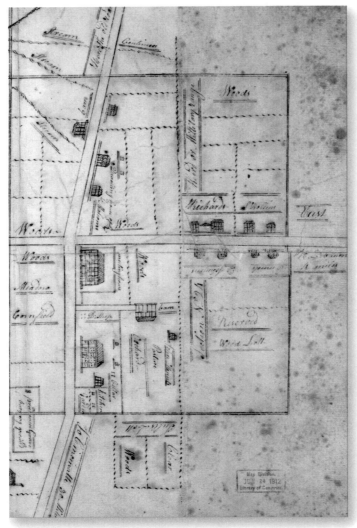

Malcolm Worley was respected by the central ministry as the first western Shaker convert. His dwelling is shown close to the meetinghouse. Worley remained a Shaker but more and more young people left the faith as the nineteenth century progressed, taking the road to Cincinnati and beyond.

"We were all fearful of giving the ark the wrong touch," McNemar wrote later.[1] Ironically, he was one of the leaders embroiled in the disharmony that ensued. Twenty years had passed since the founding of Union Village, yet distinct rivalries remained between some of the original Easterners and the western converts. McNemar felt that the Easterners never fully appreciated the contributions the Westerners made in spreading Shakerism. Bates provoked jealousy when some Believers referred to him as Father and as a patriarch of the West. The central ministry solved that problem by decreeing that the titles of Mother and Father should not be used for anyone. McNemar and Worley expressed ambivalent opinions about Bates. While acknowledging that he had special gifts, they claimed that he had been "vulgarized" by his military service, and was too concerned about being everyone's friend to be an effective spiritual leader. McNemar may also have been jealous of Bates' obvious influence in the West. Between 1825 and 1830, Bates had extended visits at each of the western communities and visited the East for guidance and support twice. He found dissenters within the Pleasant Hill community and a group of malcontents at Watervliet (Ohio) who wanted to dissolve the joint interest. Bates attributed some of the dissension and apostasy of the era to the final closing of West Union in 1827. Several members who were already struggling with Shaker beliefs used the closing as a means of attacking the integrity of the sect. The dissatisfied members rationalized that if the Believers were truly doing God's will, that West Union would have been successful.[2]

The central ministry's concerns over loyalty and dissension resulted in a flurry of correspondence in which Union Village leaders pledged solidarity with the United Society. In an 1826 letter signed by all the elders and eldresses, the Believers reassured New York of their fidelity and affirmed that they were surviving without their spiritual parents. As much as they revered Farrington and Darrow, they placed their faith in the Gospel, not in any specific individuals. They also wrote that they were pleased with King and Johnson, and reconciled to whatever the future would bring, yet there was a tone of resentment in their reassurances:

> *We apprehend the point has been so effectually gained, that not even a dog can move his tongue against the order established by Father [Joseph Meacham] and Mother [Ann Lee] and now firmly supported by their successors. In this order we have found salvation, and to it we are determined to cleave at the risk of all things. The blessed fruits of the Gospel are too manifest to admit any hesitation in maintaining it, if it should be to the laying down of our lives.[3]*

The central ministry responded approvingly, overlooking the pensive tone and reiterating the importance of unity and obedience. They expressed joy and confidence in the Believers' missionary work:

> *We are well pleased to learn that you consider yourselves as Branches of the same root with us. And when we see the Branches flourish, then we know that the root is holy. We rejoice that you do so well sustain the 'trial of being bereaved of the immediate support of your good Parents;' that it has neither shaken your faith nor marred your confidence in the work of God; that you find in the successor, all the needful gifts & graces of the predecessor, so that*

*the body is supported & kept unbroken. This is a mark of good faith, & an
evidence of being Mother's children...now to witness the wonderful increase of
Christ's Kingdom in the Western Country causes us great joy & satisfaction.*[4]

The ministry's message was clear: true Believers were part of one family, a
family that could not be disrupted by death or disobedience. Believers had to
respect the United Society's decisions, and the central ministry had to maintain
control of the western settlements to continue proselytizing successfully.

By 1830, a greater effort was made to blend the new and the old when
appointing leaders. King and Johnson, both easterners, were first in the
ministry but that was to be expected because they had been Believers
significantly longer than any westerners. King had been formally named
Darrow's permanent successor in the West in the fall of 1829. Johnson had held
her position since Ruth Farrington's death in 1821. Joshua Worley, Malcolm's
son, was second in the ministry for the men, and Nancy McNemar, Richard's
daughter, was second for the women. Another of Worley's sons, Joseph, was an
elder at the North House. James McNemar, another of Richard's sons, was an
elder at the Brick House. Charlotte Morrell, daughter of Calvin Morrell, was
an eldress at the North House. The second generation of western Believers was
being integrated into the leadership, and a more blended family was emerging.

Interestingly enough, despite the ongoing leadership crisis, no member
of the central ministry had yet visited Union Village. Although several of the
eastern Believers as well as McNemar had made the pilgrimage to New Lebanon
during the previous two decades, the visits had never been returned. That fact
surely contributed to the feelings of neglect the Believers sometimes voiced.
A prestigious visitor from the world did visit Union Village, however, shortly
after Darrow's death, and the Believers welcomed him eagerly. Henry Clay,
then Secretary of State, came to mark the groundbreaking for the Miami and
Erie Canal near Middletown, about 10 miles west of the village, in July 1825.
At the time, Clay was one of the best-known statesmen in America. He had
just lost a hotly contested four-man race for the presidency, and received the
cabinet position in return for supporting the winning candidate, John Quincy
Adams. Clay, who represented Kentucky for multiple terms in Congress, had
gained fame over the years as an orator. He completely charmed the Believers
on his two visits that summer. The church diarist found Clay "very familiar and
affable, was quite inquisitive to know the order of appointment and succession

in the ministry—wanted to know the evidence we had of miraculous gifts of healing...[we] thought he would make a good subject of the Society."[5] The renowned orator won Believers' admiration by pledging his support if the community faced any further persecution. In their enthusiasm for Clay, the Believers' rather overestimated his fitness for membership. Clay was a longtime advocate of using military might to secure personal and national freedom, going back to the War of 1812. He had also dueled with Virginia statesman John Randolph over the contested 1824 presidential election. Clay wasn't likely to fit into the pacifist mold of a Believer. Despite that, the Shakers and Clay found plenty to discuss. They empathized with his interest in healing gifts. Clay's daughter, Eliza, who had accompanied him to Ohio, had suddenly taken sick. Clay had been forced to stay over in Lebanon due to her illness. Sadly, the Believers could not help Eliza. Although Shaker literature contains several cases of miraculous healings, such events had never been commonplace. Eliza died three weeks later in Lebanon.

Consumed with his daughter's illness and his official duties, Clay did not record his impressions of Union Village. But his remarks at Pleasant Hill four years later could have applied to Union Village in 1825, a sign of the disharmony that tainted the western communities after Darrow's death. In a speech to the Kentucky Believers, Clay said that he didn't agree with their religious practices but had learned to appreciate their communal life: "It is in its social aspect that I can contemplate and have ever admired your society. The example which it exhibits of industry, economy, regularity and fidelity to engagements cannot fail to communicate a salutary influence around you.... I should regret the existence of any dissensions among you which might threaten a dissolution of your interesting community; and I sincerely hope that none such may arise."[6]

Clay's comments also mirrored a changing attitude towards the Believers. Their private lives might be nonconformist, but economically they were useful and successful in society. The canal system—Clay's reason for being in Warren County in 1825—was planned to increase commerce in the region and stimulate the weak economy. As businessmen, Shaker leaders strongly supported the canal. They saw how it could improve distribution and sales of their goods and provide easier travel between Shaker communities. More dignitaries joined Clay in Lebanon that summer. New York Governor DeWitt Clinton; Jeremiah Morrow, then Ohio governor; and General William Henry Harrison, whom Believers knew from West Union, came for the canal festivities and stayed on to visit Union Village. The visitors wanted to study Shaker Creek to determine if it and another local creek could contribute enough water to construct a lateral canal coming from Lebanon to intersect with the Miami canal. The elders approved of the use of their creek, located in what was commonly called Shaker Swamp, for the local enterprise. One of the design engineers boarded with the Believers during construction of the canal.[7] Although the lateral canal did not prove to be as successful as planners hoped, the Shakers' willingness to participate in the project demonstrated their progressive approach to commerce.

By 1830, more changes were brewing at Union Village. The population had dropped to 502 people. Women outnumbered men, 264 to 238. The majority of the members were white; only two black males and six black females were counted. The Believers attributed the decline to "the gradual wearing off of former inspiring testimony of the Word; (and) the reception of unsteady characters."[8] Action was taken to prevent further erosion. A new church

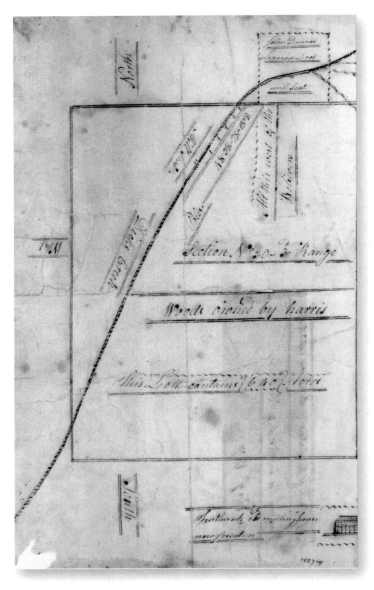

The Shakers agreed to allow local businessmen to use Dick's Creek, commonly called Shaker Creek, to develop a lateral canal to intersect with the Miami and Erie Canal.

constitution, prepared by the New Lebanon ministry, was signed by Union Village members. They were reminded of their principal obligation: "The faithful improvement of our time and talents in doing good…a duty which God requires of mankind as rational and accountable beings."[9] Specific duties of elders, deacons, trustees, and members were outlined. Elders were to watch over their respective families, instruct members as to their duties, counsel and encourage them, chastise them when necessary, and conduct worship services. Deacons and deaconesses were to oversee the domestic needs of their families. Trustees oversaw the village's temporal and financial affairs. Account books and records were to be kept scrupulously and trustees had to sign a declaration of trust affirming that all their business transactions were on behalf of the United Society and in the interest of all members.

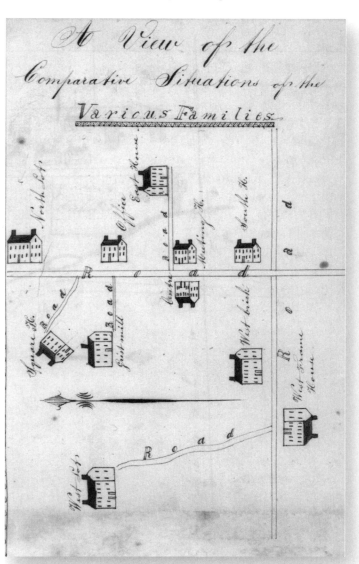

The Grist Mill section was the site of many commercial enterprises.

The important concept of clothing as a symbol of unity resurfaced in 1827, when sisters all began to dress entirely in white—"like a crowd of saints"—at Sabbath meetings.[10] The practice spread to other communities and, by 1835,

Shaker women throughout the United States appeared in white at Sunday services. What began in 1819 in New Lebanon as a laundry convenience was now viewed in a spiritual context. On a more formal level, efforts were renewed to have more people sign the church covenant, which turned over their property to the United Society and—the ministry hoped—ensured their faithfulness. By 1829, 304 adults at Union Village had signed the covenant. Between that year and 1836, McNemar was sent to the other Ohio and Kentucky communities to have as many people as possible sign the covenant. Ironically, McNemar, who had donated his property in 1805, forgot to sign the document.[11]

Despite the reassurances of solidarity, Union Village broke ranks with New Lebanon over an important issue during this period. The central ministry opposed their military veterans receiving pensions or bounty lands for prior military service, calling them blood payments. But, under the state Pension Act of 1832, Ohio leaders allowed veterans to collect their pensions, saying it was the only way they could recover militia fines paid over the years and recoup their 1812 losses from West Union. New Lebanon severely criticized Union Village for the action.[12] This may have contributed to the central ministry's ultimate decision to appoint an easterner to lead the West.

In the summer of 1834, the central ministry sent Elder Rufus Bishop to see first-hand what was happening in the West. This was the ministry's first visit. With Bishop was Brother Isaac N. Youngs. They made an extended tour of all the western communities, spending several weeks at Union Village. Bishop reserved his observations for the central ministry, but Youngs kept a journal as he

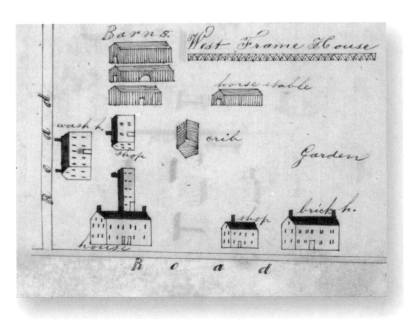

Youngs' sketch of the West Frame House family shows several agricultural buildings.

visited each family and made detailed drawings of the village. While Bishop assessed the spiritual health and leadership of the community, Youngs visited the shops, mills, and barns. He noted that he was very impressed by the village's business ingenuity and accomplishments. Agriculture in the community was thriving, with 705 acres dedicated for grazing and raising crops and produce. Corn commanded 252 acres; wheat, 140; oats, 52; rye, 10; and gardens, 45 acres. Livestock included 600 sheep, 510 swine, and 369 head of cattle.[13]

Innovations used at various shops and mills intrigued Youngs. The various communities had always exchanged information but Youngs now had a chance to personally trade ideas and record new methods to take back East. At a shop where Timothy Bonel made chairs and wheels, Youngs shared a chair-repair technique that was used at New Lebanon. He noted how horse-power was used throughout the Union Village, from running the machinery at the cooperage where barrels were made to turning a new washing machine, three and a half feet in diameter, where large loads of family laundry were washed. While visiting the East family, Youngs took special pains to record the details of an innovative loom that he saw at the Sisters' shop. At the Square House family, he studied a new device for grinding shears at the clothier's shop and a new machine for boring fence posts. At the North House, he took notice of a new type of spinning wheel called the Pleasant Spinner.

Youngs also visited the pottery, a seemingly common business that illustrates an interesting fact about the United Society. A common misconception is that all Shaker villages operated in exactly the same way and that each aspect of life was identical. Although Believers shared a common faith and lifestyle, each village was unique in many respects. Some of the most visible aspects of individual difference were the diversified industries at various communities. In southwestern Ohio, for instance, Union Village might have been recognized for pottery, Watervliet for iron wear, and Whitewater for produce. It was a very concrete way for the world to see that Believers weren't all completely alike. It might make people feel—on a secular level—that the Shakers weren't as different from them as was thought.

Union Village is believed to have had the only commercial Shaker pottery in the nineteenth century. The pottery may have begun to fill the members' needs, and then expanded into a commercial enterprise because of the availability of good clay or the presence of skilled potters in the community. Four potters lived in the West Brick Family in 1834. Account books show that clay pipes, commonly smoked by men and women of the era, were made and sold from Union Village as early as 1813. An 1824 newspaper advertisement advised customers that the Shakers were "keeping on hand a general assortment of Potters-ware warranted to be first quality; for which sugar, flax, and flax-seed will be taken in payment." A large wagonload of pottery was taken to Pleasant Hill by three brothers that same year.[14]

At the time of Youngs' visit, the pottery was a two-story building in the West Brick section. Behind the workshop was a large kiln. Youngs watched the potters turn a large vessel and a jug, and noticed other crockery and earthenware in the building. Several brothers worked fulltime at the pottery, and had a good market for their wares. Two years later, the smith shop at the West section was expanded by 45 feet, providing a total of 80 feet for a pottery. All the potters moved from the West Brick section to the North section during the winter of 1835–36. As a result of the move, two large buildings—one brick and one frame—were constructed to accommodate the pottery business. A large kiln was also added, and ware making soon began. The size of the operation and Youngs' comments indicate a healthy business. "We have now and expect to keep constantly on hand a large assortment of ware, for sale at the Union Village Pottery," noted an 1839 advertisement. An early 20th century newspaper article mentions "squat little black vases" made by Union Village potters, which suggests more decorative wares made for the world.[15]

Youngs' journal entries also reveal a bit about daily routine and life at the village. An amateur artist, he brought some drawings of New Lebanon that he

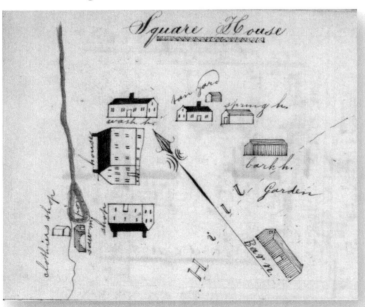

Youngs visited the clothiers' shop at the Square House family.

shared on visits to each family. Youngs also sketched views of the dwellings and shops of the respective families as he visited. He met several people who had family at New Lebanon, and was entrusted with messages to take back home. During one visit, he met Daniel Stag, a blind man, "a sound believer; much pleased to feel us; can spin mop yarn, works a good deal in the kitchen."[16] Stag lived in a one-room log cabin, where everything was

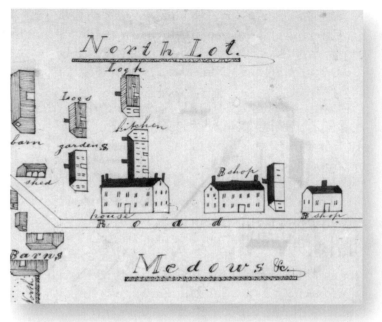

North Lot

arranged for his convenience and to accommodate his companion, a little dog. Believers typically arranged appropriate work for any handicapped or elderly person, realizing that everyone needed to feel useful. Church records note that members also cared for those who could not work because of physical or mental challenges.

The Believers showered their visitors with hospitality. Youngs and Bishop were treated to a welcome hymn, composed in their honor, and greeted with songs in several of the shops. They also participated in several meetings where Youngs was impressed by the spirited dancing and singing. At a Sabbath public meeting, their hosts introduced the visitors to a new anthem, "Be Ye Holy," and danced in both a circular march and a square order march. That evening, in a members-only meeting, the singing and dancing grew more intense:

A number of songs were sung and then they had some exercise in the quick circular, and finally, nothing would do but I must lead the ring. We had a real high, and after dancing awhile they sung some word songs, the animation grew higher and higher, and shouting and clapping of hands ensued, with hopping and skipping like so many newlights that seemed at a loss for ways to express themselves. It was enough to fill one with surprise, and make one stare, and set erect one's hair, to hear the shouts and view the exercises.[17]

Music was also part of a birthday surprise that Youngs received on July 4. On a visit to the Brick House that morning, he and Bishop were "in a sort of sly or humorous way, invited into a room where a brother or two, and some sisters, were paraded to sing a little hymn to us, and behold, it was on purpose for my birthday!"[18] He received a new pair of trousers as a gift.

The scenes of music, birthday presents, fellowship with friends, and enthusiastic worship contrast sharply with the somber view of Shakers the world held. Englishman Thomas Trollope's account of a visit to Union Village in that era contains impressions similar to those of other visitors. He found the Believers to be remarkably prosperous, well fed, and dull. Like many visitors, he saw the dancing during worship as an "uncouth" spectacle, never understanding the intent of the dancers:

They jumped and 'shook' themselves in two divided bodies [men and women]. Any spectator would be disposed to imagine that the whole object of the performance was bodily exercise. It seemed to be carried on to the utmost extent that breath and bodily fatigue would permit. Many were mopping the perspiration from their faces. No laughing or gladness or exhilaration whatever appeared to accompany or be caused by the exercise. All was done with an air of perfect solemnity. All the men and all the women seemed to be in the enjoyment of excellent health. Most of them seemed to be somewhat more than well nourished—rather tending to obesity. They were florid, round-faced, sleek and heavy in figure. I observed no laughter, and very little conversation among them. The women were almost all in the prime of life, and many young. But there was a singular absence of good looks among them. Some had regular features enough, but they were all heavy, fat, dull-looking, like well-kept animals. I could not spy one pair of bright eyes in the place.[19]

The Believers appeared increasingly somber in front of outside visitors. They may have felt that a serious attitude best conveyed their deep faith. Worship was to be a respectful time; had the Believers shown obvious pleasure in their dancing, they risked being criticized as frivolous. They might have done better to explain to their visitors why they danced, yet their attitude seemed to be:

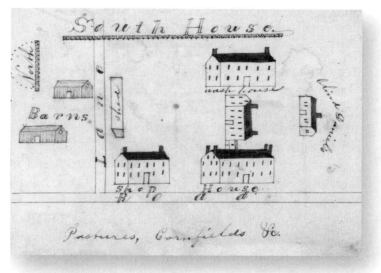

Youngs met "Blind Daniel" and drew his home as part of the South House lot.

"Accept us as we are or reject us." They may have felt such a posture was necessary to remain separate from the world. In light of the criticisms and attacks they had experienced, they may have been justifiably wary of the public's reaction. Or the visitors may not have been totally objective in their observations. If visitors had a preconceived idea of Shakers as a peculiar, repressed group of religious fanatics, they would probably interpret what they saw accordingly. Youngs, on the other hand, may have been biased in favor of the community. He knew that his journal might well be read by members of the central ministry.

After visiting other western communities, he and Bishop headed back to New York that October. A few months later, changes began at Union Village. In March 1835, Issachar Bates and Benjamin Youngs were called back to New York. Bates, 77, had been serving as elder at Watervliet. Believers seldom retired from work, but as they became elderly, they were often removed from leadership positions. Youngs, who had been first elder at South Union since 1811, was 60. Thirty years after they came west to start a new religious community, they traveled back to New York together. Bates reacted to the summons with his customary emotion: "So I wandered up and down bewailing my fate—but all to no purpose. I must go and leave my people who felt dearer to me than my natural life. For if I could have died and been buried on the ground that I purchased with my life, I could have laid my old head down...in peace."[20] Bates and Youngs began turning over their affairs to their successors and bidding farewell to their friends in anticipation of a June departure. Back in New York, Bates turned to gardening for the remainder of his life. He died at New Lebanon in 1837. Youngs continued working for the ministry in the East. With the help of Calvin Green, an eastern brother, he prepared the fourth edition of *The Testimony of Christ's Second Appearing*. This last edition of the book was published in Albany in 1856. Youngs died in 1855 at Watervliet, New York.

With all three of the original missionaries gone by the spring of 1835, the stage was set for a new leader. But the central ministry did not act immediately. Meanwhile, other difficulties plagued Union Village that spring. Caterpillars swarmed the woods in May, destroying much of the Shakers' timber. A flash flood struck on June 9, causing $10,000 to $20,000 damage. Cut lumber and timber was literally swept away and all three of the community's mill dams overflowed. The tan yard flooded and bottom fields were washed out. Half of the clothier's shop, with contents, was destroyed. A large gristmill was heavily damaged. Heavy rains and hail persisted throughout June. An unidentified man drowned in the lowlands adjoining the West family property. The wet weather was followed by an outbreak of what the locals called "Indian cholera" in the nearby hamlet of Red Lion, but the disease apparently did not spread.[21]

August brought the second visit in two years of leaders from New Lebanon. The central ministries of each community met privately to assess Union Village's future and then departed together for a visit to Watervliet, where McNemar had been temporarily assigned since Bates' departure.

Autumn brought an event that undoubtedly hastened changes at Union Village. Nathan Sharp, one of Union Village's most trusted members, ran off with a small fortune. A trustee for 23 years, he supervised the community's finances. He handled the sale of West Union in 1827 and still controlled assets from that community. On the morning of September 9, Sharp rode into Lebanon and announced to several people that he had left the community. He took property and cash estimated at $10,000, and a horse. His brother, William, an elder of the Brick family, had left the village several days earlier. A third defection followed on October 1 when Charlotte Morrell left the Believers to marry Nathan. The couple must not have feared retaliation, for they went to live at the Green Tree Tavern, just a mile north of Union Village. Sharp became the tavern keeper.[22]

The shocked members were faced with a host of new problems. Fearing they might lose the village to Sharp, the leaders turned to the East for advice and support. Seth Wells urged McNemar to keep the matter out of the civil courts. Even if Union Village won a court case, the proceedings would be lengthy and expensive, he warned. He reassured McNemar that the land comprising the village should be safe from any claims made by Sharp: "[The lands] were purchased for the benefit of the Society and most of the original purchases were paid for with monies sent from New Lebanon and other eastern Societies for that very purpose, and the Society has had peaceable possession of them nearly 30 years. This land therefore belongs to the United Society as a body of people...they are lawfully entitled to the benefits of it."[23] Wells proved correct about the land, but the Believers failed to recover all the stolen money. They had to be content with tightening the covenant's language to try to protect themselves in the future. Wells advised Believers to forget Sharp, whom he compared to Judas Iscariot: "He must sink vastly below that old traitor—doubtless too low for the pity or compassion of his much injured Brethren & Sisters ever to reach him."[24]

But New Lebanon could not forget or overlook Union Village's unsettled condition. The community that was supposed to lead the West was failing to govern itself successfully. Solomon King and Rachel Johnson were called to New Lebanon in early October. David Meacham, a son of Father Joseph Meacham and brother of John Meacham, was temporarily assigned to take King's place. Johnson's absence was filled by Betsy Hastings. Joshua Worley and Nancy McNemar were still second in the ministry. The next Sunday, the ministry decreed that the church office would be closed to outside visitors on the Sabbath. The practice of visiting with, and sometimes dining with, outsiders was thought to encourage apostates. Meacham was called to New Lebanon at the end of November to help decide Union Village's future.[25]

Union Village's diarist ended the 1835 village records with an optimistic remark: "Altho it would seem that our misfortunes or troubles had been overwhelming, yet we have unspeakable cause of thankfulness to God, who will no doubt cause all things to work for good, inasmuch as the foundation yet remaineth sure and steadfast."[26] Such faith-based optimism had seen Union Village through many trying times, and would be needed again and again in the future.

The new year brought a reorganization of the village's families, ordered by New Lebanon. Elders stated that the changes were to make Union Village compatible with New Lebanon's structure. Some families were reassigned to other dwellings, and a different building was proposed for the office. The biggest changes had to do with the Church family and the Children's Order. The Church family, which was the most influential group, was split into two families: the First and Second Families. The First Family was to be the largest and to occupy three dwellings. The Second Family was to occupy two dwellings. Each family would have its own joint interest, meaning they would work separately, pay their respective expenses, and earn their own income. The Children's Order, which had been included in the East Family, was dissolved and the members incorporated into other families. New Lebanon's intent seems to have been to increase supervision over individual families and members, and to prevent clannish loyalties from developing. The East dwelling was at the site of McNemar's old farm, and apparently many members had sentimental attachments to the area and to McNemar. Even Isaac Youngs took special care to label McNemar's old cabin in drawings he made during his 1834 visit. McNemar intimated in his writings that he had been offered the leadership of Union Village but refused it because he was so often called away to assist other western communities. Although he was frequently absent from Union Village, he retained the title of elder, usually serving at the Brick House.[27]

King, still at New Lebanon, announced his resignation as first elder, in a letter read to the Union Village Believers on February 14, 1836. The same letter announced that Freegift Wells had been appointed to the position by the central ministry. Second in the ministry at Watervliet, Wells was responsible for the publication of the Millennial Laws of 1821. Soon after arriving at Union Village in April 1836, he began preaching a series of sermons against hidden sins. At a special Sabbath meeting of the Church and Second families on May 1, a startling event occurred. At the end of the service—which included the reading of a letter from New Lebanon—McNemar surrendered the title of elder and its accompanying influence to Wells. The action implied that New Lebanon and Wells feared Believers would be more loyal to McNemar than to Wells, and that disunity would destroy the village. As part of the general reorganization, additional changes were made, from family elders to trustees. Nancy McNemar was removed as second eldress in the community and Sally Sharp took her place. The new ministry, accompanied by an eastern elder, Rufus Bryant, visited the

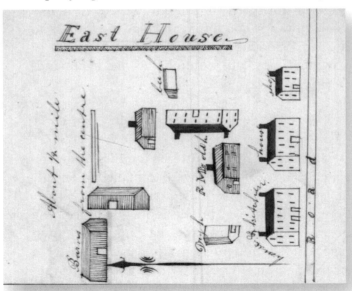

Richard McNemar's old house is shown in Youngs' sketch of the East House family.

other western societies during the spring and summer.[28]

Natural events preoccupied members that summer. Caterpillars were back for the third straight year; damage was particularly severe to oak, hickory, sugar maple, and elm trees. A devilish thunderstorm in late August damaged the First family's kitchen when lightning struck, filling the room "with a strong sulpherous stench," the church record noted. "No persons injured but some were smartly shocked."[29]

The storm proved a harbinger of the future. Wells' Sabbath talks leaned more and more toward fire and brimstone. In early August, "a powerful gift of mortification" was experienced in the church's meeting with "much bowing, shaking, etc."[30] Wells also decreed that no newspapers were to be read on the Sabbath. He prepared Believers to turn inward for a revival. The Shaker concept of mortification was central to becoming a more Christ-like person. Only by destroying the old, sinful nature could a Believer begin to live a truly holy life. In the winter of 1837, Wells preached a message that Lucy Wright had given years ago in New Lebanon, urging repentance and humiliation. That Sunday, February 5, was the start of a "refreshing" at Union Village as many members began "breaking their bands [of sin] and mortifying a proud carnal nature."[31] The service began a revival that would surpass anything Richard McNemar and Malcolm Worley had experienced in Kentucky 35 years earlier, and would change Union Village forever.

Top: During the Era of Manifestations, divine spirits sent gifts of beautiful drawings, songs, and poetry through Shaker messengers. This is a reproduction of a gift drawing called "The Tree of Life" that was drawn by Hannah Cohoon at Hancock, Massachusetts, in 1854.
Right: School children at Otterbein home.

℅ Chapter Eight ℅
Wisdom's Paradise— Spiritual Revival and Societal Upheaval

Spiritualism had a respected role in the Shaker tradition, dating back to Ann Lee's visions in the eighteenth century. Believers professed that angels and spirits of the dead revealed God's wishes through visions. Divine revelations were gifts to be treasured, not feared. Union Village members were taught to trust in visions. They knew of the vision of the beckoning arm that influenced Richard McNemar to convert in 1805. They remembered when Lee's spirit came to comfort David Darrow during the fever epidemic of

1813. Many members believed they had been visited by spirits of departed loved ones. They believed the visitations were God's way of revealing His true intentions for humanity. So when Freegift Wells read two letters telling of the "extraordinary spiritual waking up" in Watervliet, New York, in the fall of 1837, Union Village families assumed that they, too, would soon experience supernatural gifts.

The ensuing decade of intense spiritualism became known as Mother Ann's Work or the Era of Manifestations. In Watervliet, it began with children ages 10 to 12 who saw visions and heard voices while seemingly in trances. They sometimes shook, whirled around, and were thrown to the ground. Many of their visions concerned kind angels talking and walking with them in beautiful, flower-filled fields. But not all of the visions were so benign. Shaker historians wrote: "It was not all of heaven and happiness. Sometimes they (the children) were with those in suffering and torment; they seemed suffocated, as by sulphur fumes; their bodies were distorted and bore every mark of intense agony, while their screeches and cries were terrible to hear." Their agonies passed with the trance and, after sleeping, the children regained their normal demeanor. Occasionally, those in trances received imaginary gifts, such as small golden crosses. As the phenomenon spread to adults, physical manifestations became more pronounced. Adults not only danced, but also whirled around or jerked their heads and arms, seemingly uncontrollably. "The acute mortification caused by such involuntary antics was accepted as a good dose of spiritual tonic," the historians wrote.[1] The spirits called for a rededication to Lee's ways and a thorough soul-searching of each member. If Believers weren't living the holy, humble life, they couldn't help converts to do so either.

> After Wells spoke, singing started, and almost immediately, something different was felt in the meetinghouse. "Shaking commenced, and it appeared almost like electricity."

As the revival spread through the East, the western communities learned of the miraculous happenings by letter. Believers anticipated the moment that Mother Ann's Work would start in Ohio. When manifestations began at Pleasant Hill, Union Village members were disappointed that they had not yet experienced the gift. At a "very heavy" church meeting on August 26, 1838, Freegift Wells read a letter from Pleasant Hill describing some of the supernatural occurrences in that community and confidently stated that Union Village would doubtlessly be affected as well. After Wells spoke, singing started, and almost immediately, something different was felt in the meetinghouse. "Shaking commenced, and it appeared almost like electricity," wrote church scribe Andrew Houston. "The power of God seemed to shower upon the assembly, and to a number it appeared to be irrisistible. It affected a large proportion of the assembly more or less. This felt like a refreshing shower in a dry season, and we considered it a small foretaste of the great work that was rolling on."[2]

From then on, more members began to experience involuntary physical activity during meetings. As reports of more intense manifestations arrived from South Union, Pleasant Hill, and North Union, spirit activity increased at Union Village. On October 27, 1838, several members heard heavenly trumpets, and singing. A few weeks later, manifestations broke out among the Young Believers at the West Section. Houston reported having difficulty adequately describing what he witnessed. In general, Union Village members experienced the same types of phenomenon they read about in the other communities: they fell into trances, sang unfamiliar songs, and spoke in the voice and manner of a Believer who had died. As in the War-Time Revival of 1815, Believers were counseled to go to war against the Devil and against their own proud, sinful natures. The imagery in church journals grew more vivid as meetings became more physical. "Our meetings continue very animated; the beast and whore, and a self-willed high sense, are now to be purged from the consecrated ground in battles of shaking," Houston wrote.[3] Believers were literally to shake off their worldly natures.

Manifestations occurred in the public Sunday morning meetings and in the Believers' private meetings on Sunday evenings and during the week. Not everyone immediately embraced the manifestations. Houston acknowledged that some members were skeptical of the visionists' legitimacy. By late 1838, he was recording behaviors so strange that he could conceive of no other cause except a supernatural one. He struggled to describe what he witnessed. "The powerful involuntary bodily exercises; the piercing conviction, self abasement; the falling, shaking, bowing, dancing, and the many marvelous agitations of the subjects of this work, will never be fully described on paper; while the beholder is compelled to acknowledge the finger of divine agency in this work," he wrote.[4]

Adults and children were caught up in the fervor. During a public meeting on January 13, 1839, a number of adult Believers were literally knocked off their feet by powerful spirits and the accompanying physical agitation. That evening, a group of boys, ages 6 to 12, went into trances during which "they would bring and take love from and to the spiritual world," learn songs which they then taught to the adults, and "sometimes see beautiful spacious mansions, and see the Angelic hosts in their beautiful worship."[5]

In time, a pattern emerged: youngsters usually became entranced during the non-public meetings. Adults, on the other hand, experienced manifestations and visions in public and private meetings. Those who went into trances sometimes did not return to their senses for hours. They would lie on the floor, singing or speaking. At one public meeting where 20 Believers became entranced, the spell did not end with the service. The affected brethren had to be carried out to carriages and taken home. The public, who were even more amazed by the behaviors, did not always behave respectfully. After a

Sunday meeting was disrupted by rude spectators, meetings were temporarily closed to the public in early 1839.[6] That measure quickly fueled speculation about what the Believers were doing.

By that fall, meetings were reopened. A *Western Star* correspondent gave a first-person account of visionist activity in a front-page article. Like many other contemporary visitors, the writer was impressed by the members' sincerity and morality, yet dismissive of their rituals:

> *It is an impressive sight to see the long train proceeding on Sabbath morning to church in silence, in single file, the men in front with regular step and uniform dress, with broad brim hats, strait coats and collars uncravated— and all united to make a scene at once grand and imposing. To see them returning from exercise, in the same order, heated and excited by worship, with regular cadenced step, chanting in solemn unison the words, 'March on, march on, march on ye lovely bands, March on, march on, to the new Jerusalem,' give to the most skeptical an impression of their honesty and zeal, though deeply mixed with fanaticism and superstition.[7]*

Aside from their religious peculiarities, the reporter wrote, the Shakers were ideal citizens: intelligent, moral, and industrious. They paid their taxes and debts cheerfully and promptly. In light of those virtues, the writer implied, their doctrines and rites could be overlooked. But Believers were not content with benign tolerance. They kept opening meetings to the public because their mission was to save as many souls as they could. The reporter's condescending account of the visionists must have rankled Believers. Messages from Lee, which the Believers cherished as sacred and personal, were judged as ludicrous. The reporter trivialized the receiving of spiritual gifts. He wrote somewhat erroneously that the elders had previously been the only ones to receive divine messages and songs but that some of the "more holy" members now also received those gifts. In reality, the first visions had occurred among a wide assortment of members, both adults and children. His description of spirit activity certainly would have amazed Lebanon's mainstream Christians. He wrote that the visionists:

> *wheel round and round, finally swoon, are laid out on benches and covered with white garments and then in a trance they visit Mother, and...bring tidings from Heaven to the true believers on earth. While the body remains in this stupefied state the immortal spirit passes to and fro from heaven to earth, at each voyage bearing only one pious message from good Mother, and*

that generally childish and ridiculous; such as, 'Mother sends her love thus,' by patting with the hand upon the breast, which is immediately spoken and performed by all present; 'Mother says, little children be faithful;'...'Mother says we must say we are her itty babies, not her little babies;' 'Mother says kneel upon the right knee, and when you enter a door or ascend the stairs advance the right foot,' with a hundred other equally ridiculous messages.[8]

Believers were offended, and sometimes angered, by such sarcasm. Without understanding the members' deep belief in Lee as a maternal advisor and nurturer, the public did not comprehend how sacred each message was. While entranced, the visionist was aware of the public's impolite behavior and issued a sharp rebuke: "Mother says unless these spectators behave more reverently they will leave this house dead bodies..."[9] Such a violent response was uncharacteristic from Believers. It may more accurately reflect the individual visionist's pique at being ridiculed. By this time, the visionists at public meetings were frequently young women, sometimes still in their teens. In a community that was increasingly led by men, young sisters may have seen the position of visionist as a way to have a voice. That desire may have consciously or unconsciously led to their visions. The leaders may have also encouraged the young sisters' inspiration, remembering how the appearance of the first eastern sisters in an 1806 meeting had moved many cynics.

The public's skepticism was natural. Even Believers frequently struggled to understand what was happening. Through 1839, frequency and intensity of phenomenon increased. Behaviors that had been exhibited during the Kentucky Revival emerged: barking, laughing, shouting, and jerking. Sometimes the affected Believers could not remember their actions; at other times, they were aware of their actions and deeply embarrassed, but unable to control the behavior.

We are numberless times required by messages of inspiration to stoop down & eat simplicity off of the floor, and a vast many other little requisitions that have no kind of agreement with what the wise of this world call even common sense; nay, they are revolting to the wisdom and pride of man; and to this end are they given, no doubt, to mortify and subdue the haughty pride of man.[10]

As Believers began to withdraw from the world during worship, they started to receive visits from illustrious spirits. During the next few years, Jesus, Ann Lee, the 12 apostles, David Darrow, and Ruth Farrington visited often. These spirits expressed their love for Believers and encouraged them to continue the quest for holiness. Lee still played a parental role, chiding them to examine and change their hearts as well as their conduct. She counseled them against pride and urged them to be obedient to God's word. Lee's spirit also expressed a concern that was clearly on leaders' minds as the visionists began to have more credibility and influence at Union Village. She "warned the people against looking to the visionists for that counsel & protection which they ought to receive from the Elders."[11] Believers were to obey their officially chosen elders and eldresses, not the young female visionists. The leaders wanted members to be inspired and reformed by the visions and divine messages but they also wanted to maintain control. This balance became increasingly difficult to maintain as the era progressed.

In addition to holy spirits, those of different ethnic groups and nationalities visited. Some accounts of these visits reflect a naiveté about other cultures. Most are solemn; a few comedic. Susanna Cole Liddell's description of an Icelandic woman falls into the latter category. The "Icelander...skated incessantly falling at first in every attempt; but soon found the best place." The skater was joined by a French lady who was "much alarmed" by the athletics: "She thought the Shakers were all going crazy."[12] Despite the antic atmosphere of the visit, both spirits eventually "opened" their minds and confessed their sins. Most of the visits ended that way, proving to the Believers that if they couldn't be successful with the temporal world, they still could be effective in the spirit world.

Other visits reflected the sect's embracing of other races. Their abhorrence of slavery was particularly evident in the appearance of a female spirit called Dinah the African, who shared her story with them after being saved:

She was waylaid in Africa by those inhuman wretches who go there to procure that unfortunate race of beings for slaves, and caught by two men, bound and taken on shipboard; she was the mother of a family, after her separation, grief so overpowered her that she was so near dead that the wretches threw her overboard and she was eaten by a large fish while yet alive. Before her death she suffered all that confinement, starvation, and thirst could inflict; these superadded to her bereavement, delivered her from these monsters in human shape.[13]

After suffering those horrors, she wandered sorrowfully until she entered the Shaker gathering. When they asked her what she wanted from them, Dinah answered with one word: love. "What have you to receive it in?" they asked. "She held up her arms, signifying she wanted an armful." The Believers obliged and Dinah "was very thankful indeed." She confessed her sins and was saved.[14] The spirit of another black woman further confirmed what the Believers were hearing and reading about slavery in pro-abolition newspapers. This woman had been "a house servant somewhere in N. America. She was much abused by her inhuman master; She lived in the kitchen, cooked for her master and mistress, the former abused her, at times knocking her down."[15] She had died at age 16. These types of messages—and the belief that they were the spiritual rescuers of the persecuted—encouraged members to pursue their beliefs. They frequently identified with people who were outcast or discriminated against. Back in 1807, McNemar had respected the Shawnee Indians partly because they were as misunderstood and rejected by the world as the Believers.

The Shaker fascination with Native Americans continued through the Era of Manifestations. Aside from whites, Indian spirits were the largest ethnic group to visit Union Village. Almost 30 years had passed since the Believers had significant interaction with the Shawnee. Accounts of spirit visits reflect this. Indians were described in more stereotypes, probably due to the Believers' lack of contact with any Native Americans, although they were still treated with respect. George Washington accompanied one group of Indians to a meeting. Pocahontas arrived with another group.

> *They brought us presents, love.... These Indians are often seen by those who are under inspiration. They have embraced Mother's gospel in the spiritual world; and they appear in color, singing, dancing, dress...just as they did in time; at least so nearly so as to be identified.... Pocahontas...touched an inspired one (among the sisters) on the head, who forthwith began to speak in the Indian tongue; and could then, & for sometime afterwards, speak only in the Indian tongue.[16]*

Unlike Tecumseh and the Prophet, these Indians accepted the Shaker version of Christianity totally. The Believers of 1807 had been more accepting of the Indians' faith, believing it might have been just another path to the same truth. The Indians represented by the visionists were more often supplicants, beseeching the Believers to show them the way to salvation. That perception of Native Americans probably wouldn't have resulted in many converts if the Believers had an opportunity to proselytize.

In addition to demonstrating a changing attitude towards Indians, the Pocahontas vision is significant for another reason. It (as well as the visions of the African-American women) affirmed a deep Shaker belief in redemption after death. They did not believe that death meant unbelievers had run out of time to be saved. Holy spirits ministered to the dead in the spirit world. During the Era of Manifestation, the living could also minister to the unredeemed spirits. The deceased could still convert and enjoy full salvation in the afterlife.

Interaction between the temporal and spiritual worlds continued to increase in the late 1830s and early 1840s. Gifts, songs, and instructions flowed from the spirit world, sometimes at a dizzying pace. Over 60 messages were received during one meeting. Dozens of new songs were received and written down during this era. When Houston recorded some of the messages for the central ministry to peruse, he limited himself to copying 500 pages. Symbolic gifts received from the spirits included thin gold crosses that were to be placed on the tongue to show holiness, white robes, every imaginable type of fruit and flower, and even wine, which had an amazing effect:

> *Such is the influence of the invisible spirits on the natural body, that some, on receiving presents of wine from the spiritual world have & do actually get drunk on it, & reel & stagger to & fro involuntarily, just as if they had taken champagne. We seldom meet together anywhere, in these times, without a flame bursting forth & frequently at table. Surely such a time never was before.*[17]

Many of the gifts, messages, and prophecies received from the heavenly realms were depicted in vivid pictures drawn by the Believers who received them. These gift drawings are some of the most recognizable Shaker artifacts. The famous Tree of Life drawing that is frequently associated with the sect was a gift drawing received by an eastern sister in the years following the revival. Many of the objects frequently shown in gift drawings, including boxes, balls, fruits, and flowers, are mentioned in Union Village's church records. Balls of lights appeared during meetings bearing "brilliant print in writing inscribed on them, of a flame-like lustre." Writing also appeared on boxes, rolls of paper, and books received from the spirits. Each object contained the name of its giver, the recipient, the name of the gift, and an explanation of its purpose. As the phenomenon increased, other members in addition to the visionists were "blessed with spiritual sight" and able to see the gifts.[18]

Mandates for improving morals and conduct typically arrived with the gifts. Occasionally, rules of a more mundane nature were given. During a visit by Lee's spirit in the spring of 1839, several specific behaviors were addressed. Lee first presented each member present with a fine sieve "to sift our conduct, and such as would not pass thro' these sieves must be brought to the order & burnt, (i.e.) confessed." Several other gifts were given to instruct members to "curb our tempers, bridle our tongues, walk the floor light, to move our chairs easy, & shut the doors without noise." Significantly, the meeting heralded a change in the nature of Mother's Work. Houston wrote: "Heretofore it has been breaking to pieces and removing the rubbish, but now the still small noise of order begins to be whispered."[19]

As the visions increased in frequency, Wells was determined to restore order at Union Village at any cost. The community functioned as an extremely structured hierarchy with Wells as the leading elder before the Era of Manifestations brought about a more democratic tone. First, the visionists began to rival the elders and eldresses in influence. Then, many members began experiencing the visions and manifestations. Meanwhile, some of the older members, including Richard McNemar and Malcolm Worley, remained skeptical of some of the activities. McNemar and Wells had been at odds since McNemar was told to surrender his title and influence as an elder in 1836. Although neither man would admit it, they competed for loyalty and leadership. Wells was the official leader designated by the central ministry. McNemar, however, had exerted considerable influence over all of the western communities since the early days. Now, McNemar wanted to usurp Wells' authority by having the right to appeal the elder's decisions to New Lebanon. Political and spiritual concerns mingled as McNemar became the target of visionist Margaret O'Brien, a recent convert.

O'Brien, while entranced, accused McNemar of being proud and causing friction in the community. McNemar wrote that as senior members and founders of the village, he and Worley were frequently consulted by Believers on spiritual and temporal matters. He and Worley asked to reside in the Trustees' Office, rather than in the Church Family, so they could be readily accessible to all members. Wells denied their request, and ordered Stephen Spinning and Andrew Houston, elders of the Church family, to remind the two founders of their subservient position. The conflict became common knowledge and some Believers began to take sides. Unity, the cornerstone of the community, was crumbling.

McNemar complained of "jealousies and misunderstandings as to my calling and duty."[20] He maintained that he could have had Wells' job but declined so he could be more flexible in visiting and working with other Shaker communities. He wanted some public acknowledgement of his prominence in the West. Wells wasn't about to share his power with McNemar. He resented McNemar's attempts to go over his head with the central ministry, and criticized him for not signing the 1829 church covenant, something that McNemar maintained was simply an oversight.

Less obvious is why Wells disliked or feared Worley. Although revered as the first western convert to Shakerism, Worley was rarely mentioned in the church record. He does not appear as outspoken as McNemar. When Isaac Youngs toured Union Village in 1834, he visited Worley and reported only that he stayed in his room most of the time, suggesting that Worley, who was then 72, may have been in poor health. McNemar had written of Worley's extreme emotionalism and even depression at the time of the Kentucky Revival. It may also be that Wells believed Worley was not stable enough to be a positive role model for younger Believers.

The founders' children had mixed success in the community. McNemar's youngest son, Richard Jr., left the United Society in 1828. A daughter, Nancy McNemar, was relieved of her duties as second eldress in the village after Wells' arrival, but another daughter, Vincy, was noted as a visionist who received many hymns while entranced. McNemar's son, James, was also a respected hymn writer at Union Village. Worley's son, Joshua, who had been second elder in the village, was relieved of his duties in 1838, although he and two siblings remained Believers.[21]

B y the spring of 1839, McNemar was suspended from his usual duties. He claimed that no clear explanation was given for the action. During a trance, O'Brien openly rebuked McNemar for his pride, claiming the judgment came straight from Lee. There was no appeal to the sentence of a visionist. The conflict worsened dramatically when another Believer, Randolf West, wrote malicious letters about Wells, forging McNemar's handwriting. Wells believed that McNemar had written the messages and used them to support his charges of disloyalty. A second vision by O'Brien in early June declared that Worley, McNemar, and his older brother, Garner McNemar, must be removed from the community because members had treated them as idols. Garner had been mentioned a few times previously in church records. At a special meeting held on October 12, 1837, he had been accused of "writing scurrillous stuff about the Believers and conveying it to his grandson out in the world," with the intent of having the material published after his death. The writer, who may have been Houston, called Garner an "evil-minded, aged infirm man."[22]

After O'Brien's June vision, Wells immediately ordered the three men out of their church families. Garner McNemar, who was an invalid, was to board with a Shaker tenant. Worley was to be moved to a lodging in Brown County, Ohio. Richard McNemar was dropped off on the streets of Lebanon with his printing press to earn a living. Believers were appalled at the edict; several sisters burst into tears. Of the three men, Richard McNemar, then 68, was the only one in any condition to fight back. He stayed at the Lebanon home of his old friend, Judge Francis Dunlavy, for a few days to make plans. After sending the printing press back to Union Village, McNemar traveled to New Lebanon to plead his case before the central ministry.[23]

When McNemar reached New York, Elder Rufus Bishop was shocked by his appearance. McNemar seemed "to feel much tribulation" and cried often, Bishop wrote. His appearance was "very feeble... almost like a corpse." In addition to stress, McNemar was suffering from a chronic stomach complaint that would kill him within a few months. Bishop attributed McNemar's condition to being out of union with Wells. "He is like a wandering star," the elder wrote.[24] Bishop was assigned to settle the dispute. He received some unexpected help from David Darrow and Lucy Wright. Their spirits arrived via a New Lebanon visionist to comfort and counsel McNemar. The visionist urged that McNemar, his brother, and Worley be reinstated in the United Society. The central ministry agreed, and officially directed all communities to supervise visionists more closely. The elders and eldresses were to maintain control over their communities.

> McNemar had written of Worley's extreme emotionalism and even depression at the time of the Kentucky Revival. It may also be that Wells believed Worley was not stable enough to be a positive role model for younger Believers.

McNemar returned to Union Village in July in failing health. He formally reconciled with Wells at an emotional church meeting. Several young brothers carried McNemar by chair into the meetinghouse. He addressed the assembly, recalling his efforts for the western communities and pledging his love for Wells. Wells replied in kind, but the repercussions were far from over. Margaret O'Brien left the sect. McNemar's health declined rapidly. Worley and Garner McNemar continued living at Union Village under Wells' disapproval.[25]

Visions continued throughout the turmoil, provoking more mortifying behavior. Just two days after McNemar returned to Union Village, Believers were required "to stoop down and eat simplicity off of the floor. The marvelous gifts of supernatural power and revelation are constantly displayed among us; both as respects present and future, visible and invisible, heavenly and infernal," Houston wrote.[26] Disturbing revelations were balanced with messages of comfort and unity from Darrow, Wright, and Ruth Farrington. Oliver Hampton, who participated in the spiritualism at Union Village, later wrote that some of the "indiscretions" committed during the Era of Manifestations were due to unwise leadership decisions but on the whole, Hampton, a loyal Believer to the end, thought the revival helped restore many Believers' faith.[27]

The campaign against sin continued for another seven years, but it went on without Richard McNemar. He died on the evening of September 15, 1839. Houston remembered him in the church record simply as "among the first who received the gospel in the West." Years later, when Hampton was keeping the church record, he added a postscript about McNemar: "One of the most zealous and loyal Believers who ever embraced the Gospel in this Western Land. Altogether more than ordinarily intelligent."

Houston wrote nothing in the church records of McNemar's funeral or of the Believers' reaction to his death, but one mourner noted that the funeral was well attended and quite solemn. During the service, a visionist saw the spirits of McNemar and John Dunlavy, who had died in 1812, standing on the gateposts of the cemetery. Many spirits appeared in "a great retinue of loaded Chariots going in the procession to the Grave yard. [The visionist] counted a while but gave it up. She also saw many [spirits] on foot, more than there were of us."[28] The spirits seemed to give McNemar the respect that Wells denied him.

A few months after McNemar's death, the forger Randolph West inadvertently revealed his deception and left Union Village in shame. Two years later, he hung himself. Some believed that he had never forgiven himself for contributing to the turmoil in the village.[29]

Even Union Village's major building project of the era was tinged with tragedy. Late in 1841, New Lebanon instructed residents to build a large, three-story dwelling. It was to be the largest structure ever built in the community. Wells enthusiastically agreed, and village leaders set about planning the new dwelling. Leaders may have hoped the revival would bring conversions, and the need for a larger dwelling. Numbers had been dwindling since the population peaked at 634 in 1818. By 1829, the total population had declined to

500 people, and in 1836 to 330.[30] In 1841, church records show that 208 Believers signed the new covenant. The total population always remained larger than the number of covenant members, due to the presence of children and those adults who were not yet ready to sign the document. Seven adults did not sign due to old age, illness, or insolvency. Malcolm Worley was singled out as one who didn't sign, but no reason was given.

The grand Center House was begun in 1842 and completed in 1846 but it bears the date 1844. That was the year that diarist Andrew Houston fell from the third story while working on the house and subsequently died of his injuries. The Center House still stands today, renovated into Bethany Hall at Otterbein-Lebanon.

Despite the declining population, leaders planned a great house north of the Center dwelling. Several farm buildings were moved to make room for it. Cherry and oak trees were cut from the Shakers' woods, and brick production began on the grounds. More than one million bricks were fired for the building, which the Believers claimed was the largest brick dwelling at the time in Ohio. Construction continued almost four years and seriously depleted village finances, in addition to costing the community one of its most respected members. While working on the dwelling on October 7, 1844, Andrew Houston fell from the third story and died later that day from his injuries. When the building was finally completed in January 1846, it provided quarters for 112 members of the First Family, plus a large, communal dining room, and a meeting room that held 200 people.[31]

This great house may be the mansion mentioned in an intriguing manuscript thought to be from this time period. Like many of the visionists' messages, the manuscript merged the physical and metaphysical in the same way as which spirit gifts combined the symbolic with the literal. For instance, spirit brooms were received to sweep away sins, paralleling the day-to-day use of brooms to keep dwellings physically clean. The manuscript is undated and anonymous. It identifies Union Village as the birthplace of the Old Testament's Noah and the location where Noah built the ark that saved the remnants of civilization during the great flood. Whether Believers took the manuscript literally or symbolically, it was meant to encourage them. The manuscript, a 36-line poem, illustrates the Believers' special concerns during the Era of Manifestations:

> *How blest are the daughters, the virgins of Zion*
> *Who in the pure Gospel of Mother embark.*
> *And dwell in the village, the new village of Union*
> *Where Noah resided (and) builded the Ark*
> *Then oft the Good Patriarch bowed down in devotion,*
> *Imploring the mercy, the blessing of God.*
> *Where now the large mansion is built by Believers*
> *Who walk in his footsteps and tread the same sod...*
> *And now when a stench of far greater corruption*
> *Goes up from all cities, all towns, and all plains,*
> *The smiles of Jehovah encircle his people,*
> *And the Ark of his mercy with Union remains...*[32]

The poem reinforces the idea that Believers shared an ancient faith with Noah, the same way they shared the task of trying to convert people in an incredulous world. As long as the faithful stayed true, however, they would be protected and blessed. Union Village was not the only community to be associated with a Biblical occurrence. Watervliet, New York, where Ann Lee had lived, was said to be the spot where Adam and Eve were created and fell from Paradise. The Shakers believed that Lee, "the second Eve," was showing the world the way back to paradise.

The world's rejection—and mocking—of the manifestations and revelations led to meetings being closed to the public in 1842 in all Shaker communities. For those who sincerely believed they were being visited by Lee, Jesus, the apostles, and the spirits of loved ones, the world's mockery was devastating. For those whose faith was floundering, the skepticism was unsettling, sometimes resulting in abandonment of Shakerism. Trustees published a special notice in the July 22, 1842, issue of the *Western Star*, informing the public that meetings were no longer open. They cited the public's behavior at meetings as the reason for their decision:

*...we are called and required by (God's) Holy Angels to spend every day
of our lives in walking softly and humbly before Him; and to enable us to
offer acceptable Offerings of prayer and thanksgiving to a pure and Holy
God. But we regret to say, that for some years past many have thronged
our Meetings, with no higher motives, than to pass time away, and satisfy
and amuse a vain curiosity at the expense of the peace and repose of those
who assembled with sincere and honest hearts, to devote themselves to the
solemn worship of God.*[33]

People sincerely interested in learning about the Shakers' beliefs were
invited to call at the church office during the week. A sign, featuring a message
from Jesus, was placed outside the meetinghouse to warn the world: "Enter not
into this holy Sanctuary, to disturb the peace of my chosen people; but go your
way and the gospel will be preached to you in due season."[34] The revival was,
for a time, turning its back on the world that Believers hoped to save.

Spirit visitors continued to appear at Union Village throughout the 1840s
and beyond. Eternal Mother Wisdom made one of the most dramatic visits. As
the female aspect of God, she was central to the concept of a dual-natured deity,
as demonstrated in the first hymn of the 1813 songbook, *Millennial Praises*:

*Long ere this fleeting world began
Or dust was fashion'd into man,
There Power and Wisdom we can view,
Names of the Everlasting Two.*

*The Father's high eternal throne
Was never fill'd by one alone:
There Wisdom holds the Mother's seat
And is the Father's helper-meet.*[35]

Mother Wisdom's role in the revival was to judge Believers and to mark the
faithful. She first appeared at New Lebanon in the spring of 1841. Through
the visionists, she announced her mission and the dates she would visit each
community. She was scheduled to appear in Union Village on October 10.
Her visit was preceded by a day of spiritual preparation. "All our shops were
closed and all retired to their rooms and kept the day in the solemn fear of
God," noted the October 9 church record. Mother Wisdom's examination
of the ministry was held privately early on the morning of October 10. She
began examining other Believers in the afternoon during a three-hour meeting.

Thirty-six people were interviewed through an 18-year-old female visionist. After answering several questions about their spiritual lives satisfactorily, each member's respective family elder or eldress made a mark on the Believer's forehead. The mark was not described, but the Believers' reactions were:

> Union Village was called Wisdom's Paradise, a title that conveyed the respect and hope that the East held for the western bishopric.

"The powerful gift of inspiration that attended this wonderful occasion was so great, and the questions so penetrating and pointed, and at the same time, so parental and heavenly, that it made our tears flow down like water, with a deep sense of penitence and contrition."[36] The examinations continued for several more days until Mother Wisdom visited each order. Children were examined during a special session on October 12.

Heavenly spirits called for additional rituals and services, which were implemented by New Lebanon. In 1842 each community was given a spiritual name and instructed to choose a sacred spot on which to hold special feasts each May and September. Union Village was called Wisdom's Paradise, a title that conveyed the respect and hope that the East held for the western bishopric. It was perhaps the most beautiful name given to any of the frontier communities. Almost all of the names were positive. South Union was Jasper Valley; North Union was Holy Grove; Watervliet was the Vale of Peace. Whitewater, which had struggled often during its existence, received the most somber name: the Lonely Plain of Tribulation.

Was Union Village truly Wisdom's Paradise in 1842? The answer depends on perspective. Most of the community's worldly neighbors felt no motivation to join the Believers but they tolerated them much more than they had 20 years earlier. Some envied the group's prosperity while others laughed at their celibacy and way of worship. At the same time, local people increasingly turned to them for commodities ranging from herbal medicines to livestock. They wanted no part of the Believers' religious life, but they valued the products of their work ethic.

As for the Believers themselves, they consistently extolled the virtues of their village and lifestyle, even when times were rough. Their journals reveal that while they were keenly aware of some members' failures, they seldom claimed any of the responsibility. Individuals' moral weaknesses were blamed when a member left or, worse yet, defrauded the community. Only rarely did a Believer admit that more could be done to sustain the fainthearted or supervise trustees. By denying culpability, members too often missed the opportunity to prevent similar problems. Rivalries within the leadership and with other Shaker communities were almost inherent within the sect's familial hierarchy. Someone was bound to want to be the golden child and someone else to be the rebel. The majority of members seemed to accept the central ministry's leadership decisions.

For the Believers who were faithful, Union Village was a good place to live. Physical want did not exist, an important consideration that was reiterated over the decades by almost every outsider who visited. Believers had built up a creative, prosperous community that offered a free education for all children and night classes for adults. Each person had a home and a purpose. Everywhere Believers turned, they saw lush gardens and fields, and healthy livestock. In their shops, they created items that were highly functional and singularly beautiful. In their worship, they found comfort and emotional fulfillment. And, for those who strayed, the Believers offered the hope of divine forgiveness in this world or the next.

In impact on the United Society and the world, Union Village rivaled the major eastern communities in achievement. The greatest success was the creation and continuance of the five other villages in Ohio and Kentucky. Union Village maintained the sect's beliefs in the West. Population growth had leveled off but the communities remained vital. Union Village members were also justifiably proud of the literature and music that sprang from their community. Dozens of hymns, as well as *The Kentucky Revival*, *A Concise Answer*, and *The Testimony of Christ's Second Appearing* had originated at Turtle Creek. These writings provided history and theology to members throughout the United Society, and sometimes challenged other communities to publish more as well. They also spread Shaker teachings to the world.

If the people of Union Village had not quite attained paradise, they felt they were on the right path. The special services held at their sacred spot were to aid them on their journey. Leaders were to choose a site that had a high elevation or was very secluded to hold semiannual feasts. They chose Richard McNemar's former garden. They named it Jehovah's Chosen Square. At the "love feasts" held there each spring and fall, visions, songs, and gifts were received from Heaven. Believers bathed—metaphysically—in the life-giving waters of God. Prayers, songs, and testimonies were offered to and received from Heaven. Jehovah's Chosen Square also drew the faithful at other times. One Believer who was often drawn there was William Reynolds. An elder who later became first in the ministry, Reynolds found himself strangely affected by spirits during this time:

For a period of three years, every Sunday he would turn over and over like a cartwheel from the residence to the church. On leaving the church he would be seized with the same impulse, which at times would take him to 'Jehovah's Chosen Square,' notwithstanding all his power to prevent the same. At this unusual and unseemly practice, he was intensely mortified. The power controlling him was so great that at times he would turn over fences, just as though they were naught.[37]

It was this type of behavior that the Believers wanted to keep to themselves. They couldn't always grasp what was happening to them and they realized the world might laugh at such unusual actions.

Other manifestations had more understandable applications. Such was the case with an awe-inspiring spectacle that occurred during a summer meeting in 1839: "There was seen a profusion or shower of starry lights in our meeting, which were succeeded by a great company of horsemen, riding and prancing over our heads. They came to assist us in our spiritual warfare."[38] This vision, shared by many present at the meeting, reinforced the idea of aggressively battling sin, as the Believers had done during the 1815 revival. Many manifestations, such as a large scale one in the spring of 1846, offered encouragement and support to continue revival efforts. The Believers at the meeting were visited by five hundred angels, "cloth'd with Love and blessing from the heavens." Believers gathered first at the meetinghouse to hear Elder John Martin speak about what could be expected. Then:

After dancing a lively song and gaining some freedom we were inform'd that the holy Savior and Mother Ann was with us and would accompany us to the chosen square. As usual we march'd to the square to the sound of music; stopping once on our way to sound on our trumpets; on arriving at the gate we were met by a large company of holy Angels...Mother pours her love on the multitude, it is flowing all around and the company feel its invigorating influence; the blessing flows in a full stream, and the baptism becomes universal tro' the body....

Father Joseph [Meacham] now arrives, and requests six of his class to go to the tree of victory which in standing in the S. East corner of the square, and take their baskets and fill them, then bring them forward and give the Contents of them to the people.[39]

The day continued with messages from the spirits of David Darrow, loved ones, and some of the original Believers. At the close of the five-hour meeting, Believers marched back home together and went to their respective dwellings.

Visits by Christ, Ann Lee, and other first-generation Believers were clearly meant to sustain members and connect them to their spiritual roots. Receiving fruits from a tree of victory was to destroy doubt and encourage them to believe that they too would be victorious over the world. Journals and church records of that time are persistently positive and supportive of the spiritual activity. Decades later, however, at least one participant acknowledged that some of the events were frightening.

In 1901, Susanna Cole Liddell recounted the strange experiences she had as a teenager during the Era of Manifestations. Some spirit messages arrived in unknown languages and had to be translated into English before they could be passed on to the proper party. Freegift Wells received an unintelligible spirit letter from New Lebanon one day and tested Liddell to see if she could interpret it, knowing that an English translation of the letter existed in New York. He hid the spirit letter in his vest pocket, buttoned his coat over, and went into her classroom. Wells asked her what she saw, and the girl replied that she saw the letter in his vest. He then ordered her to read the letter and write out an English translation. The document was sent to New Lebanon where it was confirmed to be the same translation that their visionist had made. Wells' next order shocked and confused Liddell:

> [Wells] wrote a letter, pinned it near the left shoulder of Miss Liddell's dress, and commanded her to take it to [New] Lebanon. She was not only nonplused, but greatly grieved, and, bursting into tears, went to her eldress, and stated the case. The eldress kindly told her to go to her room and remain quiet. She obeyed, threw herself on her cot and after having composed herself, she felt her body lifted up and then passed out of the window, and rapidly glided over the earth, passing rivers, cities, and forests, until she came to…[New] Lebanon. When she arrived there no one noticed her. She passed on until she came to a very large house and entered the doorway. Here she saw two young Sisters who recognized and spoke to her. One of them unpinned the message, when Miss Liddell immediately glided back to Union Village. In due course of mail Elder Wells received an answer to the message. So delighted was he…that he sent Miss Liddell on a second errand. On her way back she became greatly frightened by being pursued by an immense animal in shape like a hog. She then absolutely refused ever to go on a similar errand.[40]

One of the many remarkable aspects of Liddell's tale is her refusal to go on any more spirit errands. Most of the accounts of spiritual activity at the time stress the participant's inability to resist or prevent what was happening to them. They might be compelled to perform embarrassing or odd actions, like Reynolds's cartwheels, or be so overtaken by spirits that songs and revelations poured out of them. Yet Liddell simply refused to cooperate when she became frightened, demonstrating that some Believers still exercised free will. Liddell did continue, however, to experience visions in which the spirits of departed Believers spoke to her.

Many of the revelations received throughout the United Society were collected in a two-volume book, published in 1843 in Canterbury, New Hampshire, called *A Holy, Sacred and Divine Roll and Book from The Lord God of Heaven to The Inhabitants of Earth.* Copies of the book were kept in each meetinghouse; they were to be read frequently. Hundreds of copies were sent to worldly leaders in the United States and Europe. One positive response was received from the king of Norway and Sweden. Among the revelations contained in the book were several messages received by Mary Ann Jennings and other unnamed visionists from Union Village. Jennings was a teenager at the time she recorded messages she said were given to her by angels. Two of the missives, written just weeks apart in the spring of 1843, stress a common theme: the faithful would continue to face trials for following God's will yet He would allow them to ultimately succeed if they followed the angels' counsel:

> *...stand ye firm and strong, and fear not what an unbelieving world may inflict upon you. But keep ye low and quiet; stand firm and unshaken, amidst storms and tribulation, for the holy hand of God will cover and protect his chosen, from every harm; Zion shall flourish, bloom, and grow, like a well watered garden; her beauty and glory shall spread far and wide, and many shall flock to her peaceful borders, to learn the holy way of righteousness.*[41]

The message was reassuring in content and style. The visionist confirmed that the Believers were God's chosen people and that they would be protected if they humbly, conscientiously obeyed Him. They were reassured that their labors were not in vain; eventually, many would enter the fold. The garden analogy was also comfortingly familiar. It paralleled well-known

Biblical metaphors, and related to their everyday pursuits in horticulture and agriculture. Jennings' second message offered more solace for the faithful but warned of imminent judgment for the unrepentant. Everyone was to follow God's commands closely because a reckoning was approaching:

And now, as the time is drawing very near, and is even at the door, I say, Blessed are ye that have hearkened to my warnings, and have kept my commandments; for it shall be well with you; And those who have not done this, must bear the reward of their own labor, and feast upon such fruit as they have gathered. For I have been merciful to all, and sent repeated and timely warnings; that all who had done wrong, and wandered from the path, might have time to see their own state, repent and come down, where they could find their union and relation to Me...those who will not obey my voice, shall perish in the dust.[42]

The tone of such messages attracted members of another unorthodox group in 1844. Believers had long welcomed inquiries from other sects and had gained some converts that way. A fanatical group called the Pilgrims came through Union Village in 1818 searching for a Promised Land. Sect leader Isaac Buller required his followers to lead lives of severe self-abasement and poverty. Believers welcomed the Pilgrims, fed them and their horses, and allowed them to preach in the village. When Buller commanded his people to move on, several of the 55 members stayed and became Shakers. Issachar Bates visited a German Christian sect called the Separatists at Zoar, Ohio, in 1824, presumably on a missionary trip. He had become dangerously ill during his travels and was in such poor health when he reached Zoar that no discussions with the Separatists were possible.[43] Still, the interest in attracting members from other small sects was present.

Another group that became interested in the Believers in 1844 was considerably larger than the Pilgrims or the Separatists. Members were called Millerites because they followed the teachings of William Miller, a New York farmer. While studying the Bible in search of assurance of salvation, Miller became convinced that he had calculated the date of Christ's return, which he referred to as the Second Advent. He and his followers lectured heavily in the eastern and Midwestern states, convincing hundreds of people to prepare for Christ's return sometime between 1843 and 1844. Millerites believed that Christ would physically return to earth then, having given humanity repeated opportunities to reform and be saved. The wicked would be destroyed by fire, and Christ and His followers would rule on earth for a thousand years.[44]

Adventists published the *Day-Star* newspaper at Union Village

Ohio became an important state for the Millerite or Adventist evangelists. Thousands attended meetings, particularly in Cleveland and Cincinnati where Adventist newspapers began to be published. Evangelist Enoch Jacobs helped publish the *Western Midnight Cry* in Cincinnati and became influential in the group. When Christ did not literally appear according to Miller's predictions, Jacobs and many of his friends began searching for a new religious base. In speaking with Shaker leaders, Jacobs became convinced of the merits of their faith. Believers taught that the Christ-spirit's return was an internal event, rather than an external one, and that the Christ-spirit could enter a Believer's heart at any time. The Believers welcomed Jacobs and other Adventists wholeheartedly, providing they accepted celibacy.

Approximately 200 Adventists joined the communities at Union Village and Whitewater. Jacobs and his family joined the gathering order at Union Village where he began to publish another religious newspaper, the *Day-Star*. Believers helped Jacobs print and distribute the paper, which presented their beliefs and courted converts.[45] Their enthusiastic embracing of divine revelations during this era encouraged the former Adventists who struggled with disappointment after the failure of Miller's predictions. An eastern sister, Prudence Morrell, a former Union Village resident who had moved east, was impressed with the Adventists she met there during a visit in 1847: "There we found a number of the Advents, both brethren and sisters, and some that were not Advent; but all appeared so simple and sincere and so much like Mother's children that we could not but love them very much.... They sung some of their advent songs which showed their former ideals very clear."[46] Morrell wrote approvingly of the prospective members' childlike natures, a quality that was thought necessary for spiritual rebirth. But celibacy was already creating a schism among the Adventists. Silas Strong, a former judge, was a promising member, who appeared "as simple as a child," but could not persuade his wife to join him in his new faith. Charles Clapp was another promising candidate who had the "misfortune to marry a very rich woman, and, of course, she cannot enter the kingdom of Heaven." When Clapp chose the Believers, he left his former life completely:

> *For when he left his family he would not accept of his clothes, nor money to bear his expenses to Union Village. His woman was one of the best kind, and loved him as she loved her own life; but her rich father would not let her come with him. He felt it his duty to forsake all and he left her. He now appears very promising whether he endures to the end or not.*[47]

Morrell heard both Clapp and Enoch Jacobs speak at public meetings. Clapp talked of the personal sacrifices he had made to gain salvation. Jacobs praised Shakerism's inclusive nature. While most worldly people prayed only for themselves and their biological families, he said, Believers prayed for all their members. Both men spoke sincerely but Jacobs was the more dynamic of the two. The elders believed both had a good gift to preach. But only one remained a Believer. Clapp continued to preach and recruit new members for the rest of his life. Jacobs left just a few months after Morrell heard him speak. Apparently the disruption to family life was untenable. He reportedly said that he would rather "go to hell with Electra his wife than live among the Shakers without her."[48] Such extreme reactions were not unusual in a faith that asked so much from its followers.

Jacobs' departure was not the only upheaval during the 1840s. More turmoil ensued related to the tumultuous tenure of Freegift Wells. He was recalled to New Lebanon in the summer of 1843 while spiritualism was still quite active. Questions remain about why Wells left. Typically, primary elders and eldresses were removed either because they were ineffective leaders or too aged or infirm to lead. Wells was neither. After returning to New York in July, he served as an eastern elder for many more years. It is possible that the central ministry was displeased with Wells' treatment of McNemar and Worley, and with the extremes of spiritualism that he had permitted. The divisions that surfaced in the community at the time certainly could have lessened his effectiveness as a leader. Church records make no disparaging remarks about Wells, however. Liddell recorded in her journal only that "Our Beloved elder Freegift Wells returned home to the East July 13, 1843."[49]

John Martin took Wells' place. A westerner and long-time Believer, Martin had been second elder of Union Village since 1838. Martin had barely been lead elder one year when he faced his first crisis, a profoundly temporal one. Malcolm Worley died on August 3, 1844, at age 82. While his friends mourned his passing, his children—Joshua, Rebecca, and Joseph—began plans to leave Union Village. They had grown up in the community, watched their father labor to spread the faith, and served in various capacities themselves as adults. Apparently they were unable to accept the way their father had been treated by Wells and his supporters. Upon leaving, they began legal proceedings to recover the land their father had deeded to the Believers in 1808.

The loss of Worley's homestead would have taken a central section of land as well as several buildings out of the heart of the village. Such a loss would have had a profound emotional effect on members as well. Martin and the trustees responded in court with a deed that Malcolm, and his wife Peggy, had signed. In the document, they relinquished any rights for themselves or their heirs to the property, giving it as a free-will offering to the United Society. The Worley children countered that their father was insane when he signed the deed. Their defense failed during four years of court proceedings that cost them $1,200. The case ended up in the Ohio Supreme Court, where former Ohio governor Thomas Corwin represented Union Village. A native of Lebanon, Corwin was well acquainted with the Believers and had visited the village more than once.[50] In his defense arguments, Corwin compared Worley to other Christian reformers:

> *George Fox wore leather breeches and did many eccentric things; Martin Luther threw his inkstand at the devil, but the Quakers will not admit that George Fox was crazy, and the Protestants will not admit that Martin Luther was crazy; neither can it be allowed that Malcolm Worley was crazy because by a deed drawn by himself he chose to give his property to this peculiar people.*[51]

Corwin won the case. The legal victory was crucial to keeping the village intact, but chinks were forming in the community's stability. The Era of Manifestations had renewed many Believers' faith and permanently converted some of the Adventists. Some not wholly committed individuals left after the most dramatic spiritualism subsided by the late 1840s, a good thing for the general unity of the village. But the defection of Worley's family showed that even prominent members who had lived in the community for decades could leave. The episode no doubt influenced others who wavered in their faith. Prohibiting the public from attending meetings twice during the era seriously hampered proselytism. Most of the Believers' neighbors remained skeptical of their beliefs and mode of worship. Within the membership, divisions had to be healed between Wells' supporters and those of McNemar and Worley. The unity that kept the village thriving economically during the revival needed to be applied to its spiritual life. Believers would accept the challenge as they began to achieve one of the most peaceful and productive periods in the history of Union Village.

"Prove all things; hold fast that which is good."

—1Thessalonians 5:21

Top: This North Family dwelling shows the typical T-shape of large Shaker homes. This photograph was taken sometime after 1918 when Otterbein administrators remodeled the home and added the front porches.
Right: Detail of Center House.

ഴ Chapter Nine ഴ
Peace and Prosperity at Mid-Century

After the extremes of spiritualism and the internal conflicts of the Era of Manifestations, the routine of daily life and work helped restore unity. In a communal society, people had to work together to succeed, and the Believers did. Agriculture and industry flourished through the 1850s, with a large number of enterprises that attest to the group's versatility.

By the middle of the nineteenth century, Americans from Illinois to Louisiana began and ended their day with products from Union Village. A

homemaker could clean house with a fine flat-headed broom, wear a stylish bonnet to market, season a stew with sweet marjoram, and quiet a child's nighttime cough by purchasing Shaker merchandise. Their quality created the demand and their salesmen provided the goods.

The Believers followed the example of their secular neighbors in supplementing their farm income with other goods and services. Rural people in the early 1800s rarely just farmed to make a living. They had to produce many of their daily necessities and building materials, and they eventually began selling some of these items. A woman might sell her surplus eggs and butter to town families, or, if the flax crop had been especially good, weave some extra cloth to be sold. Many people developed a specialty, such as building furniture or making brooms, and began selling to customers from their homes. Some of the goods, such as food, were offered on a daily or seasonal basis, while others, such as fancy work or tin ware, could be produced during the slower winter months when gardens and fields were not being worked.[1] People who had been gardeners and farmers before joining the community brought these additional skills with them. In the communal setting, they often

Storage boxes and a two-drawer chest atop a sugar chest

had the opportunity to practice their crafts extensively, allowing them to refine their own work and teach it to other members. Entrusting the care of young children to the sisters in the Children's Order freed women to concentrate on specific skills, such as food preservation and bonnet making.

Tasks usually fell into traditional patterns of the period with women performing a variety of domestic jobs in and around the dwelling, and men doing most of the heavy and outdoor work. The Believers became adept at producing goods in large quantities for their growing community, frequently developing more efficient machinery or techniques. That resulted in more economical and efficient production of goods for the secular market. Early financial assistance from the central ministry as well as the cumulative support of the village's joint interest provided the funds to try new industries or to import and breed superior livestock.

As the century progressed and individual farm families began to buy rather than produce some of their necessities, the Believers were ready to supply them. Chairs and spinning wheels were regularly sold to the public. In the last year of his life, McNemar wrote of constantly making chairs and weaving cloth. Hats, gloves, socks, and blankets were commonly made for sale. Women's palm leaf bonnets became a new manufacturing success. The Believers had been making and selling straw hats for more than two decades when Abner Bedle, a mechanic, invented a palm leaf-weaving loom at Union Village. Bonnets began to be manufactured on February 16, 1837. The loom shortened the tedious process of making the bonnets. Hat making was the type of laborious task that Shakers excelled at because of a ready labor pool. The palm leaf bonnets were a multi-step project. First, leaves were sized and dampened to make them pliable. The leaf pieces were then woven on the loom. Rough edges were singed off with a flame of burning alcohol. Each bonnet was composed of a front piece and a crown. The outer side of the hat was varnished and the inside was lined with cloth—usually silk. A four-inch "cape" of silk, attached to the bottom of the bonnet, hung over the wearer's neck. Women's bonnets sold for about $1 each; girls' bonnets were $5 for a dozen. Palm leaves were also made into fans. Several local churches and funeral homes, including a funeral parlor operated by Morris Oswald in Lebanon, purchased fans from the Believers.[2]

Bedle was also credited with inventing a silk-reeling machine in 1837. An iron vessel and furnace for this machine was invented by another Union Village brother, Thomas Taylor.[3] Silk was used primarily in clothes for sale, including handkerchiefs, ladies' collars, and the linings of capes. Sisters raised their own silkworms and grew mulberry trees to keep the creatures healthy and productive.

Improvements in daily living also continued. The North dwelling house gained running water on August 25, 1837, when a lead pipe was installed to carry water from the former Office well to the North house. A copper pump was fitted to raise the water for the sisters cooking in the kitchen. The project cost about $160. A similar project was undertaken for the Center family kitchen the following April.

New buzz saw machinery for cutting out broom handles was completed and running on November 29, 1837, indicating that broom manufacturing was well-established at Union Village by this time. The humble art of broom making was perfected by Believers with the creation of the first flat broom by a Watervliet, New York, brother. A Harvard, Massachusetts, brother is credited with inventing a machine for sizing broomcorn brush. Union Village men made brooms for many decades, and the church records are filled with references about planting and harvesting broomcorn. In accordance with the group's emphasis on cleanliness, brooms were made for every purpose, including a long-handled broom designed to clean ceilings. The Shakers themselves sometimes fitted clean white cotton hoods over the broom head to dry-polish their wooden floors.[4]

As more industries were pursued in the village, farming and livestock production was slightly decreased. At a March 21, 1841 meeting, elders and deacons decided to allow trustees to rent some West section acreage to tenants. Any livestock not needed for the Believers' own use was also to be leased to tenants. By this time, the trustees also hired more outside workers for specialized tasks, such as the raising of a dam embankment for a gristmill. A group of Irishmen did the job. Routine jobs continued to be done by the brethren. On June 7, 1841, a group of brothers repaired a series of underground earthen pipes that carried wastewater out of the Center house under the street into the orchard. The notation highlights the Believers' practicality in recycling wastewater to nurture fruit trees.

Improvements were always encouraged. Mechanic Micajah Burnett arrived at Union Village in December 1842, to build some new planing machinery for making oval boxes and half-bushel baskets. He left for Pleasant Hill the next March, leaving behind satisfied customers. The popular covered oval boxes, like brooms, were made for decades at Union Village. As early as 1819, Ruth Farrington sent an oval box filled with maple sugar as a gift to New Lebanon. Traditionally, tops and bottoms were made of pine; rims were maple. The boxes were held together by overlapping "fingers" or "swallowtails" that were secured by copper tacks. Oval boxes were usually painted; blue was a favorite color.[5]

Religious advances also occurred. Inspired by the divine revelations of the preceding 10 years, the Believers in 1847 published a pamphlet titled *Condition of Society; And Its Only Hope, in Obeying the Everlasting Gospel, as Now Developing Among Believers in Christ's Second Appearing.* The booklet shared some revelations with the public in an attempt to save more souls through conversion. On the cover was the Apostle Paul's advice to the Thessalonians: "Prove all things; hold fast that which is good." The message was meant for the world, but could also be applied to the Believers. After a decade of spiritual excesses and possible misuse of power, it was time for them to examine their actions and motivations.

The central ministry at New Lebanon published a new, more extensive list of Millennial Laws in 1845; it was partially based on divine messages received during the Era of Manifestations. Modern readers often see these rules—which cover everything from relations between the sexes to furniture finishes—as extreme and oppressive. Shaker leaders saw the Millennial Laws as a guidebook. If questions arose in a community over a member's manner of dressing or his relations with the world, answers could be found in the Laws. Many rules were

FORMER BROOM FACTORY

The broom shop was part of the North Family lot. The family's section also included a three-story carding factory, large barn, silo, main dwelling, and smaller residence for workers.

written to ensure safety in the villages, including "Orders to Prevent Loss by Fire." The rules, read annually to each membership, were a combination of divine revelations and administrative decisions based on more than 50 years of managing communal societies.[6]

Publication of all types of rules seemed to be in vogue in the 1840s. Reading them offers a view of the Believers' daily lives. On a practical level, the rules helped get work done. For instance, two New England sisters compiled rules for doing the laundry and sent them to Union Village to be shared with the other western communities. A written set of instructions was quite practical. Although a community might have one sister in charge of the laundry, her helpers often changed jobs. Sisters took turns, or tours, doing certain routine chores, such as the laundry and kitchen work. According to Amy Slater's journals of the mid-1840s, women in the Second Family at Union Village did a one-month tour of kitchen duty and then went on to do other jobs. This system gave the members a variety of skills and varied the monthly routine. Like many of the Believers' journals, Slater's is simply a brief listing of important or interesting events. Personal observations and elaborations are rare; a death in the family is recorded with the same economy of words as a thunderstorm. She wrote of the sisters' activities in their family's shop, weather conditions, and visits to and from the world. Small pleasures included taking the younger girls to play in the woods, picking the first strawberries of the season, attending weekly singing meetings, and baking green apple pies, all of which offered a break in routine.

The Second Family women were typical of other sisters in that they performed many different tasks. In less than a month in 1845, the sisters made 67 yards of carpet to be sold to the world. Before they wove the carpets, they processed and dyed the wool for them. The women also made candles, spooled yarn, plucked goose feathers, sheared sheep, whitewashed the dwelling walls, made cheese, washed and ironed the laundry, watched the silk worms emerge, and cleaned house. Four of Slater's sisters stained the floor of the grand new Center House in the summer of 1845. Slater helped paint chairs for a week in the fall of 1846, probably for sale to the world.[7]

Sisters routinely produced goods for the world, as well as for family use. The silk made by those silkworms Slater watched went mostly to fancy goods made for the public. Sisters were allowed two or three good silk handkerchiefs and a cotton and silk blend neckerchief, but most of their clothing was still made of cotton, linen, and wool. Colors of drab and butternut continued to predominate in the Shakers' everyday wardrobe; those dyes were made on the premises.

Apples were an important commodity at Union Village.

Girl's straw bonnet.

Blue coloring was also prepared by the sisters and used for blue and white striped riding gowns and checked neckerchiefs. Although sisters dressed plainly, they dressed well, with clothing provided for household work, travel, and worship. A list of clothing provided to communities by New Lebanon in 1840 shows close to 100 items of clothing per woman, including collars, mittens, and cloaks. Second Family sisters made palm leaf bonnets for themselves as well as for sale. Head coverings were important to women to preserve their modesty, and girls started wearing caps at a young age. At age seven, they began wearing net caps to meetings. At eight, they graduated to cloth caps for meetings and at age 12, they began wearing cloth caps every day. Girls' hair was cut short until they were 10 years old. As they matured, their hair was allowed to grow, but they wore it up and tucked under their caps.[8]

Believers were even given rules about bathing. Most of these rules were to ensure that people did not become ill from bathing in cold water, or from getting their feet wet—then believed to be major causes of illness. Reckless bathing was considered more dangerous than not bathing. According to rules circulated especially for the sisters and children:

No one is to wash more than their hands and face and their feet if necessary within five days after being taken unwell, and not within the same number of days before the time they expected to be taken unwell. Except it is thought necessary to soak their feet in warm water... Children should be washed all over once a week in warm weather, but let the water have the chill taken off, except it be brook or pond water, or water that has stood in the sun...Great care should be taken that children should have plenty of air; for it is a given point, that children need more air than grown people.[9]

There were also guidelines for charitable giving. In 1845, the ministry at Enfield, Connecticut, reminded Union Village residents that Ann Lee had encouraged Believers "to be kind to the poor, and to impart a portion of the good things which God hath blessed them with, to the needy and the destitute."[10] Food and clothing distributed to the poor was to be of good quality. Like other Shaker villages, Union Village was known for its charity. In a time when food pantries and shelters did not exist, a meal and a bed at a Shaker village could literally mean the difference between life and death. The community took in many people who were destitute and could not survive living outdoors. These homeless people were given food, shelter, medical care, and work. They were not expected to join the faith, but they had to live according to the Believers' rules while in the village. Some stayed for days; a few remained for several months. Most never joined the faith.

To help care for the homeless as well as their own large families, the Believers constantly improved homemaking procedures. By 1850, they provided a constant supply of water for all the dwellings from a central cistern located in the Gathering Order. A "hydraulic ram" forced spring water 700 feet up into the holding tank. Horsepower, used for so many purposes at Union Village, was now also employed to knead bread dough and wash the huge quantities of potatoes that were consumed each day.[11]

Visitors often marveled at the village's industry while criticizing the sect's family practices. An English writer's account of an 1846 visit questioned the Believers' lifestyle but praised their work ethic:

Its gardens, orchards, fields, and even woods, at the first glance, were very attractive. The buildings stood irregularly, and were of various sizes and designs, for the various purposes to which they were devoted: yet, although scrupulously clean and neat, they exhibited no marks of taste, such as vine-covered verandahs, or roses and honeysuckles...and the want of this our flower-loving friends regarded as a great failing.... Some of the dwellings were large, containing from eighty to a hundred inmates, both men and women but it was a sort of union workhouse, where parents and children, husbands and wives, were no more to each other than mere neighbors.[12]

The visitors, Harrison and Harriet Aldersen and their daughter, Florence, saw a group of children leaving the school on their way to the meetinghouse. The boys looked like miniature adults dressed in gray pantaloons, black jackets, and broad-brimmed straw hats. The girls wore brown gowns, clear muslin handkerchiefs, and straw bonnets. They walked in separate paths, two abreast in each path, just as recommended in the Millennial Laws. Mrs. Aldersen spoke with an elderly sister who heartily endorsed Shaker life: "She said that it certainly was the best that could be thought of; for that they all lived in peace, had all they wanted, and were removed from the temptations of the world."[13]

As the visitors departed, Mr. Aldersen met a brother, Zephaniah Kumbal, whom he had known before the man's conversion. Kumbal and his family joined the community after he failed as a farmer. He became comfortable with the Believers but his wife pined away for her children who had been placed in the Children's Order. The wife left the village, secured a cottage nearby, and tried to see her children when she could. "But it was a melancholy life for her, and only a few months ago she died," the author wrote.[14] The Believers appeared prosperous and frugal. The men, whom the writer described as "singularly ruddy-complexioned, with something of a jolly-friar look about them," seemed to fare better than the women, who "looked thin and out of condition." While admiring their industriousness, the writer questioned the toll taken on personal lives:

> *Their reputation for honesty was so great, that whatever was made or sold by a Shaker would fetch a higher price. Shaker seeds, Shaker herbs, Shaker carpets, etc., were all thought better than ordinary articles of the same kind.... Spite of all its worldly prosperity, however, our friends never thought of Union Village, but with somewhat of a melancholy feeling; for everything seemed to flourish there, excepting the women and children.*[15]

The Believers had heard this criticism before and were intensely sensitive about it. Silas Strong, the Adventist convert, presented statistics in an 1847 issue of the *Day-Star* refuting a common allegation that Shaker "females generally soon became sickly in appearance; and that the greatest number of them died young with a consumption, or some worse disease; the cause of which was too shocking to mention." The double-edged criticism played off two anti-Shaker attitudes. One was that celibates, living closely with the opposite sex, led unnatural lifestyles that created unwholesome stress. The other accusation was that the female Believers were actually subjected to promiscuity. Drawing on church records and other unnamed sources, he stated that the average age of death in the village from 1805 to 1817 was 24. The average age of death continued to increase from 1836–1847, until it was 57. The average lifespan in the general, non-enslaved public was quite similar—around 60.[16]

Strong's statistics, read primarily by sympathizers, did little to allay gossip about the Believers, but they do reveal the ages of Union Village residents in 1847: 41 inhabitants were under 10; 69 were between 10 and 20; 39 were between 20 and 30; 28 were between 30 and 40; 61 were between 50 and 60; 42 were between 60 and 70; 25 were between 70 and 80; and 10 were over 80. In age, they were a well-balanced group, with a similar number of adults on either side of 50. That implies a good mix of experienced members with those being trained in the faith, as well as a sufficient labor pool to sustain the physical work of the community. With more than one hundred children and young people, prospects for future membership seemed good.

Prudence Morrell's journal of her trip to Union Village in the summer of 1847 enthusiastically supported Strong's contention that the overall population was thriving. She marveled at the improvements that had been made in the village and found both sisters and brothers looking well and feeling hospitable. She visited the First Order family and met some young sisters she had not known, "but I love them very much for they appeared very pretty & loving," she wrote. In an afternoon Sabbath meeting with the First and Second Orders, Morrell rejoiced at being able to worship with fellow Believers after her long journey from New Lebanon. The spirits of David Darrow and Ruth Farrington attended the meeting along with many other spirits. Spiritual gifts were shared and then the Believers sang a welcoming song. Morrell and her traveling companion, Eliza Sharp, each received a basket of fruit during a visit to the Second Family. Soon after, they visited with the Frame House Family. "Some very pretty among both sexes," Morrell wrote.[17]

Physical improvements in the village also delighted her. The Center House was pronounced "very durable, plain and handsome." Elder John Martin took the visitors to the West Section where they observed a gristmill, carding machine, new mill house and dam, and a roping and spinning machine for wool. The spinning machine, which ran by water, impressed Morrell, because its 140 spindles turned out 50 to 70 pounds of wool a day. She went to see the women reel silk and reported that they reeled between 50 and 60 runs in a day. Equally impressive was a herd of 60 Durham cattle. "Their horns are very homely," Morrell wrote, "but they are as fat as meadow moles. A number of them give a large pail of milk at a milking."[18] Visits to various families continued, and Morrell and Sharp constantly took their sewing with them so they could continue being productive.

Morrell was also impressed by the village's spiritual life. She wrote that

Sabbath morning meetings were once again open to the world in 1847. At the June 6 meeting, spectators filled about half of the meetinghouse and another large group stood in the yard. Most of the visitors behaved well at the meetings but Morrell wrote that she didn't know if they heeded the message. While the public was tolerated at meetings, the Believers were reminded they should not be too familiar with them. One family elder cautioned against socializing with the hired hands working in the village. If visiting continued, he warned, the hired hands would be released. At times, visitors were admitted to the village for other reasons. On July 5, nine wagons full of outsiders came to Union Village to celebrate Independence Day. "Some of the world came to the office and asked liberty (permission) to go to the great mill pond on Believers land and get themselves a meal of victuals," Morrell wrote. "They bought two pounds of butter, killed a dozen squirrels, and caught a few little fishes, which, I suppose, made out their dinner with what they brought with them...this was the way they took to keep independence."[19]

Eldress Ellen Ross was a testimonial to Silas Strong's claim that Shakers flourished in their wholesome lifestyle. Ross came to Union Village with her parents in 1838 as a two-year-old. She remained a Shaker until her death in 1927.

What Morrell enjoyed most about her visit home were the special services held at Jehovah's Chosen Square. She described the site as "a beautiful square yard, ten rods each way and shaded with forest trees, ash, oak, & hickory. The fountain is in the centre of the yard, just 18 feet square and over the gate is as follows: 'Purity, Holiness, and Eternal Truth, I do require of all who enter here to worship Me, Saith the Lord.'"[20] Admittance of the world to this sacred place and service demonstrates that the Believers still actively sought converts. The pools that Morrell described were imaginary:

When we reached the sacred ground, we were informed that there were two pools of living water wherein we might bathe and be clean. After we had bathed, the gate was opened, and the people entered in.... We then went forth in the dances of those that make merry, and shook off all pride, lust, self-will, and everything that goes to hinder a free circulation of the pure spirit of Mother. One of the instruments spake a few words for the apostle John concerning the mission of our blessed Mother Ann.... Then a message was read to the spectators that was given by inspiration on purpose for strangers that attended the chosen square...we then gather'd around the fountain, bathed and received love to carry to Pleasant Hill.... The singers marched next to the Elders, and sung nearly all the way going and coming back.[21]

After visiting the other Ohio communities and Kentucky, Morrell and Sharp returned to New York in late August. Her overall impression of the western villages was quite positive; she was especially impressed with Union Village's prosperity and the promise for its future.

If hard work could make the community successful, Union Village was certainly headed for success. Morrell's habit of sewing while visiting was indicative of the effort put forth by the Believers. Work and worship were so intertwined in daily life that they were nearly inseparable. Susanna Cole Liddell's journal reflects the members' work ethic. During the first 13 weeks of 1851, the sisters in her shop made a total of 62 jackets, 43 frocks, 40 pairs of trousers, 20 shirts, three gowns, three wrappers, three coats, and one surtout. Unlike the stereotypical Shaker attitude of steady but moderate work, this time the sisters felt pressured to produce. Liddell wrote:

Every-thing was contrived in such a manner as to make the sewers feel the burden and interest of the sewing. It was hurry hurry hurry all the time till it seemed that the very atmosphere was filled with hurry hurry...I haven't spent one hour...in reading nor in doing any chores for myself whatever until last ironing day when I mended some.... The time of year has now come for the sisters to be called off for other business and the sewing company is reduced to three or four. However the brethren's woollen sewing is nearly done. There is but four jackets to begin.[22]

Women had taken over some of the tailoring duties previously performed by men, but the 1850 census still listed three men as either clothiers or tailors. One man, Robert Dulton, is listed as a lace maker. Women's occupations were not listed on the census. The range of occupations listed for Union Village men indicates that the village was fairly self-sufficient. Occupations included: minister, elder, trustee, botanist, horticulturist, gardener, orchardist, farmer, basket maker, shepherd, herdsman, carder, wool stapler, currier, shoemaker, physician, schoolteacher, miller, teamster, house joiner, mason, wood chopper, carpenter, painter, cooper, millwright, whitesmith (tinsmith), blacksmith, machinist, broom maker, bookbinder, printer, chandler (candle maker), potter, and silversmith. The village's racial makeup was less diverse. Of the 448 people living there, seven were black or mulatto. (Lebanon's population that year was 2,088, with 128 being non-white.[23]) Union Village was still progressive in that blacks and whites lived and worked together.

By the 1850s, livestock was a major business for the village. Cattle replaced hogs as the top cash livestock. The Believers had shunned pork in 1842 along with store-bought tea, coffee, tobacco and alcoholic beverages. The dietary restrictions, which were mandated throughout the United Society, were part of the purifying process that accompanied the Era of Manifestations. Shortly after dietary restrictions were ordered, pork production at Union Village ceased. Beef and dairy cattle sold well, as did blooded stock for breeding. Patton and Durham stock were in great demand. In January 1853, Trustee Peter Boyd wrote to a prospective buyer that a large white cow, Snowball, was with calf by a large red bull, named Brutus. According to the Millennial Laws of 1845, animals were not to be called by proper Christian names or nicknames but stockmen had to identify animals in some manner so names such as Spotted Mary, Red Beauty, and Amelia were used.

Buyers came from nearby as well as from other states. When a farmer from a neighboring county inquired about livestock in the fall of 1853, he was advised that several calves and heifers were for sale. In response to an inquiry from an Illinois farmer in 1854, Boyd noted that he had two fine bulls for sale. He sent their pedigree papers along with their price. The two-year-old bull was for sale for $200. The one-year-old untried bull cost $100. Several heifers were for sale, ranging from $50 to $125, depending on breed and pedigree. "If you want any bulls or heifers you had better order soon or we will not be able to supply you probably," Boyd wrote, indicating that sales were brisk.[24]

Warren County businessman Robert G. Corwin collaborated with the Believers in importing herds of thoroughbred shorthorn cattle from Scotland in 1854. In March of 1855, the Shakers sold several thoroughbred Durham cattle for a total of $8,420. They also began patronizing agricultural fairs to support the industry and promote their products. They showed their cattle at county fairs and at the state fair in Columbus. In 1852, they donated $25 to the Warren County Agricultural Society's first county fair. That same year, the Shaker-bred bull, Chillicothe, took the second place premium at the Ohio State Fair.[25] Participation in the fairs also led to more social interaction with the world. While a few brothers attended just to exhibit livestock, other brothers, sisters, and children frequently attended the Warren County Fair in Lebanon and the Butler County Fair in Hamilton purely for enjoyment.

A sale of Shaker cattle, held October 13, 1859, in Lebanon, demonstrates how important the livestock business had become. The bloodlines of cattle were meticulously delineated in an illustrated 18-page catalog. Most of the cattle were bred at Union Village, but a few were imported. Sixteen bulls and 46 heifers and calves were sold that day. The catalog noted that the heifer, Roan Beauty, had produced a calf that sold for $500 and had a young grand-calf that sold for $300. Buyers who paid cash received an eight percent discount. Credit was extended for six months without interest; buyers could also choose to pay after fifteen months at a six percent interest rate.[26] No matter how buyers paid, the Believers made a substantial profit on the livestock sales.

As principal trustee, Boyd's letters reveal which industries ceased and which thrived during his tenure. For instance, Union Village had stopped producing cooper wares for the open market by 1853, but the broom business was still strong. In response to an inquiry from a St. Louis businessman, Boyd wrote that he could supply up to 100 dozen brooms at a cost of $2 per dozen, deliverable to any location in Cincinnati.[27]

Industry was making the Shaker name and reputation for quality well known. The Believers' neighbors were becoming their customers. With familiarity came tolerance, but very few conversions.

"The garden is said to be an index of the owner's mind."

—Gardener's Manual, 1835

Top: The Trustees' Office was the village's commercial center and where the world came to do business with the Shakers.
Right: Detail of seed box.

✹ Chapter Ten ✹
Success from the Earth—
Seed and Herb Industries

Many Americans became aware of Union Village in the mid-nineteenth century through the community's garden seeds and herbal medicines. The enterprises, natural offshoots of the community's agricultural efforts, proved financially successful. The industries also show how men and women divided work at the village. Although the Believers were progressive in operating these businesses, they were traditional in how jobs were performed. Brothers and sisters performed the same jobs that men and women did on family farms. Most often, they toiled at different tasks in the same area, with men doing the heavier work, and women doing the more detailed work. During especially busy times of planting, harvesting, and packaging, they might work side by side and also enlist the help of the older children. They worked cooperatively to change the way that Americans treated nutrition and home health care. The sect is generally credited with improving the diet of Americans, especially those of middle and lower incomes.

One history of food notes that "through instinct or empiricism," Shakers were progressive in growing and eating a variety of nutritious produce that some Americans still considered dangerous.[1]

While many frontier families survived on wild game, cornbread, and milk, the Believers began to preserve foods that traveled west with the pioneers and varied the diets of those at home. Apples and corn were the first foods to be preserved in large quantities for sale to the public by Believers. Union Village did a brisk business in both. Storage rooms were knee-deep in dried corn that was sold in hogsheads. Large quantities of apple "snitts" (quarters) were processed and sold as applesauce or dried fruit.[2]

Drying houses were built around 1840 to dehydrate the corn and apples when they could not be dried in the sun. The work was first done manually, in a very rudimentary way. Corn was boiled and the kernels cut off by knife by sisters. Kernels were placed out in the sun on boards to dry naturally. Periodically, a brother or a boy raked the corn to promote even drying. Later, processing became mechanized. As more heavy machinery became used, the brothers became increasingly involved in the production. Steam-operated machines sliced corn from the cobs at a rate of 45 ears per minute. The cut corn dropped into baskets and was whisked into a kiln, where it was treated to even heat from furnaces. Dried corn passed through a mill that winnowed any remaining silk or husk. The corn then shot into a large bin and was fed into barrels through a tube.[3]

Apples were at first quartered and cored by hand by sisters until the invention of a paring machine, credited to a brother. In a two-story drying house, a large stove on the ground floor provided the heat to dry the apples, which were placed in large bins on the second floor. Once cooled, the apple quarters were stored in barrels. Union Village took pride in its orchards. By 1815, the community had nurseries that were noted for apples, cherries, and pears. Village gardeners also enjoyed experimenting with new varieties. Orchardist David Rowley recorded over 40 different types of apple trees in the West orchard in 1855. Apples considered excellent for cider included the Roxbury Russet, Snow Apple, Baldwin, Rhode Island Greening, Golden Pippin, Seek No Further, and Spitzenberg. Others considered better for cooking or making dried apples included the Gravenstein, Northern Spy, and Superior Sweet. Some variety names are self-explanatory: Early Pie Apple, Belly Bound.[4]

The development of the garden seed industry at Union Village had an even bigger impact on the community's economy and on the American diet. Believers modeled their garden-seed business on those started by New England brethren in the late eighteenth century. Evan Davies, a Boston gardener, advertised English seeds as early as 1719, but on the whole American neighbors typically traded seeds with one another to obtain new plants. Most vegetable cultivation took place in the more established communities; frontier families at first survived on seasonal food and a limited variety of preserved food. In 1784, the first major seed house in the country was started by David Landreth, who sold imported and native seeds in Philadelphia. The Believers improved on the idea. At first they sold seed from the world as well as seed they raised, but in 1819 three of the New England communities signed a covenant to sell only Shaker-grown seeds to ensure the best quality. The sole exception was melon seeds, although Union Village did sell its own watermelon seeds. By 1825, Shaker seeds were reputed to be the finest and most reliable available. When Hamilton, Ohio, shopkeeper William Blair received a "great variety" of spring seeds from the Warren County Believers in 1826, he advertised the seeds as being from Union Village rather than from the Shakers, showing that the village itself had a good commercial reputation in the region. By the 1850s, the Landreth Company—then one of the leading nurseries in the country—was buying Shaker seed to distribute.[5]

> The development of the garden seed industry at Union Village had an even bigger impact on the community's economy and on the American diet.

Union Village contributed to the blossoming seed industry with revolutionary packaging and marketing. By 1813, the community was selling seed in small but consistent amounts. Accounts for that March show a few dollars worth and sometimes just a few cents worth of seed being sold. On March 8, Calvin Morrell turned in a whopping $14 he had collected for seed. Business boomed after the Center family began to make bags to put up their seeds in 1816. Previously, seed had been stored and transported in boxes or baskets that made selling smaller quantities difficult, and also increased the risk of spoilage. Soon small paper packets, like the ones that modern gardeners buy, replaced bags. Accounts show the sale of four papers (packets) of garden seeds for 31 ¼ cents on April 9, 1816. Each packet was imprinted with the seed's variety, the community's name, the initials of the family's deacon, and sometimes planting and care instructions. Seeds could be purchased in graduated sizes from the packets, which held just a few ounces for a typical family garden, up to pound bags. The papers were inexpensive, convenient, and informative, encouraging more people to plant gardens and veteran gardeners to try more varieties of vegetables. Typical offerings included onions, beets, cabbage, lettuce, cucumbers, turnips, sage, parsnips, carrots, radishes, summer and winter squash, watermelons, muskmelons, asparagus, celery, parsley, and peppergrass. Additional types of seeds were added over the years at Union Village, including pumpkin, corn, mustard, beans, peas, cauliflower, and cress.[6]

The seed industry was labor intensive. Preparations started in late fall. Head gardeners, who were brothers, prepared an annual sales report and sometimes entertained worldly gardeners who wanted to preview the coming season's offerings. Retailers were urged to place their orders by mid-November to make sure they received the seeds they wanted. Manure was set aside for spring fertilizing. Hot beds were prepared in March for melons, tomatoes, cucumbers, and cabbage. The men also began plowing the fields in late March, and applying manure and other amendments including wood ashes or lime. They used compost extensively and prided themselves on creating the best mixture. Planting and sowing began in April. From June through August, men—and sometimes women—weeded and cultivated crops. Plants were hoed routinely to stimulate growth. Mulching was not commonly done, so weeding was a constant chore. Harmful insects were plucked off by hand. To prevent insects from returning, gardeners doused the plants with a tea of cayenne pepper, dusted them with ashes or sawdust, or showered them with tobacco juice or mild soapsuds.

Women often joined the men in the fields during harvest. After seeds were collected, they were cleaned and dried, frequently by the sisters. Packaging the seeds required first making the packages, another winter task that was done collaboratively. The trustees bought the paper, and then brothers cut and printed it. Women folded and pasted the bags, sometimes assisted by the children or the elderly in busy times. The bags were filled and sealed, and then loaded into seed boxes that the sisters had cleaned. Brothers prepared the horses and wagons for selling trips, and two or three trusted brothers peddled the seeds to the world and collected the money. Union Village salesmen followed two large routes; one in the Midwest and another through the South.[7] Any undertaking that brought members into closer contact with the public was handled by the men. Many rural people and small businessmen in the world also followed this practice.

Gardeners of both sexes used the *Gardener's Manual*, first published by Brother Charles F. Crosman of New Lebanon in 1835. Believing in the spiritual nature of all work, including gardening, Crosman offered moral advice as well as practical horticultural information. "The garden is said to be an index of the owner's mind," Crosman noted, and should be carefully tended to grow only beautiful and useful products.[8] In the world of Shaker metaphors, weeds were ugly, destructive thoughts and actions that the individual had to eradicate to allow goodness to flourish. For the secular reader, the six-cent manual and catalog provided information about the plants and advice on increasing productivity. Crosman's informative manuals were the forerunners of modern seed catalogs. Through the seed industry, the Believers—particularly the Westerners who sold to the frontier—provided a healthier variety of food to a greater number of people.

The herbal medicine industry became even more important than the seed business for the community. Believers became known nationally and in England and France as creators of herbal remedies before the American pharmaceutical industry fully developed. Like most frontier people, the Believers had long gathered and processed plants to treat illnesses and dress wounds. Many people feared traditional doctors, or had no access to them, or couldn't afford them, so they turned to self-proclaimed healers who used techniques and plants from old European, African, and Indian traditions. Another type of practitioner—the botanical or homeopathic physician—might have apprenticed with a regular doctor or studied or their own.[9] The Shaker doctors were closest to that type of practitioner who usually prescribed a systematic course of treatments for their patient. At Union Village, most of the doctors were men, and most nurses were women.

Shaker medical practices were heavily influenced by Samuel Thomson, a homeopathic practitioner of the early nineteenth century. He favored using steam to produce a cleansing perspiration in patients and herbal preparations to promote internal cleansing. All Shakers did not unequivocally accept Thomson's methods, however. David Darrow officially chastised members in 1824 for

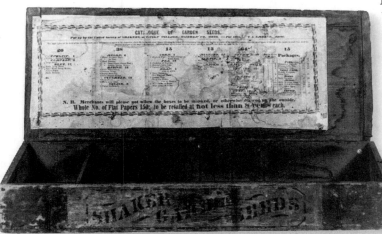

Shaker salesmen took the seed boxes out to customers and to place in stores.

arguing over the choice of "the regular, Thompsonian, or steam" system of medicine. Many botanical doctors used the same types of treatments, as did formally trained physicians. Bleeding, emetics, and laxatives were rigorously used in the early 1800s by all types of doctors to rid patients of substances that were believed to cause illness. Shakers had their share of preparations that caused dramatic results as well, but they also offered some milder ones—preventatives and remedies for chronic, non-life threatening conditions. Their cough syrup, for instance, contained rhubarb, a novel ingredient in such medicine that routinely contained wild cherry bark and morphine. The rhubarb was added as a tonic, which, the Shakers said, would prevent the need for even stronger medicine later. They presented herbal medicines to the public as part of their larger mission to improve people's lives. The poem on the cover of their 1850 herb catalogue read "Let gratitude in acts of goodness flow/our love to God in love to man below/ be this our joy to calm the troubled breast/ support the weak, and succor the distrest."[10]

> Shakers claimed to have originated the herbal business as early as 1800, with widespread commercial sales starting in 1820.

Union Village was one of six Shaker villages in the country that became widely known as producers of herbal remedies. The other five were all in the East: New Lebanon and Watervliet, New York; Canterbury and Enfield, New Hampshire, and Harvard, Massachusetts. Union Village had by far the largest herb business in the West, grossing an average of $150,000 annually during the peak years in the 1840s and 1850s. Other communities in Ohio and Kentucky also had botanical gardens, primarily for their own use. Union Village's doctors sometimes traveled to those other villages to obtain plants that they lacked. South Union, which had a thriving seed industry, also sold some herbal medicines.[11]

Shakers claimed to have originated the herbal business as early as 1800, with widespread commercial sales starting in 1820. Herb catalogs from Union Village have been found for 1847, 1848, 1850, and 1856, but herb cultivation for members' use started much earlier. Believers there were growing sage and sassafras by 1819. By 1833, village physicians Abiathar Babbitt and Andrew Houston headed the botanical department, where they began growing medicinal plants in quantity. They had previously distilled oils and "fragrant waters," and whiskey for medicinal purposes. Some of the herbs they grew had been gifts from the Shawnees during their 1807 exchanges with Union Village. When the Believers began growing herbs commercially, they focused on plants familiar to most of their clientele: foxglove, used to treat heart conditions, asthma, and nervous disorders; belladonna and poppies, used as painkillers and sedatives; wormwood, for stomach complaints and worms; henbane, to induce sleep and treat rheumatism; hellebore, to poison insect pests and vermin; rue, to ease rheumatism and aid digestion; hyssop, to treat a variety of complaints; horehound, to ease sore throats and earaches; and catnip, to aid sleep and digestion. In their 1847 catalog, the offerings were more extensive: 156 medicinal herbs, 25 extracts, nine essential oils, seven fragrant waters, and four culinary herbs.[12]

By 1850, 252 medical plants were offered, ranging from aconite, which was used to reduce pain and fever and to slow the pulse, to yarrow, used as a diuretic and tonic. Only a part of some plants was used, while multiple parts— roots, leaves, bark, seeds, flowers, and berries—of other plants were processed into medicines. Forty-six plant extracts were offered, as well as 30 powdered roots, herbs, and barks, 10 essential oils, eight inspissated (condensed) juices, seven distilled fragrant waters, and four pulverized culinary herbs: sage, summer savory, sweet marjoram, and thyme. Other items were available at the customer's request. Plant names were those commonly used in Cincinnati, St. Louis, Louisville, and New Orleans, all parts of Union Village's sales territory. Individuals could buy these products from the Believers, but most plant materials were sold in bulk to merchants, druggists, and physicians. An extra ten cents per pound was charged for packing in one or two-ounce packages. Prices were not listed in the catalog, so customers had to write to trustee Peter Boyd to learn what that season's costs were. The finest medicines and plants were guaranteed:

> *The various Herbs, Roots and Barks, are gathered in the season proper to each; the stalky and coarser part being rejected; they are then uniformly dried under shelter, after which they are neatly prepared and papered in assorted packages for the convenience of purchasers. Our Extracts are prepared by experienced persons; they are vaporized by steam, and great care is used that they are not burned or otherwise injured. Our Inspissated Juices are of superior quality and excellence.*[13]

An account of the herbal medicine department at New Lebanon in the mid 1800s provided a more detailed picture of how products were made. Union Village and South Union Believers visited there for 10 days in 1854 and spent many hours studying the operation. As they did with the seed industry, the Shakers operated the herb business under one roof to monitor quality and efficiency. The main herb department occupied a two-story building with a basement and a loft. A steam boiler and machines for pressing and grinding plants were used in the basement. Herbs were compacted into one-pound blocks, an inch thick and seven and one-fourth inches square. On the first floor, packages were printed and plant materials were sorted and stored. The second story and loft was used for drying and storing herbs. Extracts and inspissated juices were processed in the extract house, or laboratory. Plants were steamed in large boilers, and then pressed in cylinders. The resulting juices were boiled in a copper vacuum pan to extract the most concentrated form of liquid. They were sold in bottles ranging from one-ounce to five-pound sizes. Dried roots that were to be processed into medicinal powders were pulverized between one-ton granite discs. The powders were sold in small pasteboard boxes.[14]

Business was brisk at Union Village by 1852. Peter Boyd told one customer that "we have made considerable additions to our gardens & other conveniences for pulverizing" herbs to accommodate increased demand. Men and women worked cooperatively on related tasks. The men did most of the planting and cultivating as well as the heavy processing work, such as pulverizing plants and running the steam engine for vacuum processing of extracts and juices. Women helped to tend the herb gardens, harvest, pick over the plants, wash and dry them, and package them. Boyd took care of accounting and correspondence, which took a fair amount of time. Villages frequently bought or traded herbs with each other when they ran short. Union Village and Canterbury frequently depended on each other for needed plants. The many letters between Boyd and Canterbury's David Parker attest to these two communities' importance in the herb business. "The English Valerian Root arrived in good order last week, which we feel very thankful for," Boyd wrote to Parker. Parker later wrote to Union Village, inquiring about the availability of peppermint oil. "We have about 150 pounds of oil of peppermint which we hold at 4 dollars per lb.," Boyd replied. "The druggists are offering us three dollars and fifty cts., but as the market is on the rise, we hold it at 4." Seven months later, Boyd agreed to sell Parker 100 pounds of peppermint oil at $3.75 per pound. Boyd kept all accounts for the herb business and he frequently wrote to people who owed the community money, sometimes asking the postmaster of the debtor's town to recommend a collection agent. He began requiring payment with incoming orders on sarsaparilla to avoid more collection problems.[15]

Sarsaparilla was soon one of the village's primary products and one that became synonymous with the Shaker name. Five communities specialized in making the sarsaparilla syrup and once again, Union Village and Canterbury were among the sales leaders. The syrup sold for $1 a pint or $8 a gallon in the 1850s. Recommended as a treatment for everything from skin diseases to rheumatism, it became so well known that competitors tried to copy the product and imply that it came from the Shakers. In Cincinnati, Dr. S.D. Howe marketed Shaker Compound Extract of Sarsaparilla Syrup, which he led customers to assume came from Union Village's private formula.[16] Boyd took pains to disassociate his product from competitors, especially those that were starting to be peddled as patent medicines. He warned against competitors' false calms in the 1850 catalogue: "we never…obtain any patents for our medicine, or sell any receipts, or sell any medicine of which the materials are secret; any publication purporting to have obtained receipts of us, is a fraudulent attempt to obtain money on our credit."[17] To be absolutely sure of the finest quality, customers were advised to order from the community's catalog, buy from the Shakers' peddlers, or authorized dealers, or visit Cincinnati's farmers' market where products were sold weekly.

Other products that Union Village's botanical department became noted for were narcotic sedatives and painkillers including belladonna, hemlock, and opium poppies. Botanists there also developed a new plant, the hybrid colocynth. The colocynth was a bitter cucumber native to Africa and Asia. The botanists crossed the colocynth with a watermelon to produce a laxative.[18]

By selling produce, medicinal herbs, and other products, Union Village

As principal trustee for decades, Peter Boyd was responsible for the marketing and sale of everything from garden seeds to livestock. He eventually lent his image to the village's famous line of herbal medicines and sarsaparilla syrup.

remained involved in commerce in the Miami Valley and throughout the Midwest and South. Familiarity with the Believers' merchandise made the sect less threatening to many people. One sign of greater public acceptance was a product endorsement. In the 1850 herb catalog, a full-page advertisement for Shaker products included endorsements from Andrew Campbell, a physician from nearby Middletown, Ohio; R.D. Massey, a professor of surgery at the Medical College of Ohio; and the Lebanon Medical Society. The latter endorsement was still being used in the 1890s. It read: "Resolved. —that this Society have entire confidence in the purity of the Pharmaceutical preparations of the Shakers at Union Village, Ohio, and that we heartily recommend these preparations to the profession; especially the extracts of the Narcotic Plants and of Sarsaparilla."[19] The people who once mobbed the village and condemned the Believers in local newspapers now trusted them for food and medicine.

Peter Boyd, busy with the myriad industries of the community, was about to become even busier after a series of moves in the hierarchy. In 1859, New Lebanon relieved John Martin of his position as first in the ministry due to unspecified "pronounced eccentricities."[20] Aaron Babbitt, second in the ministry, succeeded Martin. Boyd was named second in the ministry, but he continued to oversee the herb business.

Economically bolstered by the sustained sales of herbs and medicines, life at Union Village proceeded relatively calmly until the start of the Civil War.

"Peace...was the principle which all true Christians lived and taught, and we can live and teach nothing else."

—William McGladeny, 1863

Top Left: Oliver Hampton
Top Right: Richard Realf
Right: Green Tree tavern

❧ Chapter Eleven ❧
Momentous Times— Union Village and the Civil War

Union Village tried to remain apolitical during the Civil War, although circumstances kept drawing its people into the conflict. In response to the turmoil, the Believers deepened their commitment to pacifism, retooled their industries to accommodate the wartime economy, and struggled to retain their young people.

Like their secular neighbors, the Believers had listened to debates over slavery for decades before the war began in 1861. Although their hearts and sympathies were clearly on the side of abolition, their commitment to unity put them on the side of preserving the Union and their faith demanded that they remain neutral. Unlike the Quakers who actively worked for abolition, the Believers tried to show through example that everyone was equal and worthy in God's sight. Their position led to speculation in the twentieth century over whether Union Village had been a station on the Underground Railroad. Unfortunately, the Believers never provided many answers.

A labyrinth of stations throughout the Miami Valley guided streams of slaves to freedom in Canada. One freedom trail passed directly through Union Village, fueling speculation that the community was a station. The idea seems logical. Shakers had always opposed slavery for religious reasons, believing that each person is equal before God. Racial equality had been practiced within the community since 1805, when a black woman became the second Western convert, and since 1807 when Richard McNemar wrote that race, sex, and age didn't matter among the Believers. Their abhorrence of slavery is mentioned frequently in their writings.

The Believers knew of the Underground Railroad and the controversy surrounding slavery. Many of them were quite well informed about local and national developments. Business dealings kept trustees, salesmen, and deaconesses in touch with the public. Even members who did not routinely leave Union Village might have had contact with hired men and visitors at Sabbath services. Members also read several newspapers. Although the number of copies received in the village decreased during the Era of Manifestations, anyone could go to the trustees' office to read a current paper.

> If Union Village was a link in the Underground Railroad, its members were singularly united in maintaining a long-term silence about it.

During the Civil War, the First Order Family subscribed to a daily newspaper, *The Cincinnati Gazette*, and to four weekly papers: *The Western Star*, published in Lebanon; *The Liberator*, an abolitionist paper published in Boston; *The Wool Grower*, a trade paper; and a German-language newspaper.[1] The war and all of its political, philosophic, and economic effects were covered in the publications.

Southwestern Ohio was home to many Underground Railroad stations and prominent abolitionists. Harriet Beecher Stowe supposedly was inspired to write *Uncle Tom's Cabin* while living in Cincinnati, after she heard tales of fugitives and saw slaves in northern Kentucky.[2] Escaped slaves crossed the Ohio River on ferries and packets, and set out through Ohio to the safety of Canada, where bounty hunters were less inclined to follow. Legend has it that secret tunnels existed in the Center House cellar to hide fugitives who waited to move on to the next station. Documented sources show the proximity of Union Village to several Underground Railroad routes. Several southern routes converged in nearby Lebanon. Jon Van Sandt, the famous railroad conductor, used U.S. Route 42 (Reading Road) in Hamilton County to move fugitives out of Cincinnati to Palmyra (Mason today) in Warren County. From Mason, Van Sandt used what is now State Route 741 to move slaves to the next stop, the Red Lion Inn, just north of Union Village. Route 741 runs through the center of Union Village, meaning that fugitives traveled straight through the village. Immediately northwest of the village was the Green Tree Tavern, where Ichabod Corwin operated a busy Underground Railroad stop on the road to Red Lion in the early 1800s.[3]

Given the Shakers' religious beliefs and their location, it is logical to assume that they supported the Underground Railroad. But documentation of their involvement is yet to be found. Railroad scholars say this is not surprising since few people were willing to implicate themselves in an illegal activity. After passage of the Fugitive Slave Act in 1850, some conductors closed their stations, fearing they would lose everything if charged and convicted.[4] Much of the Railroad's history "comes from unsubstantiated reminiscences published 50 years after the fact in newspapers and by scholars."[5] Such stories fueled speculation that Union Village had indeed actively participated in the effort. Local historians began to analyze and interpret comments in the Believers' letters and journals as supporting evidence. It has been suggested that some of the land the Shakers purchased outside Warren County was bought to establish stations farther north on the way to Canada.[6]

Proof remains elusive. Wilbur Siebert, a historian of the Underground Railroad in Ohio, wrote about numerous stations in Warren County, but not Union Village. While researching a book on the subject, Siebert attempted to correspond with Job Mullin, a Quaker from the Warren County village of Springboro, who worked with the Railroad in the early 1800s. Mullin's son-in-law, W. H. Newport, wrote back to Siebert at the elderly man's request, saying, "He cannot at his age [90] recall much of interest." Mullins had said there had been a freedom station at "Shaker Village," but he offered no support for the claim or details about operations there.[7]

If Union Village was a link in the Underground Railroad, its members were singularly united in maintaining a long-term silence about it. Even apostates, who often besmirched the community, didn't discuss the issue. Many of these backsliders committed hostile acts against their former brethren. In March 1860, apostates broke into the Second Family's building and stole large amounts of clothing and wheat. Others were suspected of numerous thefts and arsons within the village over the years, yet none of these disgruntled apostates accused the Believers of violating the Fugitive Slave Act. Perhaps the central ministry's plea for members to remain apolitical overrode their moral abhorrence of slavery. It is equally likely that the Believers simply allowed the escaped slaves to quietly pass through the village without actively sheltering them.

Although references to the Underground Railroad are conspicuously absent from Union Village documents, the church records for 1861–65 are filled with observations and news about the war. The number of black members was always small, but the practice of whites and blacks living and worshipping together as brothers and sisters was a constant reminder that the Believers were more progressive than some of their neighbors. South Union and Pleasant Hill also had black members. No one could predict how these communities would be treated in a war. As the western leader, Union Village was responsible for the Kentuckians. Yet the actual advice and help they could provide was limited. Slavery was an especially difficult burden for southern Believers because they lived with it daily. Elders constantly struggled with moral decisions: Should they employ slaves as hired help? Should they buy sugar and coffee that had been raised by slave labor? Should they keep a member's worldly inheritance if it included money generated by the sale of slaves? Each dilemma was handled on a case-by-case basis with input from New Lebanon. It was to the Ohio communities, however, that Kentuckians usually turned for fellowship and economic support. Believers throughout the west corresponded frequently and leaders visited each other fairly often. War threatened communication and travel, and raised fears for all Shakers, regardless of race.

As war fever swept the country, New Lebanon urged Believers to focus on spiritual matters and to leave secular conflict to the world. Unlike the Quakers, who actively championed abolition, the Shakers were to resist any efforts to participate in the war, either militarily or politically. This had been a challenge for Union Village even before the war started, and it became increasingly difficult after South Carolinians fired on Fort Sumter in 1861. Hardly a week passed that Union Village did not feel the effects of the conflict.

The first intimate brush with the conflict came in 1860 when 25-year-old Englishman Richard Realf arrived, seeking to become a member. Realf was one of the most controversial figures ever to live at Union Village. He started out as a poet, published a collection of verses (*Guesses at the Beautiful*) at age 18, and became romantically involved with Isabella Milbanke Gordon, the widow of Romantic poet Lord Byron. Realf came to the United States in 1854 and soon became a radical abolitionist. While reporting for the *Illinois State Gazette*, Realf met John Brown, the anti-slavery zealot who planned an assault upon slavery. Realf rapidly became an integral part of Brown's plans. When Brown's followers met in Canada in the spring of 1858 to organize a provisional government for a black state that he hoped to establish in the southern Appalachians, Realf was chosen as his secretary of state.

As Brown's plans became more violent, however, Realf decided to get out. He asked Brown's closest associates for $250 to finance a fund-raising trip to England. He claimed that he could easily raise at least $2,000 there to aid Brown's cause. He boasted of his association with Lady Byron and "others of the aristocracy and literati. I have some acquaintance with men of wealth, letters, and position; and I used to possess an influence among the more educated of the working classes," Realf wrote to Brown's co-conspirators. "I believe I have sufficient ability to collect funds without disclosing our plans, or the names of any of its adherents."[8]

Realf received the money but apparently had no intention of soliciting funds for Brown. His real motive, he later claimed, was to visit his parents to seek their blessing to join the Roman Catholic Church. Being staunch Anglicans, they refused. Realf spent almost a year in England. When he returned to the U.S., he did not contact Brown or his followers. He ended up instead in New Orleans, where he contemplated studying Catholicism to become a Jesuit.

Meanwhile, Brown was captured during his bloody, unsuccessful attempt to seize the federal arsenal at Harpers Ferry, Virginia, in order to arm a slave rebellion in late 1859. With most of his associates killed in the attempt or about to stand trial, Brown was hung as a traitor that December. Realf immediately sold his story to the newspapers, providing many details about Brown's associates. He stressed his innocence in any wrongdoing as he tried to avoid treachery charges. Two weeks after Brown's execution, Realf was questioned by a special Senate committee that wanted to know if any "subversive organizations" had conspired with Brown. Realf testified that the scheme had been solely Brown's idea. He also testified that he had never collected funds for Brown and had deserted him before the final plans for the Harpers Ferry raid were laid. Charges against Realf were eventually dropped.[9]

> Unlike the Quakers, who actively championed abolition, the Shakers were to resist any efforts to participate in the war, either militarily or politically.

Four months after the Senate investigation, Realf sought refuge at Union Village. "He was weary of the world, and wanted rest, not for his body...but for his mind," Elder Oliver Hampton wrote. On April 2, 1860, he was accepted into the Gathering Order, where all newcomers went to be introduced to the faith. Charles Hampton, Oliver's father, instructed Realf. By April 29, Realf was using his gifts of poetry and persuasion to speak to the public at the open Sabbath meeting. Realf was a dubious celebrity but Oliver Hampton referred to him as "our dear friend Richard," and wrote of his selfless efforts to establish freedom for blacks in Kansas. Meanwhile, the abolitionist drew new crowds to the village. He "still gives entire satisfaction both to the world and to Believers thus far," Hampton noted after Realf spoke publicly again that spring. "He seems to have an excellent gift to unfold truths."[10]

An anonymous correspondent to *The Western* Star was also impressed with Realf's rhetoric. Seeing Realf for the first time at a late April service, the writer described him as handsome, anxious, and prematurely aged. Realf began his talk a bit hesitantly, gained steam to dissect the shortcomings of the Anglican and Roman Catholic churches, then "gave us particular thunder." He proceeded to lecture on:

> *The curse of intemperance, the Devil's tea-kettle, the vices of fashionable life, caught such fiery and forked thunderbolts, as to make them feel weak in their knees. He manifested the deepest feeling, and spoke with the greatest pathos upon the evanescent vanities of the world. Speaking of men's aspirations for honor, place, power, fame and wealth, led me to reflect, so much truth did he infuse into this part of his subject, how he could so well portray such efforts, if by himself unattempted?*[11]

Slavery was not mentioned explicitly in the account, but the writer judged the talk a success, and urged the public to attend the next Sunday service. By early September, however, Realf's talent for preaching faltered. He spoke well on ethical matters but could not teach the Shaker principle of Christ's second appearing. Oliver Hampton's disappointment in the young Englishman was cloaked in half-hearted praise:

> *Not quite man enough for the fire of this great day. A fine moral lecturer, and a pretty good kind of man, but the world had too many charms for him.... Ambition dealt hard with him, and the thought of being a great man in the world was sore on him.... Poor boy, he has many good properties, but unfortunately for him, being a genius, he lack'd common sense.*[12]

Hampton wrote of Realf's departure in a tone approaching contempt. Pride was the young man's great weakness, and his desire to live a worldly life had led him astray. Hampton saw little change for Realf's redemption: "And when he finds himself again he will, like an infernal frog, come creeping out of the Corners of Hell, with the filth and dust of the regions below hanging to him—I love him—but he must bear the reward of his doings."[13]

The journal entry reflects a self-righteousness that would dissuade anyone from attempting to return to the Shakers. They had never been tolerant of those who strayed, but in the past they had been more willing to give backsliders another chance. Their growing unwillingness to do so can be traced to the many times they were disappointed by apostates, and as such is understandable. But this attitude made it difficult for anyone who left to return, and most probably intimidated people who might have considered joining the sect.

In the late 1800s, an aging Hampton wrote more tolerantly of Realf. The poet had been "not quite ready to shoulder the whole cross, by which we are crucified to the world." Like many others who sampled the Believers' demanding code, Realf found the total commitment of body and soul too daunting. He joined the Union Army and served honorably as a major during the war. Pride and ambition got the better of him, however, and he "became entangled in the meshes of a certain woman's wiles," Hampton later wrote. The romance went badly and Realf, in despair, committed suicide.[14]

Realf was not the only person to leave during the 1860s. Union Village's population had been gradually declining for years, and the Civil War contributed to that trend. The strain of constantly seeking moral perfection, the charms of living a more independent life, and the pressure to enlist to save the nation caused more young people to leave. As war became a reality, spiritual apathy enervated the community. Hampton later identified 1862 as a low point. At least seven or eight people left the faith that year. Those who remained grappled with indifference:

> *An almost unperceivable spirit of apathy and decaying of spiritual zeal among too many seemed to stealthily creep in and affect our spiritual travel. We cannot doubt but an inward desire for military glory was seething in the minds of some of the young, and this of itself would necessarily detract from a spiritual life and zeal in the Gospel.... Still the Ministry and Elders tried hard to maintain good order and keep up a living zeal in our worship; and often to bear a strong testimony in favor of the most Holy cause in which we had enlisted.[15]*

While war threatened to split the country, the village struggled to remain unified and to maintain various properties it had acquired. In 1856, Elder Aaron Babbitt approved the purchase of two farms totaling 1,572 acres in

Jefferson Township in Clinton County, just north of Warren County. Trustees decided to farm a portion of it and use the rest to pasture cattle and sheep. Initially, some members hoped to move there but never did. Unable to manage the property properly, they began to sell it. By 1859, their holdings had shrunk to 950 acres. A bad storm in the spring of 1860 blew down a log house, uprooted trees, and killed several cows. The following spring, wild dogs and starvation decimated the sheep, and the cattle did poorly on inadequately drained land. Trustees decided to rent part of it to other farmers at $3 an acre in the winter of 1862. Meanwhile, they acquired about 480 acres in northern Indiana, from a Mr. McWilliam of Xenia, Ohio, in trade for 12 head of "fancy" cattle. They soon discovered that the property was wet and unproductive, and apparently they did not keep it for long. The Believers persevered in Clinton County for several more years, taking cattle there for summer pasture, raising oats and broomcorn, and gathering herbs for the medicine shop. They finally sold the property in 1869.[16]

In addition to unsatisfactory land deals, a devastating fire hit the community on the night of March 4, 1861. Flames gutted the North House and destroyed several shops, including the tinsmith's, shoemakers', and carpenters'. Even more serious were losses of the sarsaparilla laboratory, which produced the best-selling sarsaparilla syrup and extracts, and the broom shop, which had generated a consistent income for the village for decades. Two hundred dozen finished brooms awaiting sale were destroyed. Total losses were estimated at $10,000. For a community already $12,000 in debt from land purchases and rebuilding from previous fires and storms, the loss seemed insurmountable.[17]

The central ministry's edict against incurring debt echoed harshly in members' minds as they began to rebuild with the help of outside masons and carpenters. Believers were no longer numerous enough or diverse enough to do all the work themselves, as they had 40 years earlier. Since they raised their own broomcorn, they had to wait for that season's crop to be harvested and processed before manufacturing could resume. Industries dependent on the seasonal growing and processing of plants could not be rushed. Botanist Charles Clapp periodically foraged in the wild for herbs that the villagers did not have in stock. Unfortunately, many customers did not wait for them to re-establish the broom and sarsaparilla businesses.

Although the fire did not damage the seed industry and livestock production, the war changed both. As early as January 1861, the businesses faced declines. Distribution and collection costs were cited as the major problems with the seed industry. Union Village had two major bulk seed routes at the beginning of the war: Illinois and Mississippi. The Mississippi route was discontinued in August 1862, due to expenses and the war. For the year, 1863, a sizable amount—$3,834—was collected from the seed business, but $1,071 of that gross went for expenses. The decline in the cattle industry may have been linked to Cincinnati's economic status. Long a leader in the meat packing industry, Cincinnati began to be eclipsed by Chicago in the 1850s.[18]

War reversed cattle sales. Union Village once again profited from its proximity to Cincinnati. By 1863, federal contracts for beef, pork, and lard, as well as clothing and shoes, were pouring into the large Cincinnati processors and manufacturers. To fill the contracts, they had to turn to local suppliers, including the Shakers, who also continued to sell blooded cattle on their own. In the fall of 1863, they sold 20 head of Durham cattle to New Yorkers for $1,050. When the central ministry issued an edict against pork, similar to the prohibition during the Era of Manifestations, the Shakers turned away from pork consumption and production. They increased sheep production in hopes of cashing in on an increased demand for wool. With wool selling for an undreamed of 90 cents a pound in

> In addition to unsatisfactory land deals, a devastating fire hit the community on the night of March 4, 1861. Flames gutted the North House and destroyed several shops, including the tinsmith's, shoemakers', and carpenters'.

New York, they resolved to gradually build their flock up to 1,000 sheep and to produce yarn for stockings. Knitting machines were introduced in 1861, allowing the sisters to produce more woolen goods. In the summer of 1864, work began at a new woolen factory in the village.[19]

Commerce received attention during the war years, but concerns over military and humanitarian service were paramount for most Union Village Believers. As the decade began, the probability of war was discussed almost daily. Members were concerned about their friends in Kentucky and public reaction to Shaker pacifism. They remembered their struggles during the War of 1812, and how many people resented them for refusing to serve in any military capacity. They were committed to staying out of the war but extremely sensitive to being identified as nonsupportive. When they were singled out in a newspaper article as not having contributed to a charity drive for soldiers' families, they sent an outraged letter to the local newspaper:

*Why were the Shakers thus singled out and all others left unnoticed? The time
has been when the public, less enlightened, and less tolerant than now, might
have been aroused to deeds of violence by such a missive...whilst [Shakers] do
not appear to give as much material aid as others...because the prosecution
of the war is contrary to every principle and tenet of their religious belief; yet
they humanely do as much otherwise to benefit society as any other portion of
the community.... And if it requires all the blankets in their possession to cover
the naked and destitute orphan children they have received from the world
and are raising, together with widows and others, is it just that they should be
singled out...as refusing to aid suffering humanity?[20]*

The writer notes that in most cases the Believers did not accept members'
military pensions yet still cared for its veterans, preventing them from
becoming wards of the county. This indicates that a change in policy had
occurred since the 1820s when Union Village was chastised by New Lebanon
for accepting military pensions. Apparently, the majority of veterans at Union
Village did not receive their pensions. The writer recalled Richard McNemar's
arguments from 50 years earlier that the right to be a conscientious objector
was rooted in American law:

*It is to be remembered that our armies are in the field to support a
Government which has...basic liberty of conscience and freedom of opinion,
and it certainly is no time now to bring public prejudice to bear upon
those who, restrained by religious convictions from entering upon war-like
measures, have yet an inalienable right to that liberty of conscience without
which our free institutions could not exist.[21]*

The correspondent also noted that Union Village might have the burden of
assisting their Kentucky brethren, who were already suffering for their loyalty to
the Union. Signed only "A Subscriber," the letter reflects Oliver Hampton's style.

Believers who had long defied convention by treating black members as
equals now defied public opinion by refusing to fight in a war fueled by slavery.
They strongly supported preserving the Union but would not bear arms to
achieve it. They believed political and spiritual changes were necessary to reunite
the country. "This is the commencement of a War between Freedom and Slavery,
which will never end...[without] the universal spread of free principles, the
extinguishment of slavery...and the introductions of hundreds into the Gospel,"
Hampton wrote in the church journal of March 1861.[22] As the war progressed, he
called slavery an "unholy curse" that mocked the country's basic principles:

There can be no rest for either the righteous or the wicked while that withering curse of the nations is suffer'd to hold up its polluted head and act the tyrant over the image of God. Only think what an impudent lie that is, now standing on the face of the Constitution of the United States, that all men are born equal, and have a just right to life, liberty, and the pursuit of happiness, while...souls are condemned to hopeless involuntary servitude under the same constitution.[23]

Hampton was also critical of what he saw as the government's views about blacks. His comments echoed Ann Lee's earliest teachings about not differentiating between people because of their color or sex. Hampton wrote:

It seems very hard for the United States government to look at the Negro as a man, they think and speak of him as a "chattel; and the secesh [secessionists] force him to fight to rend his chains—& do not expect any great victories by the federal forces until they are willing to acknowledge the African to be a man, and prove their sincerity by making him a free man, and defending his rights as a free man in a free country. Then, after they do that, they may expect victory to crown their labors, and the rebellion will soon be ended.[24]

Ironically, Union Village lost one of its most venerable members just two days before the Confederates fired on Fort Sumter. Anna Middleton, the freed slave who had been the second western convert in 1805, died on April 11, 1861. She was remembered in the church record as an "honest-minded, kind-hearted colored woman" who lived in the First Family for decades.[25]

Being committed to peace and equality, Believers prepared for public reaction to their pacifist stance. Pressure came from the world where volunteering for the Union Army was viewed as an honor and duty, and from young Believers caught up in the glory of the war effort. As a result, the Shakers compromised much more than they had during the War of 1812. Relief efforts for soldiers and their families sprang up in every township just months after the war started. Eventually, major cities began to organize Sanitary Fairs to collect money, food, clothing, and medical supplies. Cincinnati's branch of the United States Sanitary Commission opened in the fall of 1861. The city's importance as a commercial port and a gateway between North and South made it a key player in the Civil War. Kentucky declared itself a neutral state, but Confederate troops fought in the Bluegrass State, and threatened to cross the Ohio River and invade Cincinnati. War-readiness was the order of the day.

The Sanitary Commission outfitted hospital boats to travel to areas where medical care was needed, assisted in establishing eight hospitals in the greater Cincinnati area, set up a home for traveling soldiers, provided burial plots for soldiers in the city's historic Spring Grove cemetery, and held large sanitary fairs to solicit public donations.[26]

The eastern ministry recommended that Union Village contribute to the sanitary fairs. Believers gave troops things that the Army did not provide, including fruits and jellies. In the fall of 1862, the sisters provided 150 cans of fruit. Believers also donated to a large fair sponsored by the Cincinnati commission during the Christmas holidays of 1863. That fair netted $235,406. To that effort, Union Village contributed items valued at $158.20, including four and a half bushels of dried sweet corn, five barrels of dried apples, one barrel of green apples, one barrel of sauerkraut, one and one-fourth barrels of catsup, five boxes of garden seeds, 10 gallons of gooseberry sauce, five gallons of apple preserves, and eight dozen brooms. It had been decided, Hampton wrote, that they might donate "something to the relief of the sick and suffering," as long as those donations could not be converted into anything that aided combat.[27]

Believers continued to contribute to other charitable causes. In August of 1863, Union Village donated 25 boxes of garden seeds to freed blacks who were settling in Arkansas. In 1864, the village donated 20 boxes of garden seeds to the National Freedmen's Relief Association. This group was one of several established in the early 1860s to help freed blacks obtain food, shelter, medical treatment, and schooling as they began new lives.[28]

A more atypical concession to the war effort was the elders' decision in October 1863 to pay military fines for seven brothers who did not attend a required military muster. During the community's early years, David Darrow prided himself on never paying military fines, even when the government confiscated livestock in lieu of payment. But now, in the face of war fervor, the elders instructed trustee Peter Boyd to pay the fines. That's where the concessions ended, however. Believers tried to avoid the draft during the war, as did the Quakers and other conscientious objectors in Warren County. This included the village of Waynesville, which had a particularly active Quaker community. Nationally, the Quakers were the most aggressive in seeking military exemption. Their activities frequently benefited other religious conscientious objectors, including the Believers, Mennonites, Nazarenes, and Dunkards.[29] Although the Quakers led the quest for exemption, Shaker leaders also worked in their respective states as well as nationally to defend conscientious objection.

At the war's start, the governor of each Union state was charged with recruiting troops. As the number of recruits lessened and the demand for soldiers increased in the summer of 1862, a federal draft began. Congress passed the Militia Act that July, empowering President Lincoln to call out the militia for nine months. All men ages 18–45 had to report for duty if called.[30] The Believers' stand was adamant and consistent with their church history. The New Lebanon ministry, which was visiting Union Village that August, entreated all members to remain united and focused on spiritual matters. They were not to bear arms, pay fines at that time, or hire a substitute for military duty. "But if it comes to the worst, let every Shaker keep his faith, and not flinch, nor serve as a teamster, or submit to do any military duty...stand up in the integrity of free men and if they persecute us, why then bear it."[31] At the end of August, several brothers went to Lebanon to seek exemption based upon "conscientious scruples." They were not released from service.

By September 1, Cincinnati was under martial law, bracing for an imminent invasion of Confederate forces. "The whole male population from 16 to 60 years mustered into service to protect the city," Hampton wrote. "Rebels are in force in Kentucky within a few miles of the (Ohio) river, have possession of Lexington and....running legions south, stealing horses, clothing, money... burning houses, rails...shooting some men down on their premises for the crime of being Union men."[32]

Fears were strong for the Kentucky brethren. In the late winter of 1862, Shaker Reuben Wise painted a dire picture of conditions at South Union. Confederates threatened alternately to burn down the village or take it for a military hospital. Southern troops "cursed" the Believers as abolitionists. Both Confederate and Union troops placed demands on South Union's resources that spring but members were happy to share what they had with the Northerners, whom they viewed as protectors.[33] By spring, conditions in Kentucky had worsened; travel and mail were all but stopped. For a time, the fate of those in South Union and Pleasant Hill was unknown. Union Village also worried about its own future. The community had been burglarized at various times over the years due to rumors of Shaker wealth. Believers feared an attack by Confederates or by the Union faithful who might consider them unpatriotic or worse. Cincinnati called out its home guard and all able-bodied men but the Confederates did not cross the river into Ohio that year. Still, the incident proved unequivocally to the Shakers that their resolve to turn the other cheek might soon meet the ultimate test.

Ohio Governor David Tod attempted to ease the situation for religious conscientious objectors by exempting them from bearing arms upon payment of $200 per man. He wrote to Secretary of War Edwin Stanton on October 5, 1862, seeking acceptance for his plan. He purposed using the money to hire substitute soldiers and to care for the wounded and sick. The federal government eventually implemented the plan for all Union states. But for the Believers, the issue was still unresolved. New Lebanon Elders Frederick W. Evans and Benjamin Gates met with Stanton and Lincoln in Washington that fall, seeking exemptions. With them was Brother Ezra T. Leggitt of Union Village, who had been chosen to represent the western communities. They were counseled in how Believers might go about proving themselves as conscientious objectors if they were drafted. Eventually, any brothers who were drafted were put on indefinite furlough because they would not fight.[34]

M ail from Kentucky began to arrive again in October. Pleasant Hill Believers wrote on October 30 that they could hear the cannons firing just 15 miles from the village. The Confederates took six wagons and four horses from them, as well as 200 shocks of corn and several barrels of old corn to feed their horses. From September 3–11, the Pleasant Hill Shakers fed from 300 to 1,000 soldiers on any given day, placing a considerable strain on their food supplies. Another letter received November 4, and noted only as from Kentucky, described the Confederate soldiers as "starving and almost naked, barefoot and ragged, absolutely begging for a piece of bread, or any bit of cloth to hide their nakedness. Sometimes they threatened to shoot one another if they refused to divide the morsel they could obtain." Such first-hand reports were eagerly read by the Ohioans, who frequently expressed skepticism about the truth of some war reports circulated by both the North and South. "Both sides strive to make as good as story as they can and it is impossible to come to the truth of the current reports," Hampton wrote in the church journal. By the end of the year, brethren from Pleasant Hill and South Union were able to visit Union Village once again. One South Union visitor was temporarily stranded in the village after Confederate General John Hunt Morgan destroyed tracks of the Louisville and Nashville railroad.[35]

The new year brought a terse assessment of the war's effects in the church record. William McGladeny, who took over Hampton's journal writing for most of 1863, described the impact: "These times in consequence of the war there is much derangement of commercial business—no trade is permitted with those in insurrection. Currency is depreciated 40 percent. Believers need to be watchful and are often exhorted to guard against a partisan spirit."[36] They were in a delicate position. They supported national unity and opposed slavery on moral grounds, yet they were unable to take political sides in the war. They were to keep their minds and hearts on spiritual matters, and allow New Lebanon to handle any political entanglements. In May, the eastern ministry once again sent instructions on how brothers should react if drafted. In June, the ministry requested the names of all men who might be drafted. Eastern elders again visited Washington to seek exemptions. When President Lincoln called for national days of prayer and fasting, Union Village followed New Lebanon's lead in deciding whether to participate. Believers often did participate by praying for the country's healing.

> Sometimes they threatened to shoot one another if they refused to divide the morsel they could obtain.

Like other Americans, the Believers tried to maintain normality as much as possible. They continued rebuilding from the 1861 fire, planned a new nurse's house (infirmary), and hired a local dentist to train Elder William Reynolds to serve as the village dentist. They made grape, strawberry, and currant wine for medicinal purposes, both for themselves and for the public. They dined on farm-raised mutton and veal from new Queens ware china that the sisters purchased in Cincinnati. Tea, coffee, and sugar were absent from their tables due to wartime shortages. Like many of their neighbors, they began raising sorghum to replace sugar. They attended conferences on sorghum and wool productivity held in Lebanon. Shaker teachers went to Lebanon to join their worldly peers in taking a teaching examination. As they had since 1805, Union Village Believers tried to be in the world, but not of the world, a status that was becoming more difficult for some of the young people to maintain.

Perhaps because of the pressure on the young, more journal references were made of special activities and treats for the children. Outings were simple: a ride into the "big" city of Hamilton, a picnic in the woods, a walk to the millpond. "Elder William Reynolds accompanied the little girls to the pond, put up a swing, and there being a skiff on the pond took a sail which the little folk enjoyed right heartily," McGladeny wrote on June 12, 1863. Holiday treats during the Christmas of 1864 included some hard candies, a box of raisins, six coconuts, and several pounds of sugar—all luxuries during the war.

Spirituality continued to be a casualty of the conflict. "Young people encouraged to march and motion with their hands with some life and spirit. Some marched well, but by far the greater number were stiff—very stiff,"

McGladeny wrote in the spring of 1863. The freedom to dance and worship with joy and enthusiasm was dampened by the war. Proselytizing suffered as well. "There seems to be very little feeling in the world to hear the Word hence little gift among Believers to open the Testament to them," he noted that summer.[37]

That July, southwestern Ohio focused on General Morgan's Confederate cavalry unit, which was approaching Cincinnati on its unparalleled raid into the North. On July 12, Gov. Tod summoned all militia in 32 counties to immediately prepare to resist Morgan's invasion. His Raiders were said to be advancing north of Cincinnati through Butler County on their way to encamp at Union Village. The Shakers' commitment to pacifism was about to undergo its most severe test. Telegrams flew between Union officers rushing to assemble the militia and prepare for combat. The daily newspapers printed the latest bulletins as fast as the printers could set type. At Union Village, McGladeny recorded the drama:

> *Monday, July 13—Morgan is now in Ohio, said to be in Hamilton this evening and intending to come through our Village. 300 men were mustered at Lebanon and going to Camp Dennison. Our people were called upon to furnish conveyances to carry some of them to the railroad station. We concluded to do nothing...as we would thus be giving our sanction to the war in a measure, and this would be contrary to our principles, so we choose to do so and abide the consequences.*

> *Wednesday, July 15—The papers say Morgan is leaving the state as fast as he can.... Union men are after him within 5 miles of his rear.*

> *We had called a special meeting this evening to call out an expression of faith in respect to war and bloodshed, and learning the art of war. There was a strong testimony borne by Brethren and Sisters in favor of peace. That was the principle which our Lord Jesus Christ taught, and the principle which all true Christians lived and taught, and we can live and teach nothing else; let the consequences be what they may.*

They understood that the consequences this time might be more than muster fines. Confederates had threatened to burn down South Union in 1862. Because the Believers refused to aid the Union troops in any way, the faithful had no assurance that those troops would protect them if Morgan raided Union Village. They were equally concerned about being forced to serve in the militia. Tension gripped the village, and McGladeny could not sleep. At midnight, he picked up his pen:

*Thursday, July 16—It is now 12 o'clock a.m. Our Brethren all declined going
to muster according to notice and will now have to abide the issue. Momentous
times, these, living in dread lest every person who stops at our place is the
messenger of some armed posse to drag our Brethren away to muster.*

The militia and the Believers were unaware that Morgan's men had already
left the area. Realizing that Cincinnati was armed and ready to protect its
people and railroads, Morgan had purposely sent detachments in various
directions to the north of the city, creating the impression that he was marching
to Hamilton in Butler County. "He (Morgan) deceived everybody," wrote
historian Whitelaw Reid three years after the war:

*The Hamilton people telegraphed a great alarm that Morgan was marching
on their town. A fire was seen burning at Venice [Ross, Butler County], and
straightway they threw out pickets to guard the main roads...and watch for
Morgan's coming. [Union militia] sent in word of the passage of the Rebel
cavalry through that place at one o'clock, and of the belief that they were
going to Hamilton. Wise deputy sheriffs, who had been captured by Morgan
and paroled, hastened to tell that the Rebel chief had conversed with them
very freely; had shown no hesitation in speaking of his plan and had assured
them he was going to Hamilton. All this was retailed at the headquarters, on
the streets, in the newspaper offices.*

*That night, while the much enduring printers were putting such stories to
type, John Morgan's entire command, now reduced to a strength of bare two
thousand, was marching through the [Cincinnati] suburbs, within reach of
troops enough to eat them up, absolutely unopposed, almost without meeting
a solitary picket, or receiving a hostile shot.[38]*

As the Union militia discovered the deception, McGladeny explained in the
church record how Union Village had become entangled in the Morgan hysteria:

*Friday, July 17—Our people were alarmed by the report of 2 men hailing
from Mason. They said Gen. Morgan was there and heading for our village.
The work of hiding horses and sheep was vigorously prosecuted until every
hoof was snugly concealed in some glen or paw paw thicket.... The (false)
alarm was started thus: a person passing through Mason heard one of the
citizens say, 'Morgan is coming,' but the Morgan he meant was a David
Morgan who it seems was a captain of Militia who had been to Camp*

*Dennison and was coming back to Mason. From this the alarm was brought
to our village, so we were agreeably disappointed in not having a visit from
the Rebel Chief.*

The immediate danger had passed. The company into which the Shakers
were to have been mustered was discharged because of a lack of weapons. "At
the present, we are released from the war fever which has been so afflicting
to us for the last few days," McGladeny wrote on July 18. Although the entire
incident had been based on a military deception and a miscommunication,
the Believers had reacted to a perceived threat by upholding their religious
principles under tremendous pressure.

The brush with Morgan's Raiders had ripple effects throughout the
community. Union Village Trustee Ithamar Johnson was called to the
Whitewater settlement to help those Believers receive compensation for two
horses taken by Union militia in pursuit of Morgan. McGladeny and Brother
James Smith, who were from England, applied to the British consul in Chicago
for proof of their alien status so they might be exempted from any further
drafts. In August, Frederick Evans and Benjamin Gates again petitioned the
war department to exempt all Believers. That December, several Union Village
men went to the Draft Enrollment Board in Lebanon to seek exemptions for
either physical disability or noncitizenship.

While most Shakers sought to be exempted, some brothers left the faith
to join the army. Later, some tried to return. "Adolphus Katcholdt is here
sueing for another privilege," McGladeny wrote in the summer of 1863. "The
poor fellow has been in the army and seen hard times, and he feels now like
obeying his faith—if he had a privilege." Men and women continued to leave
Union Village during the war years. The church record reflects an increasing
unwillingness to readmit them. A young member of the Second Family,
Lewis Seibenthall, left in October 1863. He returned in two months, seeking
another privilege. "Small change," was McGladeny's terse comment in the
church journal. Seibenthall was next heard of the following summer when
he volunteered to substitute for a draftee from Franklin. For substituting,
he would receive $600, which was to go to his sister. Substitutes were
commonly disdained as mercenaries, and whatever Seibenthall's motives were
in substituting, the Shakers believed he had hit rock bottom. He was not
readmitted to the village.[39]

New Lebanon continued to encourage all Shakers to stay true to their
spiritual mission. Union Village members were urged not to dwell on war and
politics, to limit their reading of war reports, and to minimize communication

with the world. To implement these recommendations, the elders ordered fewer copies of newspapers and lessened contact with the public. The previous summer, they had prohibited the world from holding picnics at the millpond, because the merrymaking annoyed the Believers.[40]

Despite efforts to keep their thoughts off the war, frequent letters from Kentucky kept the conflict fresh in their minds. The South Union ministry wrote in the summer of 1864 that their people were oppressed by the war and shot at for trying to protect their property from marauding troops. In September, Joseph West of Union Village's Second Family was drafted and pleaded a physical disability to be excused. Another young man, a 19-year-old, left the faith voluntarily the same month, supposedly to join the army. In December, Union Village sent material aid to South Union in the form of 24 dozen brooms that the Kentuckians sold to raise revenue, since their own businesses had been disrupted by the war. As battles continued around South Union, its elders reported to Union Village in February 1865 that some neighbors had been killed and that guerrilla fighters plundered and burned property around them.[41]

On April 9, 1865, Hampton's notation of General Robert E. Lee's surrender to General Ulysses S. Grant was brief and without editorial comment. His comments on President Lincoln's assassination later that month were also brief, and included an admonition against the ways of the world:

> *Yesterday, the nation was rejoicing over the recently achieved victories, and today are the children of this world seen in deep mourning over...the death of their beloved President. Here we behold one of those sudden transitions from excessive joy to extreme sorrow and poignant grief that those who live after the course of this world are ever subject to.*[42]

Union Village did join in a national day of prayer and thanksgiving for the end of the war on June 1. The entire village met for a special two-hour service that day.

Believers had much to be thankful for during the summer of 1865. With former slaves and soldiers free to start new lives, hopes for the community's economy and membership improved. Rebuilding from the 1861 fire was completed and new shops were ready to produce merchandise for sale to the world. And, the community was nearly out of debt.[43] The future hinged on membership.

In addition to Anna Middleton, several other original Union Village members died during the Civil War years. Abner Bedell, who had contributed so much to the village's economy, died in April 1860. His funeral was unusual because a number of the world's people were permitted to attend the simple ceremony. That September, Nancy McNemar, an eldress and one of Richard McNemar's daughters, died. Hampton eulogized her as a compassionate and intelligent woman who served honorably in every position she held in the village. Hampton's own father, Charles, died in August 1863. Charles Hampton typified many early converts who brought their entire families into the faith and remained faithful for decades. Union Village's early records are full of family names: Worley, McNemar, Houston, Valentine, Sharp. By the 1860s, however, such whole-family conversions were rare. Lewis Valentine's death on June 15, 1865, illustrated a double concern: "We have lost our bookbinder, clock repairer, poultry man, spectacle mender," Hampton wrote. "He was the last of the Valentine family; one of the first youths who set out in the Gospel."[44] The deaths affected morale and industry within the village. When James Smith, the Englishman who started the woolen factory, left the village in June 1865, the mill shut down. Smith was also one of Union Village's broom-makers. Hampton noted that the other primary broom-maker—an elderly brother— had recently died. Smith returned to the village within two weeks, and the broom-making and wool manufacturing continued, but an important point was recognized: running a variety of businesses with only one or two people competent to supervise them was not economically sound.

As the country began a long period of mending and coping with post-war economic problems, Union Village struggled to halt the ebb in membership. The Believers would become more aggressive in courting converts and would attempt to expand their economy in new ways.

Top: Anna and Max Goepper Jr. of Morrow, Ohio, became associated with the Shakers when their uncle, Leopold Goepper, joined the community. After the Civil War, it was rare for families with young children to join the Shakers. Anna remained a Shaker and produced many spiritual writings. Max died in a drowning accident when he was 27.
Top: Detail of Marble Hall.

⑤ Chapter Twelve ⑤
An Eternal Sabbath, A Restless Peace

After the Civil War, Union Village began to face many challenges and a very uncertain future. Involvement in the "momentous times" left many Believers unsatisfied with their routine lives. Books checked out of the Union Village Library reflect a lingering fascination with the war and an increasing curiosity with the

world. Along with the expected inspirational volumes, members read *Six Years in a Georgian Prison*, *The Poor White or Rebel Conscript*, *Poor Whites of the South*, *Journal of a Residence in a Georgian Plantation*, and *The Great West*. Their interests turned outward and many members left the community. In 1870, the population was 232, down from 364 in 1860. The remaining members were white, and predominately older. There was talk of not taking in any more children because so few sisters were young enough to care for them.[1]

Elder Aaron Babbitt suggested an even more radical idea: incorporate the village under Ohio law and allow members to choose their own leaders. The central ministry quickly quashed his proposal and reiterated authority in a stern letter:

Can it be possible that [leaders] have lost sight of the only true Order of the Church of Christ, and now wish to...introduce a worldly form of Government? Should we become a body politic, appointing our officers by ballot or vote, we then should be left to drift with the worldly tide and the Powers of Earth and Hell would most surely prevail against us.[2]

A visit from the central ministry followed in the summer of 1868. Babbitt, who had been criticized for the costly Clinton County land deals, was replaced as first in the ministry by Amos Parkhurst. William Reynolds replaced Cephas Holloway as second.

The new leaders faced financial problems. One of Parkhurst's first major decisions was to discontinue the woolen mill in 1869. Despite post-war optimism, the Shakers were unable to compete with other mills in the manufacturing of stocking yarn. Fortunately, the cattle market held steady, and several head of Durham stock were sold that spring for $11,535. Then yet another financial setback occurred in the summer of 1870, when arson destroyed a grain and stock barn and its contents, valued at $25,000.[3]

Spiritually, Believers were active. Their weekly singing meetings, always a favorite with members, lead to a singing school and use of instrumental music in 1870. That spring, the Waynesville *Miami Gazette* announced that Sunday meetings would be open for the season. Determined to attract converts, the Believers also began going into the world to preach for the first time in decades. Oliver Hampton agreed to speak at a public venue in Waynesville. "The plan would be for ten or a dozen of the Shaker friends to come and sing, preach, and show our citizens the ceremonies and instruct them in the doctrines of Shakerism," the newspaper reported.[4] A small admission fee was charged to cover the brethren's expenses in traveling to Waynesville, about 10 miles away, and in securing overnight accommodations.

On Saturday, June 4, Hampton held two meetings at the town hall. Two hundred people attended an afternoon service, and 300 an evening service. Seven sisters and three brothers accompanied Hampton. If the audiences expected to see dancing or spirit visits, they were disappointed. Simple, dignified hymns surrounded Hampton's message on the sect's beliefs. He extolled the advantages of Shaker life and stressed the necessity of celibacy. His tone was firm, but amiable. The talk ended with an invitation to join the United Society: "If any of you ever feel like giving up the world with its strifes and unsatisfying pleasures, and ascending to a higher plane, come to us, and we will ensure you a welcome, no matter how low or debased you have become, and try to do you good."[5]

The next morning, the sisters and brothers attended an Episcopal Sunday School and then a Methodist worship service in Waynesville. No conversions—on any side—were noted, but the Believers gained some goodwill, according to the *Gazette* account:

> *Mr. Hampton is a very pleasant, forcible speaker, and his remarks could not do otherwise than disabuse the minds of persons who, ignorant of the Shaker principles, felt prejudiced against what they did not understand.... The speaker's courteous and charitable references to denominations who entertained different views...evinced a broad catholic and Christian spirit which all might strive to imitate with advantage.*[6]

The Believers also ventured into the world the following year when a group attended a Spiritualistic Convention in Cleveland. An interest in spiritualism swept the United States in the post-war era, but the Believers soon decided that the world was more interested in parlor entertainment than in divine revelation. Although spirit manifestations were not as frequent or intense as they had been in the 1840s, they still occurred and were regarded as sacred gifts. The messages were taken very seriously. Women still received many of the visions, but rather than receiving them in meetings or even at the dinner table, the visions came at night as dreams. They frequently were aimed at helping the dreamer deal with a common problem, such as casting off worldly influences or becoming more forgiving. Imagery in the dreams became increasingly positive and beautiful as the century advanced.

In Malinda Buchanan's 1864 vision, she heard her own reborn spirit whispering: "Life for Life." The imagery was dazzling: "I compared it in my mind to the finest polished steel and its brilliancy reminded me of the gilding on the points of the lightning rod on our house when reflecting the rays of the sun."[7] Taken to the meetinghouse in her dream, Buchanan saw star-shaped lights in the hearts of the faithful brethren.

Thirty years later, dreams and visions mingled in Anna Goepper's New Year's Eve experience. Her dream was of beautiful spring flowers and a personal message from a dear friend. Amid the tulips, lilies, and pansies, Goepper saw the faces of departed sisters. She recognized Emily Hampton, Oliver's sister. Emily's presence and message were gentle and uplifting:

*I was so overjoyed at seeing her that I burst into a flood of tears. She
smiled, and laid her hand in blessing upon my shoulder, while in her other
hand was a large crown of pure, white lilies. I could hear her say very
distinctly—'For if ye forgive men their trespasses your heavenly Father will
also forgive you. But if ye forgive not men their trespasses neither will your
Father forgive your trespasses.'*[8]

As Goepper vainly tried to awaken her roommate to share the vision,
Emily disappeared with a smile and a "Happy New Year" for the family, and a
special remembrance for her brother. The mild tone suggests that Goepper was
comfortable with her faith and with such occurrences.

Aside from the seriousness of work and worship, there was also time for
fun in the post-war era. Young villagers and children enjoyed the county fairs,
harvest and hayrides, and wagon rides when they chaperoned a brother driving
a solitary sister to the train depot, recalled George S. Driskel. He was nine years
old in 1871 when his widowed mother moved her family into Union Village, and
his memories of the community were happy ones. Meals, he said, were perfect
for boy-sized appetites. Pies and cakes were cut into quarters for the youngsters.
Table manners were enforced by driving tacks into the dining table to show each
diner his station. Discipline on the job was sometimes harder to enforce. Out in
the fields to help the brothers and hired hands, the boys spent more time fighting
off the bumblebees and pulling pranks on their adult supervisors:

*We had more devilment in us than work.... There was one man, an
Irishman, who used to say, 'Bees won't hurt good little boys.' So one noon we
managed, while he was taking his after-dinner nap under a shade tree, to
stir up and lead over him a nest of particularly fierce eye-bungers.*[9]

The Union Village Scientific and Progressive Association, founded in the
fall of 1871, aimed to offer more uplifting diversions. Across the United States,
a peacetime re-emphasis on science and the arts resulted in the creation of
many small lyceums, the forerunners of chautauquas. Union Village lyceum
members vowed to investigate and discuss scientific subjects and "all matters
pertaining to the progress of our common humanity in all its departments"
at monthly meetings. Members hoped to benefit physically, mentally, morally,
socially, intellectually, and spiritually from the assemblies. In addition to
discussions, they studied grammar, composition, and oratory. They presented
poetry recitations, and performed "comic and absurd pieces." Discussion topics
ranged from members' favorite books to the nature of war to a discussion of

whether the Chicago Fire of 1871 was a divine judgment upon that city.[10]

Philosophical discussions gave way to action in 1874 as an economic depression gripped the country. Many jobless, homeless people came to Union Village seeking food. Church records note that 4,300 meals were served to the poor that year. Believers continued to serve the needy whenever possible, and their help was always practical. They often practiced charity quietly but they, along with other groups, did receive recognition for assisting victims of the 1884 Ohio River flood. Many residents of Cincinnati and outlying areas lost everything in the February deluge. Believers joined other civic and religious groups, and individuals, in helping victims survive and recover. They gave one of their most important resources: food. Members donated 19 barrels of potatoes, 14 of corn, 2 barrels of turnips, 1 barrel each of apples and beets, and 1 bag of beans.[11]

Despite renewed preaching in the world and acts of charity, the Believers were still considered an oddity by many people. That was the attitude of a reporter who covered another public meeting in December 1874. This meeting was held about 12 miles to the southwest, in Hamilton at Dixon's Opera House. Believers from Watervliet, Ohio, also participated in the meeting. While attempting to reach out to a larger audience, they refused to compromise their beliefs to gain converts. The journalist who reported on this meeting was more critical than the *Miami Gazette* writer of 1870.

The majority of the sisters were described as pale and ghostly, "somber as the grave." They wore drab purple gowns and white shawls. The men wore drab clothes and heavy boots. They appeared before a full house. Six hundred seats were sold for 50 cents each and several hundred general admission seats for 25 cents each. The main speaker was identified as a Father Evans of Union Village. It could be that he was Frederick Evans, the influential elder from New Lebanon (now called Mount Lebanon), who traveled extensively in the United States and England in the early 1870s, seeking converts.

The article depicted the sect as radical: anti-war, anti-marriage, anti-personal property. They also opposed ministers receiving salaries and the use of traditional doctors, according to the article. Some ambiguity was expressed about the volatile topic of women's rights. One sister, who had the "most pleasing appearance...favored independence of women and spoke of their rights." Another sister said that women should "have no more to do with politics than angels. Her place is by the side of man." In discussing his opinion that married people should not hold public office, Evans said that public service "should be reserved only for 'celibates of either sex'.... The audience became uneasy after 2 ½ hours of these radical ideas, and many began to leave...."[12] No converts were noted.

A more positive picture of Union Village was presented in 1875 with the publication of journalist Charles Nordhoff's book, *The Communistic Societies of the United States*. Nordhoff visited Union Village in 1874 while studying communal or communistic groups in the United States. In addition to several Shaker communities, Nordhoff visited the Oneida Perfectionists, the Zoar Separatists, the Harmonists, the Amana Society, and others. He found the Believers the most successful of all the communal groups. His comments on Union Village were based on his own observations and conversations with Believers. The community was one of the most prosperous in the United Society, he wrote, adding that the region was known for its rich soil and agricultural productivity.

The early Believers would have been proud of Nordhoff's general assessment of their handiwork:

> *The founders of Union Village were evidently men who did their work thoroughly; the dwellings and houses...have a satisfactory solidity and are not without the homely charm which good work and plain outlines give to any building. Two of these old houses...are uncommonly good specimens of early Western architecture. The whole village is a pattern of neatness, with flagged walks and pleasant grassy courtyards and shade trees.*[13]

Nordhoff did notice the need for some repairs around the village, which he attributed to the lack of a deacon's supervision. He also noted that the community had fewer industries than it had in previous decades, but this, he was told, was because the community was so successful in their other businesses, not because they lacked enough workers. Steel, leather, hollowware (silver utensils and dishes), pipes, and woolen yarn were no longer commercially manufactured. Their major industries were still broom-making, garden seeds, medicinal herbs, medicinal extracts, and sarsaparilla.[14] Nordhoff was particularly impressed with the intelligence and intellectual curiosity he found at the village. Oliver Hampton was described as kind and intelligent, and the school where he taught as excellent. One of the older, unidentified brothers was "an uncommonly intelligent Shaker."[15] The monthly lyceum gatherings had spawned a joint weekly meeting where all members could discuss business matters and practical affairs. By involving the young people more in the community business, the elders hoped to encourage them to remain in the sect. Nordhoff was told that Believers would never change the doctrines of celibacy and confession of sin, but they could be flexible on lesser matters to retain members. If the young people wanted more books and music, they would have them. In fact, one sister told Nordhoff that she was permitted to read novels from a circulating library in Lebanon, an unheard of liberty only a few years earlier.

Weekly business meetings aroused thought, Nordhoff wrote, adding that any member could raise a topic for discussion. A concern raised by some sisters was symptomatic of the restlessness that had led many people to leave: they were bored and wished for greater variety in their daily lives. A number of sisters still made baskets and fancy work, but their main tasks

Journalist Charles Nordhoff's 1874 description of village life as a serene, eternal Sabbath is reflected in this early twentieth century postcard.

were cooking, cleaning, and laundry. They longed to contribute something more. Nordhoff also noted yearnings for more individuality: one sister wanted to do away with wearing caps and allow more natural hairstyles. But she might be considered a radical, he noted.[16] (The sister's radical proposal was approved, but not until 1895.) As frivolous as the cap issue might seem, it points to a growing interest in personal choice and a breaking away from the desire for a uniform appearance expressed by David Darrow in 1817. He believed that dressing alike in plain styles forged a bond among members and lessened sinful pride. Slowly, that thinking changed. In 1875, the brothers became embroiled in a debate over beards. Some men wanted to retain their traditional look, which called for shaving at least once a week. Other men, considered the progressives, wanted to maintain beards, which they believed would protect them from throat and eye ailments. After months of disagreements, beards were permitted, but not required.[17]

Clothing also changed slightly after the war, reflecting an even more utilitarian appearance. Men's smocks in neutral tones of drab and gray evolved into white, banded-collar shirts that could be easily bleached and boiled in the laundry. Shirts were sewn with tails long enough to tuck into trousers and worn with very plain indigo vests. Straw hats, made in the village, became the practical choice for summer wear. The women's daily costume continued to be a plain dress with a shoulder kerchief and cape, checked apron and cap.[18]

B elievers continued to be conscious of appearances, both physical and societal. As the United States celebrated its centennial in 1876, Hampton took pains in a newspaper column to express their beliefs about patriotism and temporal governments:

> We don't trouble ourselves about the Fourth of July, Presidential nominations, Centennial celebrations 'and sich,' but we do feel conscientious to keep the laws, live in peace, be industrious and religious; and this, we think, is the best possible practical plan of supporting the best government with which any people were ever blessed. On the 4th of July, there were no fights, brawls, nor drunken persons in Union Village. Can other hamlets around us say as much?[19]

Hampton noted that Frederick Evans was representing Believers at a Peace Convention that was being held near the Mount Lebanon community as part of the centennial observance. Although Union Village did not participate in the civic celebrations, Hampton's weekly column in a secular newspaper demonstrates that members were taking a more visible role in public life. Rather than allowing the world to write about them, they attempted to create a public image.

Nordhoff certainly had gained a favorable impression from his brief visit in 1874. He was told that the community was debt-free, yet the 1875 church records reveal debts totaling $20,000 on which the village paid eight to nine percent interest. Most of the debt arose from additional land purchases, which were later criticized by the central ministry. When the entire community learned of the debt, members were shocked. Changes were made in the trusteeship and Elder William Reynolds was directed to handle the situation. He arranged to borrow money, at lower rates, from other Shaker villages, to pay off the bank loans. Revenue from part of the village's businesses was set aside just to pay off the debts. Within the first year, Reynolds had reduced the debt by $2,000.

Eastern leaders placed Reynolds first in the ministry, and Amos Parkhurst in the subordinate position. They faced new financial trouble in 1876 when an arsonist destroyed the North Family's cow barn containing 39 head of cattle. Then in 1877, a bank in which they had invested failed, costing them over $7,000. The financial upheavals forced them to take stock of their holdings. Although they had lost considerable sums of money over the years, their assets were still impressive. In June 1877, they owned 4,509 acres in Warren County, and 60 acres in nearby Hamilton County. Their land was valued at $286,000, and their personal property at $31,000. Since 1865, the Shakers' annual taxes had ranged from $3,000 to $5,800. Turtle Creek Township, in which Union Village and Lebanon were located, had its land valued at $2.7 million in 1870, making it the wealthiest township in Warren County at the time. The Believers were an important part of the local economy.[20]

Unfortunately, the community's religious life experienced its own loss

The Warren County Atlas of 1875 shows the Society of Shakers as a major landowner in Turtle Creek Township.

during this period. Due to declining membership and the age of the remaining members, dancing was discontinued as a regular part of worship services in May 1880. The population was 215 when Nordhoff visited in 1874. By the time of the 1880 census, however, the population had declined to 175.[21] Since 1805, some form of dancing (spontaneous whirling, the formal square step, the ritualized circle) had been part of the Sabbath meetings. When the dancing stopped, the meetings became even more somber and of less interest to the world. Marching, the simplest dance form, was still occasionally performed during Sabbath and special services as late as 1895.

Still, the Believers seemed determined to make the best of their situation. If they could not attract large numbers of converts, they would deepen their personal faith. If they could no longer farm all the village's rich land, they would rent it to tenant farmers. If they could no longer sustain all the businesses of earlier decades, they would concentrate on the most successful. Their products still sold well, and William Reynolds was a popular leader who was slowly paying off the community's debt. And then, suddenly, Reynolds died on May 13, 1881. The next month, the central ministry arrived in the village to name his replacement. Matthew Carter, a long-time resident, was named first in the ministry. Oliver Hampton, schoolteacher, journal writer, and public speaker, was named second. Carter faced many challenges during the nine years that he led Union Village. An elder of the West Frame Family deserted the village in 1884, taking $500 with him. A decision to lend money to the Dayton Furnace Company in 1885 ultimately cost the village $16,000. Although membership was steadily declining, some converts were still added. They included James Fennessey, a 28-year-old Cincinnati man who had worked as a farm hand and mechanic. He joined the community in the spring of 1882, and soon earned positions of responsibility.[22]

Another challenge arose when a tornado devastated southwestern Warren County in the spring of 1886. The tornado hit Lebanon at approximately 9:45 p.m. May 12, and "raged most fiercely, filling the stoutest hearted with wild dismay and consternation," the local newspaper reported. "It came howling from the southwest like a demon of the air," uprooting trees, destroying buildings, and tossing some residents out of their beds.[23] Miraculously, no one was killed. One of Lebanon's major buildings, the Union School, was destroyed, with the damage estimated between $4,000 and $5,000. By 10 p.m., the winds hit Union Village:

Shakertown was dreadfully shook up. The loss at the Center Family alone will amount to five or six thousand dollars. A strange feature of the storm is exhibited in the fact that in the locality where it raged even with greatest fury, the grain was not blown down...The destruction to the big woods belonging to the Shakers on the left side is very great, nearly one-third of the trees being broken off or uprooted.[24]

Despite 20 minutes of terror while the tornado swept over the village, the only fatalities were three cows. Early the next morning, the hired hands repaired fences and herded up cattle, sheep, horses, and poultry. In addition to the damage at the Center House, several barns, shops, and sheds were demolished. Like their neighbors, all the Believers could do was clean up and start rebuilding. The local news account is interesting because it reveals a much more sympathetic view of the sect than had been published in previous years. Members were viewed as neighbors who had suffered a common loss. On the other hand, they must have been frustrated to still be identified as Shakertown after spending decades trying to establish an identity as Union Village.

After the storm, a renewed emphasis was placed on the herbal medicine and sarsaparilla businesses. They were, after all, among the village's most successful enterprises. Leaders believed they could help generate stronger profits for the community. A market had already been established among the world's people, who placed their confidence in the

> "It came howling from the southwest like a demon of the air," uprooting trees, destroying buildings, and tossing some residents out of their beds.

village's products. "What the Shakers make can be depended upon," declared the national *Shaker Almanac* of 1886. A collection of recipes, jokes, historical facts, and household hints surrounded advertisements and testimonials for Shaker products, some of them made in Union Village. The almanac was illustrated with woodcuts of members making and labeling the syrups and extracts that, respectively, could treat a variety of conditions. Shaker medicines were not elixirs sold as panaceas for all ailments. Each item was prepared to treat specific diseases. Advertising broadsheets for Shaker medicines of this era listed ingredients in each medicine, common uses, and medical references for the product. A cough syrup advertisement noted that "this is not a Patent Medicine, nor a Secret Remedy, and we make no secret of its composition...This medicine ...had been in use for a number of years among the several families of the Society of Shakers." Ingredients included wild cherry bark, squills, Seneca snakeroot, rhubarb, and small amounts of opium and antimony. What made the medicine superior was the freshness of the ingredients and the skill with which the syrup was prepared—or so the ad claimed.[25]

An advertisement for sarsaparilla made at Union Village was also informative, rather than sensational, in its approach. According to the ad, sarsaparilla root was now being imported from South America, rather than gathered or grown in Warren County. This ensured a constant supply of sarsaparilla for what was still a major industry in the village. Three medical references were listed, all attesting to the beneficial uses of the sarsaparilla syrup when used properly. The Believers did not shy from the harsher realities of worldly use of the syrup. The ad noted that the sarsaparilla was most widely used in the treatment of secondary syphilis, and cautioned patients to abstain from all alcohol and fermented drinks while taking the medication. In a milder form, sarsaparilla was also recommended for rheumatism, skin diseases, and severe coughs. To ensure that they were getting genuine Shaker sarsaparilla, customers were to look for bottles that had been embossed with the Union Village name and a facsimile of Trustee Peter Boyd's signature.[26]

During this period, personal health and environmental concerns

Union Village members wrote on topics ranging from spirituality to healthier living in the United Society's magazine.

became increasingly important to members. As medical journals started to report on the dangers of tobacco, Believers took up the cause. The production of clay pipes and custom of smoking parties had ceased by the mid-1800s at Union Village. The Believers had long stressed moderation in diet, the importance of ventilation in dwellings, and the need for adequate rest, so it is not surprising that they opposed smoking. William Reynolds had published an anti-tobacco article in 1871, stating "science...has, as usual, taken the hand of our religion, declaring tobacco no less respectable than rum, and that it is a moral and spiritual degenerator, and a physical disorganizer."[27] The community also developed a temperance policy in line with the sentiments of an 1895 *Manifesto* article that targeted both poor diet and tobacco as health risks: "Americans [need] nutritive, not stimulating food, the former is found in fruits, these are turned into body and soul ruining beverages, and thousands more of God's rich acres are wasted with the raising of the obnoxious tobacco plant—the nerve shatterer and blood poisoner of the people in this so-called enlightened age."[28] Union Village decreed that alcohol should only be taken at a doctor's order and supported a temperance movement that flickered in Warren County in the 1870s. That temperance effort—one of many over the decades—was brief and unsuccessful, lasting scarcely four months in 1874. At the time the first temperance meeting was held in Lebanon that February, only one saloon and three druggists in town sold alcohol. When the crusade ended on May 15, six saloons were operating in town.[29]

The Believers were also among the earliest conservationists in America. By the 1880s, the country's seemingly unlimited supply of lumber was being decimated, and timber was becoming scarce and expensive. Cephas Holloway, a former trustee and an agriculturist at Union Village, addressed the Warren County Horticultural Society in June 1883 about the subject. He made a plea for preserving Ohio's forests and for restoring lost timber stands. Economics and environmentalism fueled his proposal. Scarcity and high prices were powerful arguments for his point "but when to these considerations are added the probable ruin of habitable districts and deterioration of climate in a whole country, there is an imperative demand for decision and immediate action."[30] While scientists speculated on the relationship between natural vegetation and climate, Shakers considered trees not only a valuable commodity but also a part of a healthy, desirable environment.

Holloway proposed an aggressive replanting program in which large stands of trees most used for lumber—walnut, oak, poplar—would be under-planted with smaller specimens including locust, Osage orange, and Scotch larch. Or farmers could choose to under-plant with corn, potatoes, and other appropriate plants. As they replenished the forests, agriculturists would maximize the land's potential. Easily grown Osage trees were recommended as a source of inexpensive fencing for the new stands of timber. Where only trees were grown, Holloway suggested letting hogs roam as a natural way of controlling rodents that damaged trees. He ended his presentation with a plea to parents to plant trees for the future: "We feel impelled to make an urgent request to parents as an imperative duty to provide by successive planting of lumber trees for their children especially, and also as a national duty, a humanitarian duty."[31]

Seven years later, conservation was still a concern when Hampton submitted his May column for the *Manifesto's* Home Notes section. Though timber was no longer a major industry for Union Village due to the declining population, the Believers were beginning to replant their orchards and vineyards. Hampton blamed the depletion of local forests for the second successive year of drought: "...if we will persist in cutting away all the green forests, we must look for droughts and cyclones. I hope the Government will soon pass a Code of Forestry Laws, and make the same sufficiently stringent and compulsory to secure our land from utter destruction."[32] In 1901, a national Bureau of Forestry was established as part of the U.S. Department of Agriculture. One of its first efforts was the scientific farming of trees for lumber.

The Believers also became more outspoken about touting their health products. An eight-page booklet published for the community in 1889 by their agents, the Graham Brothers, summarized the sect's origins and explained its basic beliefs, but the real emphasis was on promoting the community's sarsaparilla and herbal medicine industry. The Shakers were always successful merchandisers, even in the early nineteenth century, whether they were selling seeds in Ohio or chairs in New York. Nevertheless, by the late 1800s, considerable public attention was placed on goods and services, rather than on religious beliefs. It is not surprising that Union Village is remembered more by the general public for its products and artifacts than for its theology and hymns.

The Graham Brothers' booklet presented a glowing picture of the village and praised its products:

*A visitor at Union Village will be struck with the substantial character of
everything he sees. Everything they build or make is for use rather than
show.... Their chairs are solid and durable, but comfortable. Their brooms
are made for service. Their medicinal preparations are what they represent
them to be.... The pharmaceutical preparations put up by different Shaker
communities long ago attained a high reputation throughout the United
States and have been sent to all parts of the Old World. It is worthy of note
that the great demand for their medicinal preparations grew up without the
puffing now deemed necessary to get a medicine in the market.*[33]

The booklet was designed to persuade customers that the community's
businesses were large, well established, and dependable. Illustrations included
woodcuts of the broom house, loom house, Center Family dwelling, trustees'
office, and two medical laboratories where the sarsaparilla and medical remedies
were prepared. Directions for taking the medicine were on the back page, as
well as the 1849 endorsement of the Lebanon Medical Society. Peter Boyd, with
the traditional men's hairstyle and chin-whiskers, is pictured on the cover, above
the caption: "82 years a Shaker." They were using their image for profit.

Believers were affecting society in an unintentional way as well. The anti-
Shaker law of 1811 was evolving into a law to protect spouses and minor
children abandoned by a spouse for any reason. In 1880, a revised version of
the law did not name the Shakers directly but focused on men who renounced
their marriage vows or refused to live
with their wives due to joining any sect
or denomination that required those
actions. If a husband joined such a group
and signed his property over to it to the
detriment of his wife and minor children,
his actions were void and the property
was to return to the wife and children.[34]

> The Shakers were always successful merchandisers, even in the early nineteenth century, whether they were selling seeds in Ohio or chairs in New York.

The revised measure said little about the religious group itself. Gone was the
prohibition that forbade members of the sect from enticing spouses into a life
of celibacy. The $500 fine that the sect could be forced to pay for recruiting
members was also dropped.

By 1887, the law was even more general. The measure now was included
in the statues that governed legal relationships between spouses. Neither
husband or wife was allowed to alter their marriage covenant (except for
a legal separation) but no mention of doing so for membership in a sect or
denomination was mentioned. If a husband neglected to provide for his wife,

someone else could do so, and later recover their expenses from the husband. If a woman abandoned her husband for an unjustified reason, he was not responsible for her support.[35] A law that had grown out of a religious conflict had evolved into a measure that had more general application.

Intentionally or unintentionally, the Believers were influencing society in many ways. Little by little, they were becoming more similar to their neighbors. The trend made them more acceptable to society, but in retrospect may have contributed to their demise in Warren County. In economic affairs, they increasingly adapted the methods of the world: taking out loans, using mass marketing techniques. Those strategies sometimes compromised inherent Shaker principles of self-sufficiency and modesty. The Believers were no longer the radical group that attracted people who hungered for a different kind of faith; they were becoming a part of mainstream society.

Top: Sisters working in the kitchen in July 1913 (clockwise): Lucy Hunt, Jennie H. Fish, Eldress Clymena Miner, Harriet Drought (with eggbeater), and Aida Elam. All of the women, except Miner, were Canterbury sisters who lived at the Trustees' Office with the remaining elderly Shakers from 1912–20. Hunt stayed at Union Village for the entire period, the longest of any of the sisters. Miner was Union Village's last eldress. She began her life as a Shaker at North Union, and moved to Watervliet when the northern community closed. When Watervliet closed, she brought its remaining members to Union Village.
Right: Elders' shop.

❦ Chapter Thirteen ❦
Exodus—
Leaving Ohio

While Union Village was promoting its productivity and stability, North Union was closing in northeastern Ohio. One of the last large settlements established in the West, North Union had always been about half the size of Union Village, averaging three families and a maximum of 300 members at one time. By the 1880s, the original membership was dying off and conversions were practically nonexistent. The central ministry began to face the effects of declining conversions and aging populations in 1875,

when the small village of Tyringham, Massachusetts, dissolved and its remaining members relocated to other eastern communities. North Union was the first major Western community to face extinction since West Union, Indiana, was sold in 1826. Its closing began a domino pattern of closings that would continue for more than two decades in the West.

Twenty-seven Believers remained in the Cuyahoga County community by 1889. Part of the property was rented to tenant farmers, laborers were hired to maintain the buildings and grounds, and the Union Village ministry visited periodically to provide spiritual care. That spring, members of the central ministry arrived at Union Village to discuss the situation. Matthew Carter and Oliver Hampton then traveled to North Union with the easterners in May to announce the decision. By fall, eight of the North Union members moved to Union Village and the rest to Watervliet in Montgomery County. Three years later, the property was sold to a pair of Cleveland businessmen for $316,000. The United Society retained a parcel of land in adjacent Lake County that had been cultivated as a fruit farm by the North Union Shakers.[1]

Populations at all the western communities and in several of the eastern villages were shrinking, continuing a downward trend that had increased after the Civil War. The dawning of 1890 also signaled trouble for Union Village, which had grown increasingly dependent on outside laborers. With a declining population, the village was no longer self-sufficient. If it were to avoid North Union's fate, Union Village needed a fresh, innovative plan of survival.

That year, Union Village suffered losses from crimes committed by two unstable members, who eventually went to prison. On April 12, a suspicious string of costly fires began. Arson destroyed a large woodshed and damaged a granary and a laundry on that day. A nighttime fire on April 29 destroyed the South dwelling, built in 1812, in addition to a large laundry and several small outbuildings. Sisters discovered the fire at 1 a.m., and all 19 people sleeping inside safely escaped. The three-story brick building burned slowly but steadily as the Believers, hired hands, and neighbors struggled to save as many items as possible. *The Western Star* reported sympathetically that the "young sisters worked like trained firemen in trying to save the furniture."[2] The final loss was estimated at $50,000, with only a fraction of the property covered by insurance. The South family literally broke up from the catastrophe, with members being assigned to other families. Hampton, who lived at the South House, was so distraught that he had to go to Pleasant Hill for several weeks to recover. Before he left, he published a note of thanks in the local paper. The note illustrates that Union Village was much more a part of the general community by 1890.

> We…express our sincerest thanks toward our neighbors and all those in our employ for their utmost exertions to quench the fury of the devouring fire, by which several of our shops were saved from destruction, and also for kind and

> That year, Union Village suffered losses from crimes committed by two unstable members, who eventually went to prison.

disinterested assistance in saving our household goods and furniture when it was certain the building must go. In the afternoon several teams were engaged until evening in hauling those goods to a place of safety. Such neighbors must be friends indeed who are so eminently helpful in time of need.[3]

Facing persecution brought Believers together in the early 1800s. Now, they enjoyed a closer relationship with the community, partially through shared tribulation such as the 1886 tornado and the arsons.

Trustees suspected that the arsonist was a member so they hired an undercover detective to investigate. Archibald LaFontaine, a 60-year-old doctor who had lived at Union Village for four years, was discovered trying to burn down the West Frame house. The sensational case occupied the local newspaper for a month. LaFontaine was labeled a fire fiend who boasted to the detective of setting other arsons in the past. He supposedly had dreams of becoming a leading elder, and became enraged when he was moved from the prestigious Center Dwelling to the South Dwelling, fearing that the move damaged his stature in the village. He confessed to the other arsons and was sentenced to four years in prison.[4]

A newspaper article printed in Cincinnati eight years later proposed an additional motive for the arson. The story is questionable because it cites no specific sources but the tone is interesting. As *The Western Star* became more sympathetic in reporting on the Shakers, the "big city" paper treated them more frivolously. The Cincinnati paper claimed LaFontaine was motivated by unrequited love for an eldress who lived in the Center Dwelling. The indirect sarcasm about members' celibacy was not atypical of what Believers' faced from the outside press. The reporter wrote:

By a regulation of the village, people in one house are moved to another when that house is destroyed. LaFontaine figured up how long it would, in the course of common events, take him to be promoted to the ministerial building. The result was something like 3,600 years, but his heart longed to be near the one he loved...A month would pass by and he would not get a glimpse of her. He could not stand it, and so he adopted extreme measures. First one house and then another in which LaFontaine resided would catch fire and burn to the ground, and he would be moved up one notch nearer to his Arcadia.[5]

Believers usually did not respond to such reports in the metropolitan papers. Whatever the motivation for LaFontaine's crime, it shocked members deeply.

They were further saddened by the death of Matthew Carter, who collapsed suddenly and died on July 24, 1890. While Carter was being attended to that day, farm deacon John Wilson defected from the village, taking $700 in stock. Wilson was thought to be motivated by an addiction to morphine. Although Believers had restricted the use of morphine as a painkiller since the 1830s, some people for whom it was prescribed still became addicted. After the theft, Wilson quickly sold the stock, and fled the area. By this time, trustees were unwilling to write off the loss as they had with John Wallace in 1818 and Nathan Sharp in 1835. They pressed charges against Wilson, who was brought back to Lebanon by a hired detective. He was tried and convicted in Lebanon, and sentenced to the state penitentiary. "Very little if any of the money he received by the sale of the stock ever was recovered," Hampton wrote. "John did not seem to be a very bad or immoral man, but was strongly suspected of being addicted to the habit of using morphine."[6]

With a crisis at every turn, the central ministry did something it had not done since 1836: appoint an easterner first in the ministry at Union Village. He was Joseph Slingerland, a longtime leader at Mount Lebanon who had pressed for the closing of North Union and now wanted to abandon Watervliet, Ohio. Union Village, struggling itself, accepted his arrival with trepidation. To the surprise of many residents, Slingerland started making improvements at the village. Some changes perplexed Hampton, who was still second in the ministry. Over the next three years, Slingerland remodeled the laundry, repaired the Center House and numerous barns and outbuildings, and upgraded the orchards and small fruit gardens. Because the brothers were old, outsiders were hired to do almost all of the work. This distressed veteran members, including Hampton. "This was all the more painful inasmuch as a great deal of this repairing was done in our Center House," he wrote. "This bro't us into closer contact with those who are not to be depended upon to do and say nothing injurious to our young and inexperienced members."[7]

Slingerland's most costly and controversial project was the remodeling of the Trustees' Office in the early 1890s. Many residents strongly opposed the extensive renovation, but Slingerland maintained that the community had to modernize to stay viable. A large, simply designed building was transformed into a Victorian structure with twin turrets, beveled-glass door windows, an embellished cupola, and gingerbread-trimmed porches. Inside the building, he added marble floors and sinks, and an ornately carved staircase crafted from solid butternut. Much of the remodeling of the Office and Center House was done from 1891–1893. The creation of a Union Village train depot ("a most beautiful little station") in 1892 helped ease construction deadlines because materials were sent directly to the village, instead of the Monroe or Lebanon depots, each a few miles away.[8] The renovated office, nicknamed Marble Hall in the twentieth century, contradicted the traditional Shaker habit of eschewing ornamentation and needless expense. Believers could only wonder what would happen next.

Small changes in daily life also occurred. The practice of kneeling to give thanks silently before meals was abandoned in 1894. The following year, sisters were permitted to stop wearing caps, and men were permitted to wear their hair as they liked.

Changes occurred as well in the way converts were courted and in the types of people recruited. In the early 1890s, Charles Clapp, a long-time Believer who had been a botanist and seed salesman, began corresponding with people in Illinois, West Virginia, Massachusetts, Missouri, and Arkansas. Believers had always used the mail to communicate with interested outsiders, but Clapp made a concentrated effort to enlist young men who could infuse the village with new vitality. He sent them copies of *The Shaker Manifesto*, biographies of prominent elders, and other religious tracts.

Some of those who responded

The Trustees' Office was totally transformed after the 1890s renovation. Because of the extensive use of marble in the new structure, the building has become known as Marble Hall.

to Clapp's invitations to visit Union Village sought a refuge from the world. Gustave Bock, a 30-year-old immigrant living in Chicago, expressed the feelings of several of Clapp's correspondents: "I am disgusted with life in this great city. I am a native of Germany, and was well-educated…I greatly desire to join a community who has good Protestant principles."[9] Another man, a 19-year-old from Arkansas, wrote that a physical disability prevented him from finding a job at home, but that he was sure he could be an asset to the community. "I have been raised on the farm, and am well acquainted with farm labor, have worked in the cotton, corn, and wheat fields nearly all my life," wrote H.D. Wedlock Jr., "I do not want to be a 'dead weight' on any one's hands."[10] Few of Clapp's correspondents ever visited Union Village, but Wedlock did. He lived there several years but eventually left. The community continued to accept prospective members almost until its closing. Converts were few, however, and the Believers increasingly depended on hired men to perform necessary work at the village and to assist with industries, such as their new wine business.

The large-scale marketing of Shaker wines appears to be an 11th hour attempt by Slingerland and Trustee William C. Ayer to bolster the village's economy. Union Village residents used alcohol primarily as a medicine, as did many nineteenth-century people. Their reluctance to sanction the use of alcohol as a regular beverage dates back to the days when Ann Lee's opponents accused her and her brother of engaging in drunken, rather than spiritual, dancing. Union Village was said to have a "fine grape house" as early as 1817 (and later a distillery), but when some young men—including James McNemar—became overly fond of alcoholic beverages, the distillery was discontinued, and Richard McNemar wrote a poem against the use of "such pernicious, pois'nous stuff."[11] After that, spirits were to be dispensed only by the village's doctor or nurse. Community records show that wine was made from grapes, strawberries, and currants—fruits that were commonly used by country people for homemade wines. Brandy was also made.

Commercial winemaking in Ohio started in the 1820s, just southwest of Union Village in Cincinnati where Nicholas Longworth, a wealthy land speculator and attorney, began experimenting with Catawba grapes. Longworth has long been credited as the father of Ohio wines but recent research suggests he had some direct help from Union Village. Viticulturists there held a patent on a grape named the Union Village or Shaker grape by 1856 or earlier.

Longworth is believed to have obtained the new grape variety from the village and used it in some of his early wines. The grape was described as a very large, dark purple fruit that would, according to one expert, "make a fine, light, summer drink."[12] Although Union Village may have supplied Longworth with grapes for his winery, there is no evidence that the Shakers tried to mass-market their own wines as Slingerland was now determined to do.

Wine was an important part of Ohio's economy by the 1830s and Cincinnati was the early center of commercial winemaking in the state. During the 1860s, the climate in northern Ohio, around Lake Erie, was discovered to be better for grape growing and scores of new vineyards developed in the region. The North Union Shakers acquired about 350 acres on the shore of Lake Erie in Lake County, not far from their village, in the late 1870s. They began by growing grapes and then expanded into other fruits, including apples, peaches, pears, plums, and a variety of berries. The business was so profitable at one time that they maintained a warehouse at the railroad station to help ship their products.[13] The vineyard was called Wickliffe.

Slingerland and Ayer decided to revitalize the vineyard and develop a commercial winery. Their desire to profit from the popularity of Ohio wines resulted in numerous trips to the "grape farm" near Cleveland in 1895 and 1896. Ayer, who was in charge of the grape growing, was often there for weeks. Slingerland occasionally went north to inspect the vineyards and once brought back 100 grape slips to be rooted and transplanted into Union Village's vineyard. The village began re-establishing its vineyard in 1892. It flourished, but only provided enough grapes for the Shakers' own juice, jellies, and butters.[14] Wickliffe

Shaker wine label

was counted on for producing commercial wines. Hopes for the enterprise were so high that trustees installed a telegraph line at Union Village in 1896 to communicate with the vineyard during the grape harvest.

Around 1895, Ayer printed a 14-page booklet titled *Shaker Community Wines: A treatise on pure wines, and its beneficial uses* to market wine to the public. Photographs of Slingerland in worldly clothes, the renovated Trustees' Office, and the lakeside vineyards illustrate the booklet. From the beginning, Ayer and Slingerland tried a different approach—marketing their wines as medicinal aides. Most Ohio vintners praised their wine's rich, sweet flavor but the Shakers touted their wine's health benefits. Readers were warned of the dangers of using alcohol as an intoxicant and reminded of the benefits of using wine as a healthy supplement:

> *Now, to a man not accustomed to alcohol, alcohol in a very, very small quantity is a stimulant. A little alcohol in his blood is a good thing. It starts to burn up oxygen, and Nature responds. She makes the blood get more oxygen. The heart beats faster. The blood pours more briskly into the vital organs. The whole system is 'waked up.'... [Shaker wines] are to help people get well, or to keep people well. They are wholesome. Above all things, they are not incitives to drunkenness. The alcohol they have in them is far beneath the danger line. They are a delicious way to administer a gentle stimulant—that's all—a nice medicine.*[15]

The booklet resorted to a bit of "puffing" to promote the product. Shaker wines, like the herbal medicines, were said to be purer and more economical because of the care taken in making them and the quantities of grapes available:

> *...this Shaker wine is better than other wines for these purposes, because all the processes it goes through fit it for that end. It is the result of a good grape—luscious, Ohio grown—prepared in a cleanly manner, fermented correctly and carefully stored. And that is more than foreign wines or champagne go through.... The community has more grapes every season than it can use for wine. After careful picking, sorting out of soiled grapes, wilting for 24 hours, and packing, there is a daily shipment of four carloads of table grapes.... Grapes shipped by the community are uniformly fresh, and the same grape from one end of the car to the other.*[16]

The wine cost an average of 25 cents a quart, whereas, the booklet claimed, $1.50 worth of patent medicine would be needed to yield the same health benefits. Four types of wine were offered, either in cases of one dozen bottles, a five-gallon barrel, or a ten-gallon barrel. Light and dark Concords cost $3 a case; Ives Seedling, $3.75 a case; and Catawba, $4.50 a case.[17] Despite the advertising effort, the Shakers were not overwhelmed by orders and the enterprise was eventually abandoned.

By the end of 1895, most of the Warren County farmland had been rented to tenant farmers and used for agriculture again. Believers tended only the orchards and gardens. In 1897, with the population at a low of 60 people, Slingerland proposed the most surprising plan of all: starting a colony in the Deep South. Rail travel made the South a popular vacation spot for Northerners by the mid-1890s. Advertisements for Florida gulf coast hotels dotted the pages of *The Western Star*. The Believers were among those seduced by promises of sun-drenched orange groves and year-round warmth. As early as 1894, Slingerland joined three eastern leaders in scouting Florida sites for new communities. After the easterners purchased 7,000 acres in Osceola County, Florida, Slingerland decided that Union Village should also have a settlement in the South.

S peculation about Union Village's future in the local press fueled rumors that the village was about to totally disband and head south. Slingerland considered locations in Florida, Alabama, Mississippi, Louisiana, Texas, and even Arizona, before settling on Georgia. By then Union Village had given up the disappointing wine business and sold the remaining northern Ohio property. Slingerland used a part of the profits to buy 7,000 acres in Georgia. The property, almost twice as large as what the Shakers still maintained in Warren County, was located in Glynn County, on the Altamaha River, 13 miles north of the town of Brunswick. This was not an undeveloped patch of land like Turtle Creek had been in 1805. The property encompassed two well-known antebellum plantations, Altama and Hopeton, which had been farmed by 750 slaves as early as 1815. The farms had produced sugar, then cotton, and later rice. After the war, the plantations passed from the original owners to an aristocratic family from Paris. The properties subsequently fell into disrepair. Although valued at $600,000 before the war, the land was purchased by the Shakers for $26,000 and deeded to them in April 1898. The Glynn County newspaper optimistically hoped that the properties would be restored to their former grandeur and productivity.[18]

Altama was described in genteel terms. Its two-story brick mansion had been "the social headquarters for all the rice planters and moneyed men of this section," a reporter recalled. "When the crops had been harvested people gathered from all parts of the country to enjoy the hospitality of the [owners]."[19] A quarter-mile alley flanked by trees led up to the house, which was compared to an English manor. Each year wealthy neighbors came to watch a crew of slaves sail a yacht in local regattas. Ruins of the old mills and of a hospital for the slaves remained on the property. Altama was to be the Believers' home; the main house at the neighboring Hopeton plantation had been destroyed by fire.

The Glynn County plantations presented many benefits and disadvantages. On the positive side, the mansion—once restored—would provide ample living quarters for members and converts. The original owner had ditched 1,600 acres to transform swamp into fertile fields, and there was plenty of room for raising livestock. Disadvantages included the expense of remodeling, clearing away ruins, and restarting farming operations. Six brothers and sisters, including Slingerland and Eldress Elizabeth Downey, initially went to Georgia. It was obvious that many people would have to be hired to make Altama habitable and the fields functional. Meanwhile, western communities were shrinking and dying off; there was no reason to believe that southern communities would be more successful. Glynn County was not a fertile ground for potential converts. It had not experienced a revival on the scale of the Kentucky revival, the event that first brought Believers to the West. It seemed that Slingerland chose Georgia more for the climate and farming potential than for proselyting. In addition, there was something incongruous about the Believers, who were traditionally non-materialistic and anti-slavery, reclaiming the grand "social headquarters" of wealthy slave-owners. Still, if they wanted a large property with sufficient housing, a former plantation would accommodate them.

Back in Warren County, people were surprised to hear of the land transaction. They believed that all the local Shakers would eventually move to the South. But leaders denied plans to abandon Union Village. They intimated in the press that they were colonizing in Georgia to keep the sect alive. A Cincinnati journalist painted a gloomy, yet prophetic, picture of the aging village:

Time and again the Lebanon society has been duped and humbugged, and through fraud has lost thousands of dollars. This they did not resent, and would never of their own accord have taken any of their troubles into

Court for adjustment, but what they are now seriously concerned about is a danger which threatens them immediately. It is the fear that within a few short years the society will have become extinct.

Death plows its yearly furrows across their already aged ranks and new converts...are very few and far between...There is something so strange, weird and pathetic about Union Village as it stands in all its splendor today, as to cause the weariest wanderer to halt and go around, rather than cross the 4,300 acres of fertile land....In spite of the splendid buildings, the broad turnpike which crosses it; the tiled floor of the great central building..., the gigantic stock barns, fine fences and all the other appurtenances of the vast place, there is a spirit of dreariness that broods over these children of one idea.[20]

Slingerland's southern plan clearly was not favored unanimously. After the six Believers moved south in February 1898, Oliver Hampton recorded their progress in the church journal, sometimes adding critical remarks. Multiple train cars of goods were sent to Georgia from Union Village during February and March, prompting him to write after one shipment, "How long is this going to last?" In mid-March, he wrote, "The burden of sending a car load of stock horses and cattle to the Georgia Colony rests upon us....I hope this is the last loaded car that is to go to Georgia."[21]

The Georgia colony soon had another problem—a scandal. On April 12, Sister Julia Foley and former elder William Ayer left the settlement and eloped to Savannah, disappointing and embarrassing the Believers. "Loving Shaker Twain Marry Suddenly" proclaimed a newspaper headline. Ayer and Foley were described as wealthy and prominent members. Foley, "an exceptionally brilliant woman," had been married when she joined the community but her husband died soon after. Ayer, a trustee, traveled frequently to Cleveland when he and Slingerland ran the wine business. After their elopement, rumors arose that the two had been planning their defection for some time and that Ayer had embezzled from the community.[22]

> The Georgia colony soon had another problem—a scandal. On April 12, Sister Julia Foley and former elder William Ayer left the settlement and eloped...

A few days after the elopement, the remaining Believers returned to Ohio to regroup. Slingerland left the colony's first rice crop to the management of R.T. Clark, a local man hired as their agent. He had already contracted with Clark to fence in a pasture and stock it with cattle and sheep.[23]

Despite the scandal, more Georgia land was acquired. In June the Believers negotiated the purchase of 51,000 acres for $125,000. The land spread over three counties; the largest section was in Pierce County, near the town of Hoboken. "The Shakers intend to colonize a large portion of the land," *The Western Star* reported. "Their holdings will be devoted to stock raising and breeding purposes. The remainder will be sold to Northwestern farmers of Hoboken."[24] Slingerland apparently procured the services of J. W. Crow, a Chicago investor, in marketing the Hoboken property. In a promotional article circa 1899–1900, Crow summarized the sect's history in America, stressing their success in commerce. Union Village no longer had any significant manufacturing taking place, according to the article, but was thriving in livestock production, exporting " many thousands of dollars' worth of corn-fed beef over the United States. As they handle nothing but the purest and most profitable breeds, they have a regular demand for whatever amount they can supply. Hence we may say that the location of a colony or a branch society in any community by these prosperous sturdy people must be taken as prima-facie evidence of its merit and adaptability to their chosen industrial preference."[25]

Crow wrote that the Warren County property was valued at over half a million dollars. He implied that anyone who associated with the Georgia colony would also prosper financially. He wanted to "encourage the building up of a bright, thrifty, industrial town…Tradesmen and mechanics of all kinds will be needed; also merchants; and as soon as results will warrant, canning and syrup factories will be built…Arrangements will be made for the shipment of other products, as fruits and early vegetables, in car lots to Northern markets."[26] Land was to be divided into 50-acre tracts and sold on time; buyers could take up to five years to pay off loans. All interested parties were welcomed; conversion was not part of the package. Churches and schools were to be built, and friendships cultivated among all the neighbors.

While Crow tried to interest investors, Slingerland continued to buy land. In the fall of 1898, he purchased more than 7,000 acres in Camden County, Georgia, just 20 miles from the Glynn County properties, for $16,500. The Camden County property was known as White Oak due to its proximity to a town of that name. Five Shakers, including Slingerland and Downey, again left Ohio for Georgia, that October. In January 1899, they brought approximately 11 city blocks in White Oak. That spring they acquired an additional 150 acres in the same region. Believers first lived in cottages on the rural White Oak property, then moved into a hotel located on their town property while they had a new house built in the country. Meanwhile, they borrowed $30,000 against the Altama and Hopeton plantations.[27]

At Union Village, Hampton, Trustee James Fennessey, and the others waited to see how these plans would fare. In November 1898, Sister Amy MacNeal wrote enthusiastically to Hampton about White Oak. She raved about the luxurious plants that thrived in the warm winter; the Mexican roses and oleanders were among her favorites. She marveled at being able to dine on fresh greens in February, and at the size of the local produce: four-pound sweet potatoes and 15-inch onions. She was certain the community would be a financial and religious success. Five people had joined the colony in less than a month, and three more were expected to arrive within a week. MacNeal was optimistic about the newcomers: "(They) understand the better ways of living; and are spiritually minded. We hold service every Sunday at the usual hour, but we lack good singers; however we hope some will arrive from some quarter soon."[28] She expressed hope that more Ohio brethren would visit the settlement.

By 1901, the new White Oak dwelling was completed. Built to accommodate many future members, the house was even grander than the Trustees' Office at Union Village:

*An imposing three-storied house of 'yellow pine, Georgia oak, and walnut'
set on a brick foundation, it had the gables and bow windows, the sliding
doors, built-in window seats and ornate interior columns of the period.
There was a spacious 'gathering room' and a large dining hall furnished
with eight handsome marble topped tables seating eight persons each.
There were a score of 'retiring rooms,' numerous utility and store rooms, a
well-equipped laundry, and impressive kitchen and bathroom fittings—all
walnut, copper, and marble.*

*The kitchen sink, set in polished marble, was six feet long. The smaller
scullery sink, with its marble back and copper drain board, stood upon
sturdy legs of carved wood and was decorated with blue-and-white tiles. In
the master bathroom there was a mammoth tub surrounded by marble and
raised on a platform eight inches high.[29]*

Outside, vegetables and crops thrived. Corn was the major cash crop. Pumpkins, asparagus, and melons were raised for market. At the Glynn County plantations, the rice crop for 1899 was valued at $10,000. But as the Shakers prospered materially, they faltered spiritually. Not one permanent convert was made in Camden County. Gone was the emphasis on divine revelation, simplicity, and spirituality. Although the members still practiced celibacy and confession of sins, they had discarded many of the precepts that had them unique and therefore appealing to people seeking a new faith. In "modernizing" the community, Slingerland and his supporters doomed the colony.

Yet the southern group held on, and encouraged the Ohioans to visit. At 83, Hampton was finally persuaded to visit Georgia in 1900. In addition to being second elder of Union Village, he was a member of the local Turtle Creek Township Board of Education at the time. He tried to resign from the school board before leaving for Georgia. Board members refused his resignation, and requested that he rejoin them when he returned. Sadly, Hampton did not see Ohio again. He left for Georgia that November, accompanied by Slingerland and Downing, stopping at South Union for a visit. He became ill while visiting White Oak and died on March 29, 1901. He was buried there in a simple plot, marked only by a white picket fence. A fire later destroyed the fence, and his grave became lost.[30]

Meanwhile, Fennessey started to investigate alleged financial improprieties committed by Slingerland and Downey. He filed a suit in Warren County Common Pleas Court in October 1901, charging that the two leaders had sold some of the stock from the Glynn County properties and kept the money. Eventually Fennessey discovered that Slingerland had engaged in a number of bizarre financial dealings. The elder traded some of the Georgia property to acquire a $100,000 building in Chicago, and mortgaged the Altama plantation and the Watervliet, Ohio, community to raise money for more real estate speculation. He had acquired a $67,500 mortgage on a hotel in Saint Paul, Minnesota; bought a cemetery in Memphis, Tennessee, for $75,000; and acquired debts of $50,000 in Cleveland and New York City.[31]

Watervliet did not survive Slingerland's real estate speculating. He had first tried to close the village in 1889 when, newly arrived from New York, he refused to pay the community's taxes. Instead, he sold off the Believers' livestock and some of their household belongings to pay the taxes. He abruptly closed the village in the fall of 1900 and moved its eleven members to Union Village. The property, nearly 700 acres, was sold in sections between 1900 and 1910.[32] The Watervliet Believers tried to accept Slingerland's decision philosophically. One sister wrote to a married friend two months after the closing to reassure her that she was content at Union Village, and to invite the friend to join her there if she ever found herself alone. The invitation indicates that the sister felt Union Village would be around for a while. She wrote glowingly of her new surroundings:

> *I like the new home; it is all and more than we could ask; everybody is kind and we do not want for anything. [Eldress] Hester and I often think and speak about you all, and we love you and if ever you want a home, come to us, that's if you are left alone.... You may think [it] strange that we are all so contented, but we are.... [Watervliet] was a dear old home to us, but this is all for the best.[33]*

By 1902, the Georgia colonies were abandoned. The Hoboken community never developed, and there are no records that its sale to the Shakers was finalized. The Glynn County plantations were sold to John Crow in the spring of 1902. White Oak properties were sold to a local businessman that September. Union Village lost money on each transaction. Fennessey spent years trying to repay debts from the southern scheme and sell off mortgaged properties elsewhere.[34]

The Mount Lebanon ministry arrived at Union Village in June 1902 to formally remove Slingerland and Downing as first elder and eldress. The central ministry named their replacements and announced a change in the scope of Union Village's authority. Andrew Barrett, who had been elder of the Society's Narcoossee, Florida, colony, was named first elder. Clymena Miner, who had been eldress at North Union for many years and later of the Second Family at Union Village, was named first eldress. Their authority was over only Union Village and Whitewater.[35]

Weakened by age and debt, Union Village's demise seemed inevitable. Its centennial in 1905 passed quietly with a few newspapers marking the occasion. One writer characterized the village as a haven:

> *There is welcome there for many of the homeless and disheartened, of decent character, who will accept the terms of residence. These terms are not severe, except for those who consider the prohibition of marriage a hard rule. The Shakers provide any man or woman who will obey their regulations a comfortable and even luxurious living. There are spacious rooms in the great family houses. There are tables spread with good food. There are books, magazines, and newspapers. There is a reasonable amount of work to be done, but no one seems to be hard driven. There are beautiful*

*views for lovers of nature. The people seem to be remarkably happy and
entirely peaceful.*[36]

Despite these benefits, few people were enticed to join the Believers. By
1910, only 24 people lived in the village. Their average age was 76. Still, daily
life went on, and members enjoyed the remodeled buildings, new orchards, and
vineyards. With the fields rented, the members had primarily domestic chores
to perform. They were joined by a handful of Whitewater residents when the
central ministry dissolved that community in 1907. Whitewater, which once
comprised nearly 1,500 acres in northwestern Hamilton and southwestern
Butler counties, still had 43 members in 1903. Between that year and 1907,
Slingerland tried to remove Whitewater's two elders from authority, but the
members resisted his efforts. The central ministry then stepped in to close the
village, and began selling parcels of the property. At some point, a few of the
Whitewater people returned to the village. Six Believers were still living there
in 1916 when negotiations for the sale of the last 207 acres were taking place.[37]

Unaware of the internal turmoil, another journalist painted a pastoral
picture of the village in 1909. Believers rose at 5:30 a.m. and breakfasted
an hour later. Sisters spent the day cooking and keeping house. Brothers
tended the garden and poultry, and helped the women with the heavier work.
The writer praised the brethren for their charitable work and ethical lifestyle.
He welcomed the change in their religious habits:

*The past quarter century especially has brought about great changes,
especially one, the mode of worship. Whereas years ago, marching,
whirling, shaking and exhortations of a pronounced nature was indulged
in, today a more intelligent spirit is manifested in forms of singing, reading,
and remarks, heralding the essentials of life and duties that tend toward
the bettering of selfhood, home and humanity. For in these days of religious
skepticism, the Shakers know that reference to rules, creeds, and ceremonies
of the past fail to benefit mankind or perpetuate the gospel of Christ. Also,
that active Christian works in daily life…are the works necessary to benefit
humanity and by which the Christian's standard of love and service is
exemplified, God's love is most administered in these ways and thoughts,
the little band of Shakers toil on, awaiting the final change from earth's
community to the one unseen.*[38]

Greater conformity to traditional Christian worship brought greater admiration from the public, but diluted the unique Shaker perspective in Union Village. Believers were viewed as a quaint, well-meaning group who ascribed to the standards of local society in their old age.

In many ways, the Believers were behaving more like their neighbors. As Fennessey completed paying off the village's debts, some small luxuries became possible. A few sisters left for Florida in the fall of 1909 to spend the winter with the Shaker colonists there. Fennessey, who had always been frail, also spent time in Florida, recuperating from the stress of managing village affairs. By 1911, the community purchased an automobile, which members used to enjoy day trips.[39]

But the inevitable could not be postponed any longer. Pleasant Hill had been dissolved by the central ministry in 1910, and Fennessey realized that Union Village would probably be next. Concerned about the community's ultimate fate, he wanted to donate the property to a charitable institution that would continue the Believers' tradition of service. Mount Lebanon resisted giving away property that was valued at $615,000, and

Union Village was signed over to the United Brethren Church on March 5, 1913. It's impossible to determine by appearance which men are Shakers. Standing (left to right) are Charles B. Dechant, attorney-notary; Dr. John R. King, superintendent of the Otterbein Home; Elder Arthur Bruce and Elder Irving Greenwood of Canterbury. Seated (left to right) are Dr. Joseph M. Phillippi of the United Brethren Church; Lee W. James, the church's legal advisor; Judge James A. Runyan, the Shakers' attorney; United Brethren Bishop G. M. Matthew; church treasurer L.O. Miller, and Dr. William Funk of the Otterbein Home.

a legal battle ensued between the West and the East. Unable to handle the pressure, Fennessey asked for the village to be placed in the receivership of James A. Runyon, a local judge. The request was granted, but a higher court later reversed the decision. Mount Lebanon sued to be recognized as the legal owner of Union Village and all its holdings.

Fennessey believed the local members should decide their community's fate. Since 1909, the United Brethren Church had been secretly negotiating with Fennessey for the property. Granville Hixon, an employee of the United Brethren's publishing company and a nephew of Susanna Cole Liddell, suggested that church officials visit Union Village. The visit turned into a series of meetings in which church officials explained to Fennessey that they wanted to use the property as a charitable home for orphans, missionaries' children, the elderly, and retired clergy. Fennessey, who had been orphaned as a youngster, was ready to sign the village over to the United Brethren until Mount Lebanon took the ownership issue to court. Both Shaker communities felt betrayed. Feelings ran strong as charges and counter-charges were published in the secular press. One newspaper reported that the accusations became so sensational that attorneys for both sides advised their clients to burn copies of the original documents. That advice was taken.[40]

Meanwhile, several uses were proposed for Union Village. A group of Cincinnati investors offered $400,000 for the community. They planned to build a racetrack and gambling resort on the site, a scheme that horrified the Believers. The State of Ohio wanted the property for a large agricultural college. Fennessey had reportedly agreed to give the land to the state, until Mount Lebanon won its lawsuit. With Mount Lebanon leaders involved in the negotiations, an agreement was reached in 1912. The agreement was signed at Union Village on October 15, 1912. Fennessey signed on behalf of Union Village. Three easterners—Arthur Bruce, Irving Greenwood, and Elder Joseph Holden of the central ministry—signed on behalf of the United Society. William R. Funk and Joseph A. Phillippi signed for the United Brethren. The United Brethren would pay $325,000 for the 4,005 acres that then comprised the village proper. They paid $50,000 cash, with the rest to be paid over the next ten years. The remaining Believers were allowed to live in the Trustees' Office for up to ten years, with the use of water and heating facilities, a horse barn, carriage shed, laundry, wood shed, orchard and garden. At the time of the sale, the village contained between 40 and 50 buildings. Some had stood unused for several years.[41]

The rejuvenation of the property by a new religious group was welcomed by most of the public. One area newspaper wrote approvingly of the plan and of the historical significance of Union Village:

The old church still stands, a marvel of workmanship, finished in black walnut, having been used as a store house for grain and fruits since the inmates became too few and too aged and infirm to maintain divine worship. It will not be long until divine services again are started in this building, dedicated years ago to the worship of God. In later years, the Shaker village has become an attractive place for tourists. As a type of a disappearing communistic life in the past, it possesses an interest and a charm beyond any other place in the state; if, indeed, the entire United States can boast of its equal.[42]

As the United Brethren prepared the village for its new life, the remaining 17 Believers had the choice of living in the Office or being provided with other accommodations. In general, the sisters remained at the village, while the brothers moved to other homes. Fennessey sought out different lodgings but at least twice stayed at the new United Brethren facilities, renamed the Otterbein Home. Between 1912 and 1920, 10 sisters from the Shaker community at Canterbury, New Hampshire, came to Ohio to care for the aging sisters. By 1920, only a handful of original Union Village sisters were still at Otterbein. With the orphanage and old people's home growing steadily, more room was needed. The sisters agreed to vacate the Office three

A small family circle in 1913: (clockwise, starting from far left) Harriet Drought, Lucy Hunt, Jennie H. Fish, Eldress Clymena Miner, Moore Mason, James Fennessey, and Aida Elam.

years early and retire to Canterbury. The press continued to treat Fennessey as a spokesman for the Union Village Believers although he asked to be released from the United Society in 1920. He remained interested in Otterbein and endowed a small scholarship to enable orphans to attend Otterbein College in Ohio.[43]

A month before his death, Fennessey reflected on his life as a Believer during a newspaper interview. He never regretted his 30 years at Union Village and was "full of rich memories of the peaceful, quiet, happy life he lived there." But he also acknowledged Slingerland's financial malfeasance and his own role in restoring the community's financial health. Still stung by the 1912 disagreement with Mount Lebanon, Fennessey offered some critical remarks about the United Society. "The Shakers could not continue to progress because there was no reward for ambition, no allowance for progress. During the many years I spent there I never received one cent for my labors," he told a reporter. "For the young there were limited educational facilities, which made them anxious to go into the outside world for more learning. There were other handicaps that did not permit keeping pace with progress, but it took me several years to see it."[44]

Fennessey's secular assessment of the community hardly stands as its final testament. Like so much written about the Believers over the years, even the last interview contains paradoxical statements. Whatever his final feelings, Fennessey is forever linked with the Believers. His death at a private home in Lebanon in September 1928 made headlines in the local papers. At the time of the ownership conflict with Mount Lebanon, several of the Union Village Believers had been so upset with the central ministry that they decided they would never be buried in the community cemetery. A large plot was subsequently purchased in a Lebanon city cemetery, and their wishes were carried out at their deaths. A total of 16 Believers were buried there, including Clymena Miner, Susanna Cole Liddell, and Fennessey.[45] His grave bears a separate marker. One large tombstone marks the other graves.

One hundred and twenty-three years after its founding, Union Village seemed an anachronism. It would take another generation for the world to realize the importance of the Believers, and yet another to understand that they represented much more than herbs and architecture. The people who created a community at Turtle Creek in 1805 were positive that everyone could have a relationship with God. Optimism is apparent in the theology that the Believers published in 1808 and in the thousands of pages of correspondence, journals, songs, poetry, and meditations written at Union Village over the years. Believers avowed that people could change, and that they could help society to improve. Individuals had self-determination; age, sex, and race did not matter. These were radical beliefs in nineteenth-century America, and the Shakers spread them through preaching, publishing, the legal system, and sheer perseverance. The true Believers stayed the course through the rough times and clung to what they believed was right. What is surprising is not the number of Shakers who left the faith, but the many who remained.

The Union Village covenant of 1841 stated, "The faithful improvement of our time and talents in doing good, is a duty which God requires of mankind as rational and accountable beings." Believers were taught to be accountable for their thoughts, words, and deeds. Life was to be lived deliberately, not haphazardly. Shaker precepts were twisted by the unscrupulous or self-aggrandizing over the years, but at the heart of the faith was a profound concern for the soul and life of each individual. Their lives mattered, both in personal terms and in the impact they could have on others. Their goals of sacrifice for the good of many, respect for people regardless of sex or race, and charitable service transcend any particular era or sect. In living their daily lives, the Believers set an impressive standard for equality and religious tolerance.

Top: White Water in 2004
Right: Watervliet barn at Kettering-Moraine Museum

Afterword

The closing of five western Shaker villages between 1889 and 1912 was a prelude to similar closings in the East. Two longtime eastern villages closed by 1912, and five additional eastern settlements closed between 1913 and 1938, leaving only four communities in the 1940s. By 2000, one village remained: the Sabbathday Lake Believers at New Gloucester, Maine.

Many factors that caused the western closings also affected the eastern communities: a turning away from the demanding requirements of the faith; the desire for a personal family life and individual independence; and more educational and occupational opportunities in society. Eastern villages fared better for a longer period because of more cohesive leadership and a longer, more ingrained tradition of communal life. Although Union Village provided strong leadership for its members and those of the western settlements in many instances over the years, there were critical periods (especially after Darrow's death in 1826 and after the Civil War) when leaders stumbled. Joseph Slingerland's gross financial mismanagement in the 1890s simply hastened the inevitable. South Union managed to hang on until 1922, mainly because there were so many questions about how to provide for the Believers remaining there.

The site of Union Village has undergone multiple transformations since the United Brethren Church purchased it in 1912. The centerpiece of the original 4,500 acres is the Otterbein-Lebanon Retirement Community, operated by the United Methodist Church. The western-most part of the old property, containing Shaker Creek, abuts a weekend flea market. To the southeast, across State Route 63, two medium-security prisons loom on what was once prime Shaker pasture and farmland. One prison still operates a small farm there and a horticultural program for inmates. A brick outbuilding on the property is believed to be Shaker. Farther south, in the parking lot of a state transportation office, a historical marker commemorates Beedle's Station. To the north, nothing but grass and brush grows where the Turtle Creek Church once stood. Farther to the northwest, along State Route 741, is a steel company's employee park. Across the road, modern farmers till the quarter sections originally owned by Richard McNemar and Malcolm Worley.

Amid the physical changes over the years, a thread of continuity has kept the Believers' principles and lifestyle in the public consciousness. The most tangible legacy of Union Village resulted from James Fennessey's desire to sell the property to a religious group for use as a home. Otterbein has provided shelter in a

Center House at South Union

spiritual setting to thousands of people over the decades. "When the United Brethren purchased this land in 1912, it was to be an old folks' home, and later, an orphanage," said Mary Lue Warner, Otterbein-Lebanon archivist. "In those days, people had no pensions, no Social Security. The Church took care of them whether they came here with $1 or $100."[1] No longer a charity home, Otterbein still provides practical care and spiritual support to the elderly.

Two large Shaker buildings remain, plus a boiler house that dates to the renovations of the 1890s. Both of the primary buildings have been remodeled numerous times to accommodate modern living. Bethany Hall was the "new" Center Family Dwelling built in the 1840s under the direction of Freegift Wells. The huge brick building has been greatly changed in recent decades, with renovations and additions to accommodate more residential apartments, dining rooms, and communal meeting spaces, yet it retains its Shaker profile and 1844 inscription.

Marble Hall was the old Trustees' Building (the original 1810 Center House). The Victorian façade is the result of Joseph Slingerland's extensive renovations in the 1890s. Marble-topped tables, vanities, and floors account for the building's name. In the basement, the original thick walnut beams and built-in cupboards washed in a faint bluish hue speak of the longevity of Shaker workmanship. A section of the foundation, made of bricks fired on the site, has been left exposed. Upstairs, the modern dining room, once the Believers' kitchen, is set off from adjacent rooms by two built-in cabinets. The bottoms of each cabinet hold storage shelves. The upper section features shelves with glass doors that now hold mementoes. When the Shakers lived there, the shelves were an open area where food was passed directly from the kitchen into either of the small adjoining dining rooms. One of the dining rooms is now an Otterbein Museum and the other is the Shaker Museum.

Artifacts there range from dolls dressed in Shaker costumes made by Otterbein residents to large metal numerals that were once affixed to the buildings to show the year of construction. Copies of Richard McNemar's early maps of Union Village hang on the wall as well as two panoramic photos showing the whole village. Objects of everyday life fill the small space: a wooden yarn winder, apple peelers, a hayfork, a barrel hoop, pieces of pottery pipes, crockery. More items are displayed in the attic. Warner, who came to Otterbein 30 years ago to work in the admissions office, attempts to save everything possible after renovations, including hand-forged nails, shutters, and window frames. The attic also affords a view of Shaker practicality: a 10,000-gallon iron reservoir that once collected water from the building's eaves. A series of underground pipes carried the water to several other dwellings in the village. The Shakers were the first people in the area to have hot and cold running water.[2]

By the time Warner came to Otterbein in 1970, most of the Believers' papers and belongings were long gone. Two train-car loads of furniture and domestic goods followed the last sisters to New Hampshire in the 1920s. An unspecified number of pieces, including bureaus, cupboards, and tables, then collectively valued at $500, were donated to Otterbein in 1915 for the residents' use. Otterbein auctioned many of those pieces in 1965 to raise funds for the organization's charitable work.[3] Many written records, journals, and letters also went to New Hampshire or Mount Lebanon. Local writers and historians salvaged some papers and donated them to the Ohio Historical Society in Columbus and the Western Reserve Museum in Cleveland.

Other artifacts were acquired at auctions and sales by local people, either for practical, aesthetic, or historical reasons. Around the time of Fennessey's death, a pair of young newlyweds began picking up Shaker pieces to furnish an inn they had purchased in Lebanon. Robert and Virginia Jones planned to restore the Golden Lamb Inn, a historic building that had a long association with the Shakers. The inn stood on the site of the old Black Horse Tavern, where in 1803 the Warren County Court, presided over by Francis Dunlavy, granted Richard McNemar a license to preach in Ohio.[4]

Over the next few decades, the Joneses sought out locally made pieces and traveled to the East to purchase other Shaker items, all the while gaining an appreciation of the Believers' contributions to local culture and of their importance within the United Society. Many pieces were used and displayed daily in the Golden Lamb, but the couple eventually donated most of their collection to the Warren County Historical Society Museum in Lebanon. After the museum moved into its current home in 1961, an exhibit of Shaker pieces was assembled. Otterbein placed more than 100 pieces on long-term loan to the museum. Other local residents also donated items that they had acquired from the Shakers in the past or at auctions.

When an addition was built onto the county museum in the early 1980s, a generous loft-style area called the Robert and Virginia Jones Shaker Gallery became the home of the combined Shaker collections. In addition to Union Village artifacts, the gallery displays items and furniture from a number of western and eastern communities. Shaker pieces are still occasionally donated by local people.[5] The museum's library contains many contemporary and modern works by and about the Believers. Some records are available on microfilm, along with many copies of contemporary newspapers. Programs and speakers about the Shakers are frequently presented at the museum.

The Golden Lamb, still owned by the Jones family, continues to display some artifacts and pieces in the inn's dining rooms and public areas. Everyday items from kitchens and shops, as well as some ephemera are displayed from pegboards in the Shaker Dining Room. Two rooms on the third floor contain permanent exhibits representing a retiring room and kitchen.

Interest in Union Village continues locally. Several New England Believers visited Warren County and the Whitewater site in 1974 as Shakerism observed its bicentennial. In 1989, Otterbein-Lebanon and the Warren County Historical Society hosted a large seminar featuring many Shaker scholars and writers. More recently, a Western Shaker Study Group has come together to discuss, research, and publish information about Union Village and the other western communities. The group maintains an active site on the World Wide Web and holds regular meetings, often gathering at the Otterbein-Lebanon complex.

The other western villages still make their presence felt in Ohio and Kentucky. For many people in the Midwest and South, the word Shaker evokes one image: Pleasant Hill. A non-profit corporation revived the Shaker Village at Pleasant Hill as a 2,700-acre historical site in the 1960s and 1970s. The most completely restored Shaker settlement in the West offers educational and cultural programs about the original village. The Shaker Museum at South Union tells that community's story through displays and exhibits in the Center House, one of a handful of buildings left on the original site.

North Union's site was sold to developers and eventually developed into a section of Cleveland known as Shaker Heights. Nothing remains of the original village but the Shaker Historical Society Museum keeps its memory alive. The Watervliet site was also

Meetinghouse at Pleasant Hill

lost to commercial development, but the Kettering-Moraine Museum near Dayton has two restored Shaker buildings on its grounds and a large Shaker exhibit inside the main museum. A state historical commemorative marker was placed at the site of the original village in 2003. Whitewater contains the most extant Shaker buildings in the state. The meetinghouse, a dwelling, the trustees' office, a broom shop, and several other smaller structures still stand. The property has been a part of the Hamilton County Park District since the 1990s but the buildings have not been restored to be accessible to the public. A state historical commemorative marker was placed at the site in 1999. The Friends of White Water Shaker Village hosted the first major exhibit about the community in 2003.

Much of the public interest in the Shakers focuses on their craftsmanship, entrepreneurship, and communal lifestyle. Their idealism, charity, and commitment to religious choice are also worthy of further study.

Appendix A:
Union Village Timeline

1805   Shaker missionaries arrive in the West
First westerners convert to Shakerism at Turtle Creek
First lyrics composed for sacred music

1806   First Shaker residence is built
Sisters arrive from the East

1807   Mission to the Shawnee Indians
The Kentucky Revival published

1808   First Shaker school opens
A Concise Answer published
The Testimony of Christ's Second Appearing published

1810   Largest mob uprising against the Shakers

1811   Ohio legislature passes family desertion law aimed at Shakers

1812   Community formally named Union Village
Covenant signed with central ministry
Merino sheep introduced

1813   Shakers defend pacifism
Fever claims many lives
Numerous contributions made to first Shaker songbook

1814   Chairs sold to the world

1815   Revival sweeps the community

1816   Garden seeds first packaged for sale
Poland-China hogs developed

1817 Shakers petition Ohio legislature for militia exemption

1818 Ohio legislature passes militia law aimed at Shakers
Population peaks at 634

1819 *The Other Side of the Question* published

1821 First Millennial Laws introduced

1825 Leadership crisis follows death of first elder

1827 Women begin dressing in all white for Sabbath meetings

1829 New church constitution signed

1832 Army veterans allowed to receive pensions

1833 Herbs grown for commercial medicines
A Selection of Hymns and Poems published

1834 First visit by central ministry

1835 Flash flood destroys shops
Trustee swindles community

1836 Palm-leaf loom invented

1837 Era of Manifestations introduces intense spiritualism
Silk-reeling machine invented

1840 Drying houses built for corn and apple industries

1841 Land is rented to non-Shaker tenants

1842 Wisdom's Paradise becomes community's spiritual name
Sabbath meetings closed to the public
Dietary restrictions mandated

1845 Second Millennial Laws introduced

1846   *Day-Star* newspaper published

1847   Sabbath meetings reopened to the public

1848   Ohio Supreme Court upholds covenant

1849   Sarsaparilla becomes an important commodity

1850   Population is 448

1854   Thoroughbred Scottish cattle imported

1856   Two farms purchased in Clinton County, Ohio

1860   Population is 372

1861   Massive fire destroys major industries

1862   Mississippi seed route discontinued

1862-63   Donations to Cincinnati Sanitary Fairs support war relief

1863   Militia fines paid for first time

1869   All Clinton County land sold

1870   Instrumental music introduced
        Arson destroys livestock and grain
        Population is 232

1871   Scientific and Progressive Association formed
1874   Over 4,000 meals served to poor and homeless
        California journalist researches communal life

1880   Population is 175
        Most dancing discontinued

1886   Tornado damages village

1889   Telegraph lines installed

1890   A Shaker imprisoned for multiple arsons within village

1892   Train depot opens

1895   Shaker Community Wines marketed to the public

1897   Population is 60

1898   Colony started in Georgia

1899   Georgia colony abandoned

1900   Remodeling of Trustees' Office is completed
        Population is 44

1910   Population is 24

1912   United Brethren Church buys the village

Appendix B:
Site Information

Please contact these sites for visitor information.

Otterbein-Lebanon Retirement Community
585 North State Route 741
Lebanon, Ohio 45036
513/932-2020

Warren County Historical Society Museum
105 South Broadway
Lebanon, Ohio 45036
513/932-1817

The Golden Lamb Inn
27 South Broadway
Lebanon, Ohio 45036
513/932-5065

The Western Shaker Study Group maintains an Internet web site about all of the western communities at: www.shakerwssg.org.

Appendix C:
Western Shaker Sites

Call for times/tour information.

Miami Whitewater Forest
Oxford Road
Harrison, Ohio 45030
513/367-4628

Kettering-Moraine Museum
35 Moraine Circle South
Kettering, Ohio 45439
937/299-2722

Shaker Historical Society Museum
16740 South Park Boulevard
Shaker Heights, Ohio 44120
216/921-1201

Shaker Village of Pleasant Hill
3501 Lexington Road
Harrodsburg, Kentucky 40330
800/734-5611

South Union
State Route 1466
South Union, Kentucky
800/811-8379

The Western Shaker Study Group
www.shakerwssg.org

Key to Collections

DPL
Dayton and Montgomery County Public Library

LOC
Library of Congress

NYSL
Emma B. King Library, Shaker Museum, Old Chatham, New York

OAR
Otterbein-Lebanon Archives, Lebanon, Ohio

OHS
Ohio Historical Society, Columbus

WRHS
Western Reserve Historical Society, Cleveland

WCHS
Warren County Historical Society, Lebanon, Ohio

Chapter Notes

Introduction

1. Marguerite Fellows Melcher, *The Shaker Adventure* (Cleveland: The Press of Western Reserve University, 1960), 239.
2. Nardi Reeder Campion, *Mother Ann Lee: Morning Star of the Shakers* (Hanover, New Hampshire: University Press of New England, 1990), 9.
3. Campion, 24.
4. Benjamin Seth Youngs, *The Testimony of Christ's Second Appearing Containing a General Statement of All Things Pertaining to the Faith and Practice of the Church of God in This Latter Day*, 3rd ed. (Union Village, Ohio: B. Fisher and A. Burnett, Printers, 1823), 409–13.
5. Campion, 35.
6. Youngs, *Testimony*, 568.
7. Edward Andrews, *The People Called Shakers* (New York: Dover, 1963), 32–34.
8. Andrews, *People Called Shakers*, 14–16, 57.

Chapter One

1. Susanna Cole Liddell, *Reminiscences* (Union Village: private papers, 1903), 13, OHS, MSS 119, Series VIII, Box 23, Folder 1
2. Liddel, *Reminiscences*, 13; Richard McNemar, *The Kentucky Revival* (1807: reprint, New York: Edward O. Jenkins, 1846), 88–89.
3. McNemar, *Revival*, 88.
4. McNemar, *Revival*, 81.
5. McNemar, *Revival*, 30–31; David Spinning, *A Short Sketch of the Life of David Spinning* (Union Village: private papers, 17 September 1841) 4–5, OHS, MSS 119, Series III, Box 2, Folder 13.
6. McNemar, *Revival*, 31.
7. New Lebanon Ministry to Turtle Creek Church, 20 December 1804, WRHS IV A 31.
8. Josiah Morrow, "Turtlecreek Township," *History of Warren County, Ohio* (Chicago: W.H. Beers, 1882), 434–35, 440–41; Gardner H. Townsley, *Historic Lebanon* (Lebanon, Ohio: The Western Star, 1946), 5–6.
9. Oliver Hampton, *A History of the Principal Events of the Society of Believers at Union Village*, 4, LOC Container 13, Reels 11–12.
10. Stephen Middleton, *The Black Laws in the Old Northwest*, (Westport, CT.: Greenwood Press, 1993), 4–5, 12, 15–17.
11. Hazel Spenser Phillips, *Richard the Shaker* (Oxford, Ohio: Typo Print, 1972), 19
12. Spinning, 10.
13. Phillips, *Richard the Shaker*, 47.
14. Richard McNemar, *Diary*, 201, LOC Container 21, Reel 19.
15. Liddell, 14–18; John P. MacLean, *A Short Sketch of the Life and Labors of Richard McNemar* (Franklin, Ohio: Franklin Chronicle, 1905), 22–23.
16. Edward Andrews, *The Gift To Be Simple* (New York: Dover, 1962) 9–11; Daniel W. Patterson, *The Shaker Spiritual* (Princeton: Princeton University Press, 1979) 133; Harold E. Cook, *Shaker Music* (Lewisburg: Bucknell University Press, 1973) 65, 76–77; Phillips, 5–6.
17. Melcher, 221.
18. John Meacham, Benjamin Youngs, and Issachar Bates to central ministry, New Lebanon, New York, 5 June 1805, WRHS IV B 34.
19. Ibid.
20. Meacham, Youngs, Bates letter, 5 June 1805; Spinning, 4–5; Andrews, *People*, 84.
21. Meacham, Youngs, Bates, letter 5 June 1805.
22. Benjamin Youngs to Lucy Wright, 16 August 1806, WRHS IV A 66.
23. Andrews, *People*, 54–55, 70–71, 95–97.
24. Melcher, 69–70.
25. John Meacham and David Darrow to David Meacham, central ministry, 19 March 1806, WRHS IV A 66.
26. Ibid.
27. Ibid.
28. John Meacham and David Darrow to central ministry, 5 June 1806, WRHS IV A 66.
29. Jean M. Humez, *Mother's First-Born Daughters* (Bloomington: Indiana University Press, 1993), 148–49.
30. Humez, 108–109.

31. Ibid.
32. Youngs, letter, 16 August 1806.
33. Humez, 145–46.
34. Meacham and Darrow, letter, 5 June 1806.
35. Humez, 108–09.
36. Lucy Wright to Turtle Creek Believers, 9 October 1806, WRHS IV A 31.
37. Lucy Wright to Ruth Farrington and the sisters, 9 October 1806, WRHS IV A 31.
38. Ibid.

Chapter Two
1. David Darrow and Brethren to Lucy Wright, 13 August 1806, WRHS IV A 66.
2. Ibid.
3. Rachel Johnson to Sisters Deborah and Susanna at New Lebanon, 12 September 1807, WRHS IV A 67.
4. Ibid.
5. Spinning, 10–11.
6. Oliver Hampton, "Sacrifice," *The Manifesto*, October 1895, 221–22.
7. Spinning, 11.
8. Darrow and Brethren to Lucy Wright, 16 August 1806, WRHS IV A 66.
9. Ibid.
10. Darrow, 16 August 1806; Andrews, *People Called Shakers*, 64–67, 95, 318 n.140.
11. Darrow, 16 August 1806.
12. Andrews, *People Called Shakers*, 81, 91.
13. Lucy Wright to Turtle Creek Brethren, 9 October 1806, WRHS IV A 31.
14. Youngs, *Testimony*, 411–13.
15. John P. MacLean, *Shakers of Ohio* (Columbus: F.J. Heer Printing, 1907), 273–74.
16. Andrews, *People Called Shakers*, 85; MacLean, *Shakers of Ohio*, 272–75, 282.
17. Turtle Creek Elders to Mercer and Shelby Counties, Kentucky, 7 April 1806, WRHS IV A 66.
18. Andrews, *People Called Shakers*, 80, 83–84, 100; Phillips, *Richard*, 75–76.
19. Stephen Stein, *The Shaker Experience in America* (New Haven: Yale University Press, 1992), 73–74, 79–81.
20. Andrews, *People Called Shakers*, 100–01.
21. Darrow, "How Union Village Received Its Name," n.d., WRHS VII A 20.
22. Anna White and Leila S. Taylor, *Shakerism: Its Meaning and Message* (1904. New York: AMS Press, 1971), 124; Andrews, *People Called Shakers*, 83–84, 88–89.
23. Ruth Farrington to Rachel Spencer at New Lebanon, 21 April 1819, WRHS IV A 69.
24. MacLean, *Shakers of Ohio*, 223–24; Andrews, *People Called Shakers*, 84.
25. MacLean, *Sketch of McNemar*, 26–27; Melcher, 72–73.
26. Constant Mosely, *A Journey by Issachar, John Dunlavy, Matthew Houston, Malcham Worley & James Hodge Through Kentucky and the Wabash. 2.2.5:1808*, 4, LOC Container 9, Reel 7.
27. Mosely, 5; MacLean, *Shakers of Ohio*, 286.
28. Andrews, *People Called Shakers*, 85–86.
29. Issachar Bates to Union Village Ministry, 13 December 1811, WRHS IV A 68.
30. Ibid.
31. MacLean, *Shakers of Ohio*, 286–87.
32. Bates, 13 December 1811.
33. Darrow, "Account of Believers Leaving Busro," 1812, WRHS IV A 68.
34. David Thomas, *Travels Through the Western Country in the Summer of 1816*, (Auburn, New York: David Rumsey, 1819), 149.
35. MacLean, *Shakers of Ohio*, 115–18; Caroline B. Piercy, *The Valley of God's Pleasure* (New York: Stratford House, 1951), 75.
36. MacLean, *Shakers of Ohio*, 230–33; Edwards, *People Called Shakers*, 87–88, 291.

Chapter Three
1. Gwendolyn Milbern, *Shaker Clothing* (Lebanon, Ohio: The Warren County Historical Society, 1974), 3, 13.
2. Milbern, 5–9, 12; Jack Larkin, *The Reshaping of Everyday Life 1790–1840* (New York: Harper Perennial, 1988), 182–85.
3. David Darrow to the ministry, 1807, WRHS IV A 66.
4. Campion, 141.
5. John Meacham and David Darrow to ministry, 5 June 1806, WRHS IV A 66.
6. Hazel Spencer Phillips, *Shaker Architecture* (Oxford, Ohio: Typoprint, 1971), 5–6.
7. Humez, 153.

8. Peter Pease, *Union Village Church Record*, 11 April 1807, WRHS V B 230.
9. Andrews, *People Called Shakers*, 197–99; Fred J. Pauley, *The Shakers: A History of Union Village* (1903; Warren County Historical Society, 1994 reprint), 11; Robert P. Emlen, *Shaker Village Views* (Hanover: University Press of New England, 1987), 36.
10. Hampton, *History*, 17.
11. Phillips, *Shaker Architecture*, 6, 17.
12. Hampton, *History*, 10; Paul Monroe, *Founding of the American Public School System, Vol.1* (New York: MacMillan, 1940) 130–31, 464–66.
13. Hampton, *History*, 27; Monroe, 98–99, 346–47.
14. Townsley, 18.
15. McNemar, *Diary*, 8 January 1828, 9; *A Compendium of English Grammar Selected From Wells, Kirkham, Murray, Perry, &c* (Union Village, 1831), LOC Special.
16. Monroe, 266–68.
17. Andrews, *People Called Shakers*, 56–59.
18. Andrews, *People Called Shakers*, 66–69.
19. Youngs, *Testimony*, 463–64. Andrews, *People Called Shakers*, 47–49, 66–69.
20. Pease, *Church Record*, 31 August 1805.
21. "Investigator's Application," Union Village, n.d., WCHS.
22. Hampton, *History*, 128.

Chapter Four

1. Phillips, *Richard the Shaker*, 60.
2. Campion, 62–63.
3. Bil Gilbert, *God Gave Us This Country: Tekamthi and the First American Civil War,* (New York: Atheneum, 1989), 215–18.
4. John Sugden, *Tecumseh* (New York: Henry Holt, 1997), 120–21, 137–38.
5. McNemar, *Kentucky Revival*, 123.
6. McNemar, *Kentucky Revival*, 125–26.
7. Ibid.
8. McNemar, *Kentucky Revival*, 127.
9. McNemar, *Kentucky Revival*, 128.
10. Ibid.
11. McNemar, *Kentucky Revival*, 129.
12. McNemar, *Kentucky Revival*, 130.
13. Central Ministry to David Darrow, 11 July 1807, WRHS IV A 67.
14. Ibid.
15. McNemar, *Kentucky Revival*, 131.
16. *Church Record*, 29 August 1807.
17. McNemar, *Kentucky Revival*, 131.
18. McNemar, *Kentucky Revival*, 132.
19. Gilbert, 211–12.
20. McNemar, *A Concise Answer to the General Inquiry, Who, or What Are The Shakers* (Union Village, 1825), 5–6.
21. MacLean, *Sketch of McNemar*, 31; Phillips, *Richard the Shaker*, 87.
22. Benjamin Youngs, *Transactions of the Ohio Mob* (Miami Country, Ohio, August 31, 1810), 1–2.
23. Youngs, *Mob*, 3; "We are informed…," *Western Spy* [Cincinnati], 1 September 1810, 3.
24. *Warren County History*, 359.
25. Youngs, *Mob*, 3.
26. Youngs, *Mob*, 6–7.
27. Youngs, *Mob*, 7–8.
28. Youngs, *Mob*, 9–10.
29. Ibid.
30. Youngs, *Mob*, 11.
31. MacLean, *Shakers of Ohio*, 379; *Western Spy*, 1 September 1810, 3.
32. Thomas Freeman, "Deposition," *The Western Star*, 29 September 1810, 3.
33. Ibid.
34. James Smith, "For *The Western Star*. James to Richard," *The Western Star*, 29 September 1810, 3.
35. Ibid. *The Western Star*
36. "From the *Cincinnati Advertiser*. (Published by Request)," *The Western Star*, 13 October 1810, 1.
37. "An Extract from the *Columbian*, a New York paper of July 23, 1810," *The Western Star*, 13 October 1810, 1.

Chapter Five

1. Joseph R. Swan, ed., *Statutes of the State of Ohio* (Cincinnati: H.W. Derby, 1851), 870–72; Andrews, *People Called Shakers*, 207–08.
2. "Caution," *The Western Star*, 26 December 1821, 3.
3. *Warren County History*, 446.
4. Stein, 101.
5. *Warren County History*, 447.
6. *Warren County History*, 448
7. James McBride, "A Visit to Union Village," *Cincinnati Historical Society Bulletin*, Vol. 29, Summer 1971, 129+.
8. Andrews, *People Called Shakers*, 136–37, 179–80.
9. *Union Village Church Record*, 15 January 1812; Andrews, *People Called Shakers*, 61–64; Hampton, *History*, 20.
10. Hampton, *History*, 20.
11. Issachar Bates to Richard McNemar, 13 December 1811, WRHS IV A 68.
12. Phillips, *Richard the Shaker*, 69.
13. McNemar, *Diary*, 25 October 1826.
14. James M. Upton, *The Shakers as Pacifists in the Period Between 1812 and the Civil War* (Washington, D.C.: Privately reprinted from the *The Filson Club History Quarterly* 47 (July 1972), 268.
15. Rita Buchanan, *The Shaker Herb and Garden Book* (Boston: Houghton Mifflin, 1996), 118–28.
16. David Darrow to New Lebanon ministry, 20 April 1813, WRHS IV A 68.
17. Ibid.
18. Ibid.
19. *Church Record*, 12 May 1813, 16 December 1813.
20. MacLean, *Shakers of Ohio*, 379–80.
21. Darrow to New Lebanon ministry, 21 September 1816, WRHS IV B 34.
22. "An Agreement of Parents respecting children," 25 December 1815, LOC Container 26, Reel 21.
23. "Copy of a Declaration Concerning the heirship of children and youth, Made by the fathers and mothers at Union Village in 1816," LOC Container 26, Reel 21.
24. *Warren County History*, 344, 347.
25. Darrow to Richard McNemar, 8 November 1813, WRHS IV A 68.
26. Upton, 268–69.
27. Darrow to McNemar, 1813.
28. Ruth Farrington to Sister Rachel, 7 December 1813, WRHS IV A 68.
29. *Quaker Historical Collections: Springfield Friends Meeting, 1809–1881* (Wilmington, Ohio, 1959), 87.
30. Upton, 268–69
31. Patterson, 165–67.
32. Darrow to McNemar, 1813.
33. Farrington to Sister Rachel, 1813.
34. *Church Record*, 12 February 1815; MacLean, *Shakers of Ohio*, 68–69.
35. Darrow and Farrington to Archibald Meacham, 18 February 1815, WRHS IV A 69.
36. Stein, 105.
37. Darrow to New Lebanon ministry, Spring 1818, WRHS IV B 34.
38. Ibid.
39. Upton, 279–80.
40. Upton, 280.
41. Upton, 280–81.
42. Robert M. Taylor, Jr., ed., *The Northwest Ordinance 1787: A Bicentennial Handbook* (Indianapolis: Indiana Historical Society, 1987), 56–57.
43. Darrow, 1818 report.
44. Ibid.

Chapter Six

1. John T. Kirk, *The Shaker World: Art, Life, Belief* (New York: Harry N. Abrams, 1997), 78–79.
2. David Darrow to New Lebanon ministry, 31 July 1821, WRHS IV B 34.
3. Darrow and Ruth Farrington to New Lebanon ministry, 28 November 1812, WRHS IV A 68.
4. Cook, 76–77.
5. Edward and Faith Andrews, *The Shaker Order of Christmas* (New York: Oxford University Press, 1954), n. pag.
6. Richard McNemar, *Diary*, 21.
7. McNemar, *Diary*, 37.

8. Ibid; Darrow to Rufus Bishop, 10 March 1817, WRHS IV B 34.
9. Daniel Miller, *Journal of Passing and Important Events at Union Village*, 23 March 1818, WRHS V: B 237; Mary Lue Warner, interview with Cheryl Bauer, 8 April 2000, Otterbein-Lebanon Retirement Community.
10. MacLean, *Shakers of Ohio*, 60.
11. "Religious," *The Western Star*, 29 August 1825, 3.
12. Humez, 182.
13. Humez, 187.
14. Humez, 187–88.
15. Milburn, 6.
16. Darrow to Rufus Bishop, 20 October 1817, WRHS IV B 34.
17. Kirk, 47–48.
18. Darrow, 20 October 1817 letter.
19. Ibid.
20. MacLean, *Sketch of McNemar*, 33–34. Phillips, *Richard the Shaker*, 79–80.
21. Darrow and Farrington to New Lebanon ministry, 28 November 1812, WRHS IV A 68.
22. Daniel Miller, *An Account of the buildings at Union Village*, 21, LOC Container 26–27, Reel 22; Phillips, *Shaker Architecture*, 10–11.
23. Martha Edmiston, "Historic Shaker Building Withstands 'Fire Drill,'" *The Journal-Herald* [Dayton, Ohio] 11 October 1965, 18.
24. Miller, 21–24; Phillips, *Shaker Architecture*, 7–14.
25. MacLean, *Shakers of Ohio*, 66, 380–81; Phillips, *Richard the Shaker*, 103; Hampton, *History*, 30–32.
26. Abram Van Vleet, "Shakerism Developed," *The Western Star*, 3 September 1817, 3; "Shakerism," *The Miami Herald* (Hamilton, Ohio), 10 October 1817, 3.
27. Phillips, *Richard the Shaker*, 103–04.
28. Hampton, *History*, 32–33.
29. Eliza Sharp, "Experiences of a Veteran Sister," *Shaker Manifesto*, August 1879, 178.
30. Hampton, *History*, 35; Union Village Church Record, 12 February 1818.
31. Stein, 107–08.
32. Darrow to New Lebanon ministry, 31 July 1821, WRHS IV B 34.
33. MacLean, *Shakers of Ohio*, 69–70.
34. *Warren County History*, 448; *Church Record*, 24 May 1825.
35. Neal, 69, 85.
36. *Church Record*, 20 September 1824.
37. Darrow to New Lebanon ministry, 15 August 1820, WRHS IV B 34.
38. Hampton, *History*, 34.
39. Robert Leslie Jones, *History of Agriculture in Ohio to 1880*, (Kent, Ohio: Kent State University Press, 1984), 141; *Warren County History*, 448.
40. George C. Crout, *Middletown Diary Volume II*, (Middletown, Ohio: The Middletown Journal, 1968), 164.
41. *Warren County History*, 322; Melcher, 128; *Church Record*, 25 August 1819.
42. "The Poland China Hog," *The Ohio Poland China Association Record* (Cincinnati: Peter G. Thomson, Arcade Bookstore, 1880), 5–7, 13–14; Joseph Davis and Harry Duncan, *The History of the Poland China Breed of Swine* (Poland China History Association, 1921), 13.
43. *Financial Accounts of the Shaker Community in the Miami Valley, Ohio*, LOC Container 11, Reel 9; Phillips, *Richard the Shaker*, 107; Charles R. Muller, *The Shaker Way*. (Worthington, Ohio: Ohio Antique Review, 1979), 69–71; Hazel Spenser Phillips, interview with Rob Portman, 3 March 1973, Lebanon; Edward and Faith Andrews, *Religion in Wood* (Bloomington: Indiana University Press, 1966), 93.
44. Kirk, 45.
45. Stein, 94–95.
46. Kirk, 261.
47. John Haver, ed., *Memoirs of the Miami Valley* (Chicago: Robert U. Law, 1901), 289–90.
48. Stein, 116–17.
49. Hampton, *History*, 50–51.

Chapter Seven

1. Richard McNemar, "Papers," 41, LOC Container 26, Reel 21–22.
2. McNemar, "Papers," 47, 58–59, 94–95; Issachar Bates, *Sketch of the Life and Experience of Issachar Bates*, 101–108, WRHS VI B 18.
3. Union Village Ministry to Central Ministry, 3 July 18, WRHS IV B 35.

4. Central Ministry to Union Village Ministry, September 1826, WRHS IV B 35.
5. *Union Village Church Record*, 16 July 1825, 25.
6. Melba Porter Hay, ed., *The Papers of Henry Clay: Supplement 1793–1852*, (Lexington: University Press of Kentucky, 1992), 228–29.
7. "Public Dinner to Mr. Clay," *The Star and Gazette*, (Lebanon, Ohio) 18 July 1826, 3; *A History of the Ohio Canals*, (Columbus: Ohio State Archaeological and Historical Society, 1905) 39; Issac N. Youngs, *Tour thro the States of Ohio and Kentucky during the Summer of 1834*, 2 July 1834, 46, NYSL.
8. MacLean, *Shakers of Ohio*, 73–74.
9. MacLean, *Shakers of Ohio*, 81–88.
10. Milbern, 12.
11. Melcher, 271–72; *Warren County History*, 448.
12. Upton, 282.
13. Issac N. Youngs, 29 June 1834, 43.
14. Muller, 98–100; "Notice," *Hamilton Intelligencer and Advertiser*, 23 March 1824, 3.
15. Issac N. Youngs, 7 July 1834, 52; Phillips, *Shaker Architecture*, 16; Issac N. Youngs, 7 July 1834, 24 September 1834, 52; "Potter's Ware," *The Western Star*, 19 April 1859, 3; Findley P. Torrence, "Following the Gift That Failed," *Springfield [Ohio] Daily News*, 29 January 1911, n.pag.
16. Issac N. Youngs, 5 July 1834, 47.
17. Issac N. Youngs, 6 July 1834, 51.
18. Issac N. Youngs, 4 July 1834, 46–47.
19. Frances Trollope, *Domestic Manners of the Americans*, ed. Donald Smalley (1832; reprint, New York: Knopf, 1949), 139–40 n.10.
20. Bates, "Farewell to the West, 1835," *Sketch*.
21. *Church Record*, May—July 1835.
22. *Church Record*, 9 September 1835; Phillips, *Richard the Shaker*, 108; Stein, 143–44.
23. Seth Wells to Richard McNemar, 10 November 1835, WRHS IV A 71.
24. Ibid.
25. MacLean, *Shakers of Ohio*, 90–91.
26. *Church Record*, 14 December 1835.
27. MacLean, *Sketch of McNemar*, 52–53.
28. Ibid.
29. *Church Record*, 28 August 1836.
30. *Church Record*, 7 August 1836.
31. *Church Record*, 5 February 1837.

Chapter Eight
1. White and Taylor, 222–28.
2. *Union Village Church Record*, 26 August 1838.
3. *Church Record*, 18 November 1838; 7 December 1838.
4. *Church Record*, 25 November 1838.
5. *Church Record*, 13 January 1839.
6. *Church Record*, 3 March 1839, 31 March 1839.
7. Blossom, "The Shakers," *The Western Star*, 20 September 1839, 1.
8. Ibid.
9. Ibid.
10. *Church Record*, 18 July 1839.
11. *Church Record*, 27 April 1839.
12. Susanna Cole Liddell, *Daybook*, 2 December 1843, LOC Container 28, Reel 24.
13. Liddell, *Daybook*, 3 December 1843.
14. Ibid.
15. Ibid.
16. *Church Record*, 9 May 1839.
17. *Church Record*, 30 April 1839.
18. *Church Record*, 6 October 1839.
19. *Church Record*, 22 May 1839.
20. MacLean, *Sketch of McNemar*, 52–55.
21. MacLean, *Sketch of McNemar*, 60.
22. *Church Record*, 12 October 1837.

23. MacLean, *Sketch of McNemar*, 60–61
24. Patterson, 193–94.
25. *Church Record*, 16 July 1839; MacLean, *Sketch of McNemar*, 62.
26. *Church Record*, 21 July 1839
27. MacLean, *Shakers of Ohio*, 396–97.
28. Patterson, 194.
29. MacLean, *Sketch of McNemar*, 56.
30. *Church Record*, 22 December 1841; *Warren County History*, 448–49.
31. Phillips, *Shaker Architecture*, 16–17; MacLean, *Shakers of Ohio*, 96–97.
32. "Union Village Believed To Be The Birthplace of Noah and The Place Where The Ark Was Builded," n.d., WRHS VII A 20.
33. MacLean, *Shakers of Ohio*, 399–400.
34. Ibid.
35. Andrews, *People Called Shakers*, 158.
36. *Church Record*, 9 May 1841; 9, 10, 11, 12 October 1841.
37. MacLean, *Shakers of Ohio*, 397.
38. *Church Record*, 15 August 1839.
39. MacLean, *Shakers of Ohio*, 408–10.
40. MacLean, *Shakers of Ohio*, 397–98.
41. Philemon Stewart, *A Holy, Sacred and Divine Roll and Book*, (Canterbury, N. H.: The United Society, 1843), 367.
42. Stewart, 370.
43. Hampton, *History*, 35–36; *Warren County History*, 413–15; Bates, *Sketch*, n.pag.
44. N. Gordon Thomas, "The Millerite Movement in Ohio," *Ohio History,* Vol. 81 (1972), 97–98.
45. Andrews, *People Called Shakers*, 223; Thomas, 100–01.
46. Prudence Morrell, "Journal of a Visit to the Western Societies in 1847," *Shaker Quarterly*, Vol. 8 (1968), 43.
47. Morrell, 43–44.
48. Ronald Numbers and Jonathan Butler, *The Disappointed*, (Bloomington: Indiana University Press, 1987), 183.
49. Liddell, *Daybook*, 161.
50. MacLean, *Shakers of Ohio*, 97; Phillips, *Richard the Shaker*, 108; Malcolm Worley's Deed, 1808, WRHS I A 19.
51. Phillips, *Richard the Shaker*, 108.

Chapter Nine

1. Larkin, 39–42, 48–49.
2. *Union Village Church Record*, September 1836, 10 February 1837; Edward Andrews, *The Community Industries of the Shakers*, (Albany: The University of the State of New York, 1933), 202–05; Milbern, *Shaker Clothing*, 10–11; Edward Andrews and Faith Andrews, *Work and Worship: The Economic Order of the Shakers*, (Greenwich, Ct: New York Graphic Society, 1974), 123.
3. *Church Record*, August 1837; Andrews, *Community Industries*, 42.
4. Kirk, 106–07.
5. Kirk, 140.
6. Stein, 183.
7. Amy Slater, *A Register of Work Performed by Second Family Sisters, Together With the Most Important Passing Events*, March 1845–November 1846, LOC Container 10, Reel 8–9.
8. Eldresses Dana and Cassandra, "Rules for washing clothes," 1846; "A List of what is thought proper for all the Sisters wearing apparel," 8 September 1840; "Rules for dressing the little girls heads," n.d., LOC Container 27, Reel 22–23; Slater, *Register*.
9. "Rules respecting the Sisters Washing and bathing in hot weather," 1846, LOC Container 27, Reel 22–23.
10. Enfield (Connecticut) Ministry, "A few words respecting what we give to the poor," 11 February 1843, LOC Container 27, Reel 22–23.
11. June Sprigg, *By Shaker Hands*, (New York: Knof, 1975), 126, 184.
12. Marjorie Byrnside Burress, ed. *Whitewater, Ohio—Village of Shakers 1824–1916* (Privately published, 1979), 77–79.
13. Ibid.
14. Ibid.
15. Ibid.
16. Silas G. Strong, "Statistics," *The Day-Star*, 17 March 1847; Larkin, 72–74.
17. Prudence Morrell, "Journal," 41–42.
18. Morrell, 46.

19. Morrell, 50.
20. Morrell, 42.
21. Morrell, 56–57.
22. Liddell, *Daybook*, 6 April 1851.
23. *Warren County History*, 332; "Shakers of Union Village," *Heir-Lines*, Summer, 1985, 42–47.
24. Peter Boyd, 6 January 1853; to William Wright, Preble County, Ohio, 10 October 1853; to James Crawford, Whiteside County, Illinois, 20 March 1854, LOC Container 20, Reel 17–18.
25. *Warren County History*, 322, 328, 449.
26. *Catalogue of Short Horn Cattle Owned By The Shakers At UNION VILLAGE, WARREN CO. OHIO* (Union Village, Ohio, October, 1859), LOC Rare.
27. Boyd to Jones & Chissler, 5_____1853, to W. Wightman, St. Louis, 29 May 1852.

Chapter Ten

1. Waverly Root and Richard de Rochemont, *Eating in America: A History*, (New York: Ecco Press, 1981), 218–19.
2. Edward Andrews, *Community Industries*, 82–86, 205; Margaret Ann Ahlers, "Memories Give Boy's View," *Dayton Journal Herald*, 3 May 1963.
3. Andrews, *Community Industries*, 82–84.
4. Andrews, *Community Industries*, 205–206; Jones, *Agriculture in Ohio to 1880*, 217; David Rowley, "List of Fruits—West Orchard. August, 1855," LOC Container 27, Reel 23; Annie Proulx and Lew Nichols, *Sweet and Hard Cider*, (Pownal, Vermont: Garden Way Publishing, 1980), 95–101.
5. U.P. Hedrick, *A History of Horticulture in America to 1860*, (New York: Oxford University Press, 1950), 40–41, 114–15, 205; Andrews, *Community Industries*, 66–73; "Seeds," *Hamilton* (Ohio) *Advertiser*, 16 May 1826, 4.
6. "Financial Accounts;" White and Taylor, 315; Galen Beale and Mary Rose Boswell, *The Earth Shall Blossom: Shaker Herbs and Gardening*, (Woodstock, Vermont: The Countryman Press, 1991), 66–69; "Catalogue of Garden Seeds Put Up By the United Society of Shakers at Union Village, Warren County, Ohio for 1875," WCHS.
7. *Annual Catalogue of Herbs, Medical Plants; Also Extracts, Essential Oils*, (Union Village, Ohio: G. H. Vandever, 1850), LOC Rare; Beale and Boswell, 36–38; 66–69; Margaret Frisbe Somer, *The Shaker Seed Industry*, (Old Chatham, New York: The Shaker Museum, 1972), 17–22, 26–27, 35.
8. Beale and Boswell, 64–65; Hedrick, 483
9. Andrews, *Community Industries*, 91–92; Larkin, 86–87.
10. Buchanan, 102–03; Church Record, 2 October 1824; Larkin, 87–89; "Shaker Cough Syrup, LOC Container 36, Reel 30; *1850 Herb Catalogue*.
11. Andrews, *Community Industries*, 103; Buchanan, 108.
12. Andrews, *Community Industries*, 87–88; *A Brief History of the Shaker Community of Union Village, O.* (Union Village, Ohio, 1890), 3–4, LOC Rare; Beale and Boswell, 29–30; Amy Bess Miller, *Shaker Herbs: A History and a Compendium* (New York: Clarkson N. Potter, 1976), 95–96; Buchanan, 112, 123–25, 129, 148–49; Claire Kowalchile and William H. Hylton, editors, *Rodale's Illustrated Encyclopedia of Herbs* (Emmaus, Pa.: Rodale Press, 1987), 71–72, 335–37, 433–35.
13. *1850 Herb Catalogue*.
14. Beale and Boswell, 24–25; Miller, 26–37.
15. Boyd to David Parker, 6 December 1852, 4 February 1853, 8 August 1853, to Postmaster of Hopkinsville, Kentucky, 23 March 1852, to William Glanny, 11 February 1851; Beale and Boswell, 205, LOC Container 20, Reel 17–18.
16. Beale and Boswell, 139–40; Miller, 49; Boyd to Jerome Jackson, 6 December 1852.
17. *1850 Herb Catalogue*.
18. Beale and Boswell, 207.
19. *A Brief History*, 8.
20. MacLean, *Shakers of Ohio*, 99–100.

Chapter Eleven

1. William McGladeny, *Union Village Church Record*, 8 July 1863.
2. "Where Harriet Beecher Stowe Witnessed the Scenes So Graphically Depicted In Her Famous Creation of 'Uncle Tom's Cabin', *The Cincinnati Enquirer*, 3 November 1895, 17.
3. Oloye Adeyemon, "Underground Railroad Links to the Shakers of Union Village," (Cincinnati, Ohio: National Underground Railroad Freedom Center, unpublished report, 2000), 1–5.
4. Wilbur Siebert, *The Mysteries of Ohio's Underground Railroad*, (Columbus: Longs College Book Co., 1951), 49–50.
5. Adeyemon, 1.

6. Georgeanna Thomas, *Black History in Warren County*, (Lebanon, Ohio: Warren County Historical Society, 1976),10; Martha Boice, Dale Covington, and Richard Spence, *Maps of the Shaker West*, (Dayton, Ohio: Knot Garden Press, 1997), 99–104; Edwina Essex, "Two 'Underground' Routes Led Into Lebanon," (Lebanon, Ohio: *The Western Star*, 1973), 6–7.
7. W.H. Newport to Wilbur Siebert, 16 September 1895, OHS, Wilbert Siebert Collection, Box III, Vol. 11.
8. Edward J. Renehan Jr., *The Secret Six: The True Tale of the Men Who Conspired With John Brown*, (New York: Crown, 1995), 167.
9. Stephen B. Oates, *To Purge This Land With Blood: A Biography of John Brown*, (Amherst: University of Massachusetts Press, 1984), 243–46, 359–60.
10. Oliver Hampton, *Church Record*, 29 April, 13 May 1860.
11. "The Shakers," *The Western Star*, 3 May 1860, 3.
12. Hampton, *Church Record*, 5 September 1860.
13. Ibid.
14. Hampton, *History*, 147.
15. Hampton, *History*, 154.
16. Hampton, *Church Record*, 26 April 1859, 10 May 1859, 21 May 1860, 19 May 1861, 1 December 1862, 3 December 1862, 28 March 1864, 11 April 1864, 19 July 1864, 7 March 1865; Beth J. Parker Miller, Clinton County Historical Society, letter to Elva R. Adams, Warren County Historical Society, 2 April 1988, WCHS; Boice, et al. 97–104.
17. Hampton, *Church Record*, 4 March 1865.
18. Hampton, *Church Record*, 1 January 1861; 31 August 1862; 22 May 1863; 29 February 1864; 23 May 1864; Daniel Hurley, *Cincinnati: The Queen City*, (Cincinnati: Cincinnati Historical Society, 1982), 60.
19. Louis Leonard Tucker, *Cincinnati During the Civil War*, (Columbus: Ohio State University Press, 1965), 20–21; MacLean, *Shakers of Ohio*, 101; Hampton, *Church Record*, 6 March 1863, 13 May 1863, 27 October 1863, 25 July 1864, 20 August 1864, 10 November 1864.
20. Dallas R. Bogan, *Warren County's Involvement in the Civil War*, (Privately published, 1991), 55–56.
21. Bogan, 56.
22. Hampton, *Church Record*, March 1861
23. Hampton, *Church Record*, 3 September 1862.
24. Hampton, *Church Record*, 12 November 1861.
25. Hampton, *Church Record*, 11 April 1861.
26. Eugene H. Rosebloom, ed., *A History of the State of Ohio: The Civil War Era*, Volume IV, (Columbus: Ohio State Archaeological and Historical Society, 1944), 442–43.
27. Rosebloom, 442–43; Hampton, *Church Record*, 15 August 1862, 25 September 1862, 25 February 1864; McGladeny, *Church Record*, 17 December 1863; MacLean, *Shakers of Ohio*,100.
28. McGladeny, *Church Record*, 17 December 1863; Hampton, *Church Record*, 25 February 1864; Kenneth Estill, ed., *The African-American Almanac*, (Detroit: Gale Research, 1994), 724–25.
29. Edward Needles Wright, *Conscientious Objectors in the Civil War*, (New York: A.S. Barnes & Co., 1961), 104–105.
30. Eugene C. Murdock, *Ohio's Bounty System in the Civil War*, (Columbus: Ohio State University Press, 1965), 4–5.
31. Hampton, *Church Record*, 15 August 1862.
32. Hampton, *Church Record*, 10 August 1862, 15 August 1862, 1 September 1862, 5 September 1862.
33. Reuben Wise to Hervey L. Eads, 13 March 1862, OHS, Shaker Collection, Mss 119, Series II, Box 2, Folder 8.
34. Wright, 52–53, 135–36; Stein, 201; Hampton, *History*, 154.
35. Hampton, *Church Record*, 30 October 1862, 4 November 1862, 25 July 1861, 13 December 1862, 29 December 1862.
36. McGladeny, *Church Record*, 28 February 1863.
37. McGladney, *Church Record*, 12 April 1863, 12 July 1863.
38. Whitelaw Reid, *Ohio in the War*, Volume 1, (Cincinnati: Moore, Wilstach & Baldwin, 1868), 139–40.
39. McGladeny, *Church Record*, 20 August 1863, October 1863, December 1863, 15 August 1864.
40. McGladeny, *Church Record*, 13 June 1863, 24 June 1863; Hampton, *Church Record*, 17 January 1864.
41. Hampton, *Church Record*, 24 July 1864, 27 September 1864, 29 September 1864, 14 December 1864, 24 February 1865.
42. Hampton, *Church Record*, 15 April 1865, 1 June 1865.
43. Hampton, *Church Record*, 4 March 1865.
44. Hampton, *Church Record*, 26 April 1860, 11 September 1860, 15 June 1865.

Chapter Twelve

1. "Books Borrowed at Union Village, 1865–1868," LOC Container 27, Reel 22–23; *Warren County History*, 332.
2. MacLean, *Shakers of Ohio*, 102.
3. MacLean, *Shakers of Ohio*, 102–03.
4. "Shaker Meeting," *Miami Gazette*, 25 May 1870, 3.
5. "Religious," *Miami Gazette*, 8 June 1870, 3.
6. Ibid.
7. Malinda Buchanan, "A Singular View. A Vision," WRHS VIII A 55.
8. Anna B. Goepper, "A Dream," *The Manifesto*, May 1894, 122.
9. Ahlers, "Memories."
10. "Constitution Minutes…of the Union Village Lyceum," 2 October 1871, LOC Container 27, Reel 22–23.
11. MacLean, *Shakers of Ohio*, 104; *Report of the Relief Committee of the Cincinnati Chamber of Commerce and Common Council of Cincinnati. Flood of 1884*, 109.
12. George Crout, "Shakers' meeting drew 600," *Middletown Journal*, December 1988.
13. Charles Nordhoff, *American Utopias*, (Stockbridge, Mass.: Berkshire House, 1993), reprint of *The Communistic Societies of the United States*, 1875, 204.
14. Nordhoff, 201.
15. Nordhoff, 202–03.
16. Nordhoff, 203–04.
17. MacLean, *Shakers of Ohio*, 104–05.
18. Milbern, 10–11.
19. Hampton, "Union Village," *Miami Gazette*, 9 July 1876, 3.
20. MacLean, *Shakers of Ohio*, 103, 105; *The Passing Hour*, Vol. 1, No. 5, June 1877, Union Village, 2, LOC Container 36, Reel 29–30.
21. Nordhoff, 200; *Warren County History*, 332.
22. MacLean, *Shakers of Ohio*, 106–08.
23. "Wrecking Winds," *The Western Star*, 20 May 1886, 4.
24. "Terrors of the Tornado," *The Western Star*, 20 May 1886, 4.
25. "The Mystery Explained," *Shaker Almanac*, 1886, LOC Container 36, Reel 30; "Shaker Cough Syrup."
26. "Shaker Sarsaparilla," LOC Container 36, Reel 30.
27. Stein, 317.
28. "Vegetarianism," *The Manifesto*, August 1895, 174–75.
29. *Warren County History*, 505–06.
30. Cephas Holloway, "Forest Culture," *The Manifesto*, November 1882, 259.
31. Holloway, 261.
32. Hampton, "Union Village, Ohio," *The Manifesto*, June 1891, 138.
33. *A Brief History*, 3–4.
34. *Revised Statues of Ohio*, 1880, Vol. I, 809.
35. *Laws of Ohio*, 67th General Assembly, 1887, Vol. 84, 132–33.

Chapter Thirteen

1. Stein, 243–45.
2. "Another Shaker Fire," *The Western Star*, 1 May 1890, 5.
3. "The Shaker Fire," *The Western Star*, 8 May 1890, 1.
4. "Arrested—The Fiend Who Set Fire to the Shaker Buildings," *The Western Star*, 15 May 1890, 5; "The Shaker Fire," *The Western Star*, 22 May 1890, 1; Hampton, *History*, 212; MacLean, *Shakers of Ohio*, 108.
5. "Shakers Will Not Go To Georgia," *Cincinnati Enquirer*, 18 February 1898, 17.
6. Hampton, *History*, 210–11.
7. Stein, 280–82; Hampton, *History*, 216.
8. *Union Village Church Record*, 1891–93; MacLean, *Shakers of Ohio*, 109; Stein, 281; "Splendid Shaker Furnishings Are No Dream," *The Western Star*, 2 January 1974, B-1.
9. Gustave Bock to Charles Clapp, 10 November 1891, LOC Container 36, Reel 29–30.
10. H.D. Wedlock Jr. to Charles Clapp, 2 May 1891, LOC Container 36, Reel 29–30.
11. Phillips, *Richard the Shaker*, 104–05.
12. Charles W. Burkett, *History of Ohio Agriculture*, (Concord, N.H.: Rumford, 1900), 84–86; Root and de Rochemont, 168; Darryl Thompson, *Shaker Originated Plant Varieties and Strains*, (University of New Hampshire, Master's thesis, 1990), 46–47, 57.
13. Crisfield Johnson, ed., *History of Cuyahoga County, Ohio*, (Cleveland: D.W. Ensign, 1879), 531–32; *Here is Lake County, Ohio*, (Lake County Historical Society, 1964), 99; Robert Leslie Jones, *Ohio Agriculture During the Civil War*, (Columbus: Ohio State University Press, 1965), 14.

14. *Church Record*, 1892–1896.
15. *Shaker Community Wines*, (Union Village, circa 1895), 2–5, LOC Rare.
16. *Community Wines*, 10–13.
17. *Community Wines*, 11.
18. Herbert A. Wisbey Jr., "Olive Branch: A Florida Experiment," *The Shaker Messenger*, Fall 1980, 4; Russell H. Anderson, "The Shaker Communities in Southeast Georgia." *Georgia Historical Quarterly*, Vol. 50 (1966), 163–64.
19. Anderson, 165–66.
20. "Shakers Will Not Go To Georgia."
21. Anderson, 167.
22. "Loving Shaker Twain Marry Suddenly and Surprise Members of Their Community," *The Western Star*, 21 April 1898, 3; "A Shaker Elopement," *The Lebanon Republican*, 20 April 1898, 3.
23. Anderson, 167–68; Susanna Cole Liddell, "Account of another group leaving Union Village for Georgia," 25 October 1898, LOC Container 39, Reel 32.
24. "Exit Shakers: To Colonize in Georgia," *The Western Star*, 16 June 1898, 1.
25. John. W. Crow, "Hoboken, Georgia, Shaker Colony," *Chicago and the South*, circa 1899–1900, 11–12, LOC Container 35–36, Reel 29.
26. Crow, 11.
27. Anderson, 168–69; Hampton, *Union Village Church Record*, 25 October 1898.
28. Amy MacNeal to Oliver Hampton, 24 November 1898, LOC Container 39, Reel 32.
29. Burnette Vanstory, "Shakerism and the Shakers in Georgia," *Georgia Historical Quarterly*, Vol. 43 (1959), 362–63.
30. Dale W. Covington, "Oliver C. Hampton, Chronicler of Union Village," *The Shaker Messenger*, Winter 1989, 9; Robert F. W. Meader to Mary Lue Warner, 27 May 1986, OAR.
31. "Some misunderstanding or dissension among the Shakers," *The Western Star*, 31 October 1901; Stein, 283.
32. MacLean, *Shakers of Ohio*, 223–24; Stein, 280.
33. Mollie McBride to Maggie Keemen, 23 December 1900, DPL, The Shakers Collection, Box 5, Folder 2.
34. Anderson, 168–69; M.C. Hutchinson, "Shaker Colony is Extinct With Passing Of Leader," *Cincinnati Enquirer*, 16 September 1928, 32.
35. *Church Record*, 26 June—29 June 1902.
36. "Century Since the United Believers Gathered Under Mother Ann Lee's Leadership," *Cincinnati Enquirer*, 20 May 1905, 17.
37. MacLean, Shakers of Ohio, 228–29, 269; "Colony of 'Shakers' Soon Will Disappear," *Cincinnati Times Star*, 17 October 1916, 1.
38. "Union Village: A Glimpse of Shaker Life," *The Western Star*, 2 September 1909, 5.
39. "Union Village: To Sunny Southland," *The Western Star*, 25 November 1909, 11; "Shakers Want To Try Air Flights," *The Cleveland Plain Dealer*, Scrapbook, NYSL.
40. Andrews, *People Called Shakers*, 291; "Buying a Big Farm," *Otterbein Home Annual*. Vol. 1, 1915, 4; "Judge Runyan is Appointed Receiver of Shaker Society," *The Western Star*, 31 March 1910; "Shakers Want To Try Air Flights;" James Fennessey, "A Satisfactory Transfer," *Otterbein Home Annual*, Vol. II, 1917, 75–76; W.R. Funk, "Relation of Joseph M. Phillippi Ph.D., D.D. to the Otterbein Home," *Otterbein Home Annual*, Vol. XII, 1927, 5–6.
41. "Agreement Between the Church of the United Brethren in Christ and the United Society of Believers, Union Village, Ohio, 15 October 1912," OAR; "Sold At Last: Great Shaker Land Holdings in Warren County Goes to U.B. Church," *News–Democrat*, Georgetown, Ohio, 24 October 1912, 2.
42. "Sold At Last."
43. Mary Lue Warner, "Service of Canterbury Shaker Missionaries to Union Village Shakers at Otterbein Home From December 1912–July 1920," OAR; "Shakers Left Union Village Early," *Otterbein Home Annual*, Vol. VII, 1921, 44–45; John R. King, "A Friend of Humanity," *The Otterbein Home News*, September/October 1935, 2.
44. "Savior of Ohio Communist Colony Declares Sect Failed To Continue Because Beliefs Hindered Progress," *Cincinnati Commercial Tribune*, 5 August 1928, Section 3, 3.
45. "Shakers Monument in Lebanon Cemetery," *Otterbein Home Annual*, Vol. II, 1917, 22–23.

Afterword

1. Mary Lue Warner, interview with Cheryl Bauer, Otterbein-Lebanon Retirement Home, 8 April 2000.
2. Ibid.
3. "Furniture Donated," *Otterbein Home Annual*, Vol. 1, 1915, 76; "Public Auction," 1965, WCHS; Warner to Bauer, 8 January 2001.
4. Phillips, *Richard the Shaker*, 32.
5. Mary Payne, WCHS, interview with Bauer, 9 January 2001.

Bibliography

Special Collections
Dayton and Montgomery County Public Library, The Shakers Collection.
Library of Congress, Rare Books Division.
Library of Congress Manuscript Collection: Shaker Collection, Records of the United Society of
Believers in Christ's Second Appearing.
Otterbein Archives, Otterbein-Lebanon Retirement Community, Lebanon, Ohio.
Shaker Manuscript Collection, Ohio Historical Society, Columbus.
Shaker Collection, Shaker Museum, Old Chatham, New York.
Shaker Collection, Warren County Historical Society, Lebanon, Ohio.
United Society of Believers Collection, Western Reserve Historical Society, Cleveland.
Wilbur Siebert Papers, Ohio Historical Society.

Newspapers
Cincinnati Commercial Tribune
Cincinnati Enquirer
Cleveland Plain Dealer
Day-Star (Union Village)
Dayton Journal Herald
Hamilton (Ohio) *Intelligencer and Advertiser*
Lebanon Republican
Miami Gazette (Waynesville, Ohio)
Miami Herald (Hamilton, Ohio)
Middletown (Ohio) *Journal*
News-Democrat (Georgetown, Ohio)
Springfield (Ohio) *Daily News*
Star and Gazette (Lebanon, Ohio)
Western Spy (Cincinnati)
Western Star (Lebanon, Ohio)

Books
A History of the Ohio Canals. Columbus: Ohio State Archaeological and Historical Society, 1905.
Andrews, Edward. *The Community Industries of the Shakers*. Albany: University of the State of New York, 1933.
 —*The Gift to Be Simple*. New York: Dover, 1962.
 —*The People Called Shakers*. New York: Dover, 1963.
Andrews, Edward and Faith Andrews. *Religion in Wood*. Bloomington: Indiana University Press, 1966.
 —*The Shaker Order of Christmas*. New York: Oxford University Press, 1954.
 —*Work and Worship: The Economic Order of the Shakers*. Greenwich, Connecticut: New York
  Graphic Society, 1974.
Beale, Galen and Mary Rose Boswell. *The Earth Shall Blossom: Shaker Herbs and Gardening*.
 Woodstock, Vermont: Countryman Press, 1991.
Bishop, Rufus and Seth Wells. *Testimonies of Mother Ann Lee*. (Albany, New York: Webb, Parsons, and Company, 1888.)
Boice, Martha, Dale Covington, and Richard Spence. *Maps of the Shaker West*. Dayton: Knot Garden Press, 1997.
Bogan, Dallas R. *Warren County's Involvement in the Civil War*. Privately published, 1991.
Buchanan, Rita. *The Shaker Herb and Garden Book*. Boston: Houghton Mifflin, 1996.
Burress, Marjorie Byrnside, ed. *Whitewater, Ohio—Village of Shakers 1824–1916*. Privately published, 1979.
Campion, Nardi Reeder. *Mother Ann Lee: Morning Star of the Shakers*. Hanover: University Press of
 New England, 1990.
Clark, Thomas and F. Gerald Ham. *Pleasant Hill and Its Shakers*. Pleasant Hill: Shakertown Press, 1968.
Cook, Harold E. *Shaker Music*. Lewisburg: Bucknell University Press, 1973.
Crout, George C. *Middletown Diary: Volume II*. Middletown, Ohio: *Middletown Journal*, 1968.
Davis, Joseph and Harry Duncan. *The History of the Poland China Breed of Swine*. Poland China History Association, 1921.
Eads, H.L. *Shaker Theology*. New York: *The Shaker Manifesto*, 1879.

Emlen, Robert P. *Shaker Village Views*. Hanover: University Press of New England, 1987.

Estill, Kenneth, ed. *The African-American Almanac*. Detroit: Gale Research, 1994.

Gilbert, Bil. *God Gave Us This Country: Tekamthi and the First American Civil War*. New York: Atheneum,1989.

Haver, John, ed. *Memoirs of the Miami Valley*. Chicago: Robert U. Law, 1901.

Hay, Melba Porter, ed. *Papers of Henry Clay: Supplement 1793–1852*. Lexington: University Press of Kentucky, 1992.

Hedrick, U.P. *History of Horticulture in America to 1860*. New York: Oxford University Press, 1950.

Here is Lake County. Lake County, Ohio, Historical Society, 1964.

History of the Ohio Canal. Columbus: Ohio State Archaeological and History Society, 1905.

History of Warren County, Ohio. Chicago: W.H. Beers, 1882.

Humez, Jean M. *Mother's First-Born Daughters*. Bloomington: Indiana University Press, 1993.

Hurley, Daniel. *Cincinnati: The Queen City*. Cincinnati Historical Society, 1982.

Jones, Robert Leslie. *History of Agriculture in Ohio to 1880*. Kent: Kent State University Press, 1984.

—*Ohio Agriculture During the Civil War*. Columbus: Ohio State University Press, 1965.

Johnson, Crisfield, ed. *History of Cuyahoga County, Ohio*. Cleveland: D.W. Ensign, 1879.

Kirk, John T. *The Shaker World: Art, Life, Belief*. New York: Harry N. Abrams, 1997.

Kowalchile, Claire and William H. Hylton, eds. *Rodale's Illustrated Encyclopedia of Herbs*. Emmaus, Pennsylvania: Rodale, 1987.

Larkin, Jack. *The Reshaping of Everyday Life 1790–1840*. New York: Harper Perennial, 1988.

MacLean, John P. *Shakers of Ohio*. Columbus: F.J. Heer Printing, 1907.

—*A Short Sketch of the Life and Labors of Richard McNemar*. Franklin, Ohio: *Franklin Chronicle*, 1905.

McNemar, Richard. *A Concise Answer to the General Inquiry, Who, or What Are The Shakers*. Union Village, 1825.

—*The Kentucky Revival*. 1807. Reprint. New York: Edward O. Jenkins, 1846.

Melcher, Marguerite Fellows. *The Shaker Adventure*. Cleveland: The Press of Western Reserve University, 1960.

Middleton, Stephen. *The Black Laws in the Old Northwest*. Westport, Ct.: Greenwood Press, 1993.

Milbern, Gwendolyn. *Shaker Clothing*. Lebanon, Ohio: The Warren County Historical Society, 1974.

Miller, Amy Bess. *Shaker Herbs: A History and a Compendium*. New York: Clarkson N. Potter, 1976.

Monroe, Paul. *Founding of the American Public School System*. Vol. 1. New York: MacMillian, 1940.

Muller, Charles R. *The Shaker Way*. Worthington, Ohio: *Ohio Antique Review*, 1979.

Murdock, Eugene C. *Ohio's Bounty System in the Civil War*. Columbus: Ohio State University Press, 1965.

Neal, Julia. *By Their Fruits: The Story of Shakerism in South Union, Kentucky*. Chapel Hill: University of North Carolina Press, 1947.

Nordhoff, Charles. *Communistic Societies of the United States*. 1875. Reprint. *American Utopias*. Stockbridge, Massachusetts: Berkshire House Publishers, 1993.

Numbers, Ronald and Jonathan Butler. *The Disappointed*. Bloomington: Indiana University Press, 1987.

Oates, Stephen B. *To Purge This Land With Blood: A Biography of John Brown*. Amherst: University of Massachusetts Press, 1984.

Pauley, Fred J. *The Shakers: A History of Union Village*. 1903. Reprint. Lebanon, Ohio: Warren County Historical Society, 1994.

Patterson, Daniel W. *The Shaker Spiritual*. Princeton: Princeton University Press, 1979.

Piercy, Caroline B. *The Valley of God's Pleasure*. New York: Stratford House, 1951.

Phillips, Hazel Spencer. *Richard the Shaker*. Oxford, Ohio: TypoPrint, 1972.

—*Shaker Architecture*. Oxford, Ohio: TypoPrint, 1971.

Proulx, Annie and Lew Nichols. *Sweet and Hard Cider*. Pownal, Vermont: Garden Way Publishing, 1980.

Quaker Historical Collections: Springfield Friends Meeting, 1809–1881. Wilmington, Ohio, 1959.

Randall, J.G. and David Donald. *The Civil War and Reconstruction*. Boston: D.C. Heath, 1961.

Reid, Whitelaw. *Ohio in the War. Vol. 1* Cincinnati: Moore, Wilstach & Baldwin, 1868.

Renehan, Edward J. Jr. *The Secret Six: The True Tale of the Men Who Conspired With John Brown*. New York: Crown, 1995.

Root, Waverly and Richard de Rochemont. *Eating in America: A History*. New York: Ecco Press, 1981.

Rosebloom, Eugene H., ed. *A History of the State of Ohio: The Civil War Era. Vol. IV*. Columbus: Ohio State Archaeological and Historical Society, 1944.

Siebert, Wilbur. *The Mysteries of Ohio's Underground Railroad*. Columbus: Longs College Book Co., 1951.

Somer, Margaret Frisbe. *The Shaker Seed Industry*. Old Chatham, New York: The Shaker Museum, 1972.

Sprigg, June. *By Shaker Hands*. New York: Knopf, 1975.

Stein, Stephen J. *The Shaker Experience in America*. New Haven: Yale University Press, 1992.

Stewart, Philemon. *A Holy, Sacred, and Divine Roll and Book*. Canterbury, New Hampshire, The United Society, 1843.

Sugden, John. *Tecumseh*. New York: Henry Holt, 1997.

Swan, Joseph, ed. *Statues of the State of Ohio*. Cincinnati: H.W. Derby, 1851.

Taylor, Robert M. Jr., ed. *The Northwest Ordinance 1787: A Bicentennial Handbook*. Indianapolis: Indiana Historical Society, 1987.

Thomas, David. *Travels Through the Western Country in the Summer of 1816*. Auburn, N.Y.: David Rumsey, 1819.

Thomas, Georgeanna. *Black History in Warren County*. Lebanon, Ohio: Warren County Historical Society, 1976.

Townsley, Gardner. *Historic Lebanon*. Lebanon, Ohio: The Western Star, 1946.

Trollope, Frances. *Domestic Manners of the Americans*. 1832. Reprint. New York: Knopf, 1949.

Tucker, Louis Leonard. *Cincinnati During the Civil War*. Columbus: Ohio State University Press, 1965.

White, Anna and Leila S. Taylor. *Shakerism: Its Meaning and Message*. 1904. Reprint. New York: AMS Press, 1971.

Wright, Edward Needles. *Conscientious Objectors in the Civil War*. New York: A.S. Barnes & Co., 1961.

Youngs, Benjamin. *The Testimony of Christ's Second Appearing*. 3rd ed. Union Village, Ohio: B. Fisher and A. Burnett, Printers, 1823.

　　—*Transactions of the Ohio Mob*. Miami Country, Ohio, 1810.

Articles

Anderson, Russell H. "The Shaker Communities in Southeast Georgia." *Georgia Historical Quarterly*. Vol. 50. 1966.

"Buying a Big Farm." *Otterbein Home Annual*. Vol. 1. 1915.

Covington, Dale W. "Oliver C. Hampton, Chronicler of Union Village. *Shaker Messenger*. Winter 1989.

Fennessey, James. "A Satisfactory Transfer." *Otterbein Home Annual*. Vol. II. 1917.

Funk, W. R., "Relation of Joseph M. Phillippi Ph.D., D.D. to the Otterbein Home." *Otterbein Home Annual*. Vol. XII. 1927.

"Furniture Donated." *Otterbein Home Annual*. Vol.1. 1915.

Hampton, Oliver. "Sacrifice." *Manifesto*. October 1895.

　　—"Union Village, Ohio." *Manifesto*. June 1891.

Holloway, Cephas. "Forest Culture." *Manifesto*. November 1882.

King, John R. "A Friend of Humanity." *Otterbein Home News*. September/October 1935.

McBride, James. "A Visit to Union Village." *Cincinnati Historical Society Bulletin*. Summer 1971.

Morrell, Prudence. "Journal." *Shaker Quarterly*. Vol. 8, 1968.

"Poland-China Hog." *The Ohio Poland-China Association Record*. 1880.

"Queries—Answer." *Shaker Manifesto*. August 1879.

"Shakers Left Union Village Early. *Otterbein Home Annual*. Vol. VII. 1921.

"Shakers Monument in Lebanon Cemetery." *Otterbein Home Annual*. Vol. 11. 1917.

"Shakers of Union Village." *Heir-Lines*. Summer 1985.

Sharp, Eliza. "Experiences of a Veteran Sister." *Shaker Manifesto*. August 1879.

Thomas, N. Gordon. "The Millerite Movement in Ohio." *Ohio History*. Vol. 81, 1972

Upton, James M. *The Shakers as Pacifists in the Period Between 1812 and the Civil War*. Washington: Privately reprinted from *The Filson Club History Quarterly*. July 1972.

Vanstory, Burnette. "Shakerism and the Shakers in Georgia." *Georgia Historical Quarterly*. Vol. 43. 1989.

"Vegetarianism." *Manifesto*. November 1891.

Wisbey, Herbert A. Jr. "Olive Branch: A Florida Experiment." *Shaker Messenger*. Fall 1980.

Other Sources

Adeyemon, Oloye. "Underground Railroad Links to the Shakers of Union Village." Cincinnati: National Underground Railroad Freedom Center, unpublished report. 2000.

Miller, Beth J. Parker, Clinton County Historical Society. Letter to Elva R. Adams, Warren County Historical Society. 2 April 1988.

Payne, Mary. Warren County Historical Society. Interview with Cheryl Bauer. 9 January 2001.

Phillips, Hazel Spenser. Interview with Rob Portman. Lebanon, Ohio. 3 March 1973.

Thompson, Darryl. *Shaker Originated Plant Varieties and Strains*, Master's thesis, University of New Hampshire, 1990.

Warner, Mary Lue. Interview with Cheryl Bauer. Otterbein-Lebanon Retirement Community. 8 April 2000.

　　—Letter to Bauer. 8 January 2001.

　　—"Service of Canterbury Shaker Missionaries to Union Village Shakers at Otterbein Home From December 1912–July 1920." Otterbein-Lebanon Retirement Community, unpublished report.

Index